Politicizing Gender

Doris Y. Kadish

POLITICIZING GENDER

Narrative Strategies
in the Aftermath of the
French Revolution

Rutgers University Press

New Brunswick and London

Library of Congress Cataloging-in-Publication Data

Kadish, Doris Y.
Politicizing gender : narrative strategies in the aftermath of the French Revolution /
Doris Y. Kadish.
p.   cm.
Includes bibliographical references and index.
ISBN 0-8135-1708-7
1. French fiction—19th century—History and criticism.
2. France—History—Revolution, 1789–1799—Literature and the revolution.   3. English
fiction—19th century—History and criticism.   4. Revolutionary literature—History
and criticism.   5. Literature, Comparative—French and English.   6. Literature,
Comparative—English and French.   7. Women and literature—History—19th century.
8. Political fiction—History and criticism.   9. Sex role in literature.   10. Narration
(Rhetoric)
PQ653.K3   1991
843'.709358—dc20   91-16792
CIP

Contents

Illustrations

Acknowledgments

To the many colleagues both at Kent State University and at the annual nineteenth-century French studies colloquium who have helped to provide me with a supportive intellectual and professional environment for writing this book, and who moreover contributed ideas and references to materials that immeasurably facilitated my task, I wish to acknowledge my gratitude. I hope that those of them who read this book will recognize their contribution and know how much I appreciate it.

I would like to express special thanks to Dorothy Kelly, William Kenney, and Charles Stivale for their incisive criticisms of the text in manuscript form; to Leslie Mitchner at Rutgers University Press for her encouragement at all stages of the project; to Françoise Massardier-Kenney for her assistance with difficult translations and ideas about George Sand; and to Manuel Fontes for his willingness to relieve me of my administrative duties during the sabbatical leave that enabled me to complete this book. Most of all I want to acknowledge a profound debt of gratitude to my husband, Raymond Woller, whose unstinting efforts as resident editor, computer specialist, and companion made writing this book a labor of love.

A section of chapter 2 also appears as "Narrating the French Revolution: The Example of Corinne," in *Germaine de Staël: Crossing the Borders*, ed. Madelyn Gutwirth, Avriel H. Goldberger, and Karyna Szmurlo (New Brunswick, N.J.: Rutgers University Press, 1991). A section of chapter three also appears as "Inclusion and Exclusion of Femininity in David's 'Marat assassiné,'" *Rethinking Marxism* 3, nos. 3–4 (1990): 202–217.

1

Introduction

AN ANOMALOUS AND SEEMINGLY insignificant detail appears near the beginning of Honoré de Balzac's *Le Père Goriot* where the reader learns that the sign on the Vauquer boardinghouse specifies "Pension bourgeoise des deux sexes et autres." So anomalous is this "sign"—this telling written notice and semiotic detail—that instead of its literal translation ("Lodgings for both sexes and others") baffled translators have chosen either to omit it ("Family Boardinghouse for Ladies and Gentlemen") or mistranslate it altogether ("Lodgings for both sexes; meals)." [1] Although anomalous, these "others" are not unimportant, especially in the light of the problematic sexual practices of the evil genius Vautrin in *Le Père Goriot* and Balzac's numerous deviant characters in other works. Through them, Balzac furthers his conservative argument that postrevolutionary society no longer displays pure categories but has deteriorated into impure admixtures of gender, class, and politics. Balzac's conception of the pervasively contaminated nature of French society was also often expressed at the time as a reversal of genders and social groups. Thus early in the revolutionary period the eighteenth-century poet André Chénier accused Jean-Paul Marat's assassin Charlotte Corday of "an inversion of the sexes" that he then related to "that generalized inversion that the revolution has turned out to be." [2]

Balzac's novel is quite representative of the works considered in this book and many other nineteenth-century novels in dwelling obsessively on a story that stems from fathers' relinquishing patriarchal authority, in this case Goriot's divesting himself of his fortune. The novels begin symbolically with the fall from power of the king. What follows are descriptions of degraded sexual relationships within small social units such as the family or the boardinghouse—although Goriot is called the "Christ of paternity," hints of incest between him and his daughters abound in *Le Père Goriot*, as in so many other nineteenth-century novels—aberrant sexuality serving to dramatize disorder in society after its patriarchal anchor has been removed. Finally in the novels that reenact this often-told tale of the symbolic fall of the king and subsequent sexual degradation of characters from the nineteenth century, society reaches a symbolic state of disorder or destruction represented historically by the Terror, the onset of which corresponds chronologically to the opening of the pension Vauquer. The strong father (king) has disappeared, and control of the boardinghouse "for both sexes and others," a microcosm of the degraded family and postrevolutionary society, lies in the hands of Mme Vauquer, a corrupt, feminine, unworthy substitute. At the close of the novel, Vautrin's criminality is divulged and thus the violence inherent in his aberrant sexuality comes to the surface, as the violence inherent in the revolution surfaced historically during the Terror.[3]

Teasing out this story from *Le Père Goriot* enables me to introduce three basic ideas that underlie the chapters of this book and provide their theoretical and methodological underpinnings: that gender and politics went hand and hand in the nineteenth century; that nineteenth-century works can often be read as retellings of the French Revolution and that the political meaning of these works can be gleaned through the study of narrative strategies that I will be calling a semiotic reading. Each of these ideas requires some further elaboration, which can help explain the importance of the three key phrases in my title: politicizing gender, the French Revolution, and narrative strategies.

Balzac's "others" and similar impure admixtures belong to a protean semiotic system in the nineteenth century, whose various literary forms— allegorized women, feminized men and masculinized women, incestuous sisters, bad mothers, politicized marriages—reflected and reinforced the widespread political unease experienced in the aftermath of the French Revolution. Such consequences of the revolution as its blurring class distinctions, undermining tradition, resorting to violence, granting new roles to women, and acknowledging the demands of the lower classes triggered a profound ambivalence about social roles that haunts the nineteenth century in France and England.[4] This political ambivalence found its way into French and English novels in the late eighteenth century through the semiotic process of linking femininity and revolution that I refer to as "politicizing gender." I use the terms *femininity*, *masculinity*, and *gender* to emphasize *socially* defined categories, in this case as defined in nineteenth-century culture, as opposed to the terms *female*, *male*, and *sex*, which emphasize *biologically* determined differences, which are timeless and essential. The process of politicizing gender at the time of the revolution lived on to produce a rich and varied narrative legacy in the nineteenth-century novel. That process has a number of elements that will be studied in this book, such as names, nationalities, family roles, clothing, acts of writing. By identifying and explaining them, this book attempts to provide a series of readings of major French and English works that are "political" in the sense that they make explicit the attitudes implicit in those works regarding social class (working, middle, elite classes), systems of government (monarchy, republic, empire), and ideology (conservatism, liberalism, socialism).

My readings dwell on the semiotic strategy commonly deployed at the time of the revolution of using gender as a vehicle for dealing with a host of larger social issues. As Mona Ozouf observes: "The lesson of the Revolution was conveyed by a swarm of allegorical figures. Many of these figures were female."[5] For women to function symbolically was of course not new; as Marina Warner points out, whereas historically men have been treated as specific individuals, women have tended to be treated as generalizations and abstractions, especially in France where, "from the *ancien régime* through a succession of Republics, kingdoms and empires, French governments have used the human form, and especially the female form, to decorate the seats of authority and prestige." She adds, "'La France' traditionally personified royal France, while Marianne bodied forth La République, representative of liberty."[6] Lynn Hunt observes in a related vein that during the revolutionary period, it was necessary to promulgate certain symbols, notably female symbols of the republic, in order to provide a basis for the new class. The need arose because of the absence of any stable French constitution or tradition of common law that would anchor the nascent political forces.[7]

The strategy of politicizing gender thus served many functions. Gender operated at the time of the French Revolution to articulate representations of revolution, to form the nineteenth-century public sphere, to constitute bourgeois ideology, to distance the unruly masses, to mention just a few of the connections that revolutionary and postrevolutionary writers established between gender and politics. The reason that gender played such a predominant role at that time undoubtedly had much to do with availability: familiar and omnipresent, at a time when class and other distinctions were uncertain, gender provided a convenient and universally understandable analogy to be used, even if pure examples of masculinity and femininity were becoming increasingly difficult to find. Other reasons for predominance include the long-standing historical link between women and revolution or even perhaps some deep-seated psychological link between the two.[8]

Pervasive associations between the ancien régime and feminized aristocrats or boudoir politics also explain why republicans felt the need to differentiate and articulate their politics in terms of gender. In *Women and the Public Sphere in the Age of the French Revolution*, Joan Landes stresses that women's cultural inclusion in eighteenth-century salons provoked fears that women would usurp the social privilege and linguistic authority of upper-class men to determine truth and the law. Influential women in salons triggered what was widely viewed on the Left as well as the Right as an aristocratic feminization of the public sphere by feminized courtiers and powerful women. Landes traces the fears provoked by eighteenth-century women during two phases of the revolutionary period: an early liberal phase prior to the Terror, which merely called into question the role of women and associated them with the aristocracy; and a later repressive, republican phase starting in 1793, which actively excluded women politically and associated them with the people: "The political and legal banishment of women from the public sphere occurred as a response . . . to the ('disorderly') participation of women of the popular classes in the radical revolution."[9]

Even the surface romantic interest in many nineteenth-century novels is not unrelated to the political issues arising from the revolution. As Nancy Armstrong shows in *Desire and Domestic Fiction*, focusing on a woman, defining her, and describing her amorous conflicts served political ends in nineteenth-century novels by and about women: through such activities, writers "seized the authority to say what was female, and that they did in order to contest the reigning notion of kinship relations that attached most power and privilege to certain family lines . . . the female was the figure, above all else, on whom depended the outcome of the struggle among competing ideologies." Armstrong credits Michel Foucault with enabling us to see "sexual relations as the site for changing power relations between classes and cultures as well as between genders and generations."[10] To unify the interests of nonaristocratic groups; to reject the aristocratic values of status, and material versus moral worth; to assert the worth of a new economic model: these are according to Armstrong some of the issues at stake in the treatment of love, marriage, and gender in nineteenth-century novels. As Armstrong helps us to understand, instead of being viewed as outside politics, domestic issues too can be seen as political history, as much as battles, treaties, legislative policies, and the like. Nancy Miller reminds us in a similar vein that one of the chief contributions of feminist literary criticism is providing a model for taking "the personal and the political, the private and the public *together* as concatenated scenes of operation."[11]

Regarding the retelling of the story of the French Revolution, there seems little doubt that the historical events of that upheaval had a unique and unprecedented impact on the political unconscious of the nineteenth century. For decades after, reverberations of those events can be heard that illustrate Germaine de Staël's great insight into herself and her contemporaries: "Whenever our train of thought brings us to ponder human destiny the Revolution inevitably comes to mind."[12] Not surprisingly, then, the collective story or master narrative of the revolutionary drama was retold and refashioned throughout the nineteenth century, even in ostensibly nonpolitical works. Critics have observed, "The French Revolution marks the point at which politics begins to appear in non-political texts in a systematic way, in a ubiquitous politicisation of literary and aesthetic discourses."[13] The reason writers returned so obsessively to political events surrounding the revolution may lie in fear, especially in England, where one can single out Edmund Burke's highly polemic treatise *Reflections on the Revolution in France*. That work raised the fear of the revolutionary menace's crossing the channel by spreading such lurid anecdotes as that of the queen nearly naked fleeing the insurrectionaries in the middle of the night. Fredric Jameson speaks of "the primal nineteenth-century middle-class terror of the mob—chief actor in the various climactic 'days' of the French Revolution," a profound social and historical fear that novelists seek to mediate through symbolic expression.[14]

Mediation does not only affect the novel, of course. As such constructs as Louis Althusser's absent cause or Jacques Lacan's Real help us to understand, history is never directly accessible but must pass through a variety of mediated forms: rumors, polemics, images, stories, and the like. After all, history too is a semiotic process. The revolution was given meaning in political speeches, in the organization of bread riots or festivals, and in novels. Even "real" events had to pass through collective patterns and semiotic systems to be understandable. Consequently it is not surprising to see a similar semiotic process at work in novels. The literature of and about the French Revolution thus need not be relegated to some peripheral realm unconnected with the vital social, political, and economic activities of the time.

The repeated retelling of the story of the French Revolution needs to be understood also as part of the ongoing attempt to come to grips with class conflict in the nineteenth century. That attempt was integral to the thought of Karl Marx, who reflected on the class implications of the revolution throughout his career.[15] Many of the basic ideas that he was later to have on this subject echo in the pages of the nineteenth-century novel. Thus, for example, in George Sand's *Nanon*, to be considered later, the revolution marks the end of feudal order, as it did for Marx. In Balzac's novels, it institutes the rule of the bourgeoisie as owners of the means of production, as Marx thought it did. Another example is provided in Jacques-Louis David's *Marat assassiné*, a painting to be included in this book as paralleling the novels' semiotic workings. In that painting, the revolution strives to emancipate the people, after having accomplished the limited goal of restoring to those who produce the benefits of their gain, as Marx was to argue. Other examples could also be adduced to show that the writers themselves shared Marx's fascination with the French Revolution because of profound issues of class, not merely because of surface matters of high drama or anecdote.

The presence of the French Revolution in the nineteenth-century novel assumes many forms, from direct accounts of the events, to works focusing on key revolutionary moments, to representations that function like palimpsests, in which the story of the revolution is a dimly discernible stratum overlaid with tales of more recent disruptive events or political regimes. To decipher these palimpsests as stories of the revolution is not to distort their meaning but instead to restore one deeply embedded level and, in doing so, to provide a model for a political reading of their more obvious or accessible levels.

A few words regarding method are required now. This book attempts to discover patterns of relations that recur in the narrative literature of the nineteenth century. Those patterns can be detected in small narrative details such as Balzac's "others," as well as in the larger structures to which those details belong. An appropriate label for the method that will be adopted in these pages is semiotics, "which seeks to identify the conventions and operations by which any signifying practice (such as literature) produces its observable effects of meaning" and which "appeals to distinctions that are thought to underlie and make possible a range of interpretive possibilities."[16]

The semiotic method developed in this book is illuminated by Clifford Geertz's talk of culture as "an historically transmitted pattern of meaning embodied in symbols, a system of inherited conceptions expressed in symbolic forms by means of which men communicate, perpetuate, and develop their knowledge about and attitudes toward life."[17] The cultural patterns and systems at issue in this book are those that were developed at, around, and after the French Revolution and that served nineteenth-century writers as convenient ways of treating political issues in novels. My definition of culture, following Geertz, encompasses far more than the higher intellectual or aesthetic activities commonly referred to as "culture." In this broader sense, culture is a discourse or semiotic activity in which meaning is produced through systems of signs. Culture includes traditions, value systems, ideas, and institutions. Although literature, music, and art constitute notable examples of such semiotic activity, culture is not their purview alone. All of the arenas of culture in the broad sense that Geertz adopts similarly produce meaning and thus are similarly susceptible to being read and interpreted as languages. As one critic aptly remarks of Foucault's conception of culture, "The state, the body, society, sex, the soul, the economy are not stable objects, they are discourses." [18] It is in this broadly cultural sense of discourse that Balzac's "others" call for interpretation in terms of the discourses of sex and society in the revolutionary period.

One means of access to culture as discourse is interpreting small, seemingly insignificant and disparate details, like "others," in a method that Geertz, following Gilbert Ryle, calls "thick description." [19] For Geertz, the part should not be sacrificed to the whole, and social elements should be studied in depth in all their heterogeneity, as bearers in their own right of complex signifying practices. Geertz explains that thick description strives to stay clear of behaviorist, cognitivist, and historicist tendencies to reduce culture to, respectively, events, mental phenomena, or causes; he adds that it "is (or should be) guessing at meanings, assessing the guesses, and drawing explanatory conclusions from the better guesses." [20] As the emphasis here on meaning reveals, cultural studies inspired by Geertz and Foucault pay close attention to material, semiotic forms of expression, especially language.

"Guessing at meanings" and interpreting small details in all their semiotic materiality and heterogeneity are tantamount to resisting premature closure and refusing to rely unduly on just one unifying political, psychological, or historical explanation. One important result of the application of a semiotic method is the new light shed on issues of gender. That method is not concerned only with events and motives, as are standard historical and psychological explanatory modes; instead it carves out a new space in which to consider such matters as how events are seen by various groups, including marginal or disempowered ones. Those groups are seen as competing for authority, power, and legitimacy in their attempts to impose values and conceptions of the social world. Not surprisingly, semiotic criticism has proved to have a natural compatibility with feminist concerns. According to an intriguing prospect opened up by Naomi Schor, it is even possible to consider that paying attention to small semiotic details, and delving thickly into their significance, poses fundamental gender issues because details themselves often participate "in a larger semantic network, bounded on the one side by the *ornamental*, with its traditional connotations of effeminacy and decadence, and on the other, by the *everyday*, whose 'prosiness' is rooted in the domestic sphere of social life presided over by women." If modern methods like semiotics or such closely related theoretical frameworks as poststructuralism focus on details, it is because the study of the partial and the marginal belongs, as Schor helps us to understand, to a larger project of dismantling metaphysics, of calling into question the prioritizing of the general over the particular.[21]

Scrutinizing small details enables modern critics to grasp the relations among symbols involved in the process of representation. Roger Chartier defines representation as "the production of classifications and exclusions that constitute the social and conceptual configurations proper to one time or one place"; along the same lines, he observes,

> Structures of the social world are not an objective given. . . . They are all produced historically by the interconnected practices—political, social and discursive—that construct their figures. It is such differentiations and the schemata that fashion them that are the objects of a cultural history that has come to rethink completely the relation traditionally postulated between the social realm (identified with a very real sort of reality, existent in itself) and the representations that are supposed to reflect it or distort it.[22]

Classifications, differentiations, conceptual configurations, schemata, representations: these terms help to clarify the kind of relations that this book seeks to examine and that Balzac's "others" participate in forming. The present inquiry looks beyond small details to relations among them in an attempt to discover the larger structures governing collective literary practices. In its emphasis on relations and its deemphasis of the individual as the main origin of meaning, semiotics allies itself then with such closely related movements in literary criticism as structuralism, poststructuralism, deconstruction, and Lacanian psychoanalysis. All of these similarly highlight the production of meaning as a social, collective process, which goes beyond the idiosyncratic will of the individual.

The semiotic method adopted here is by nature interdisciplinary inasmuch as the practices it considers arise similarly in many different cultural arenas. Gender was politicized at the time of the French Revolution and its aftermath in literature, art, political discourse, and a wide range of other cultural products: festivals, statues, illustrations, coins, medals. Thus although this book focuses primarily on novels, the semiotic method of looking at "narrative strategies" it develops has relevance beyond the strict boundaries of works that fit traditional definitions of narrative literature. To emphasize the interdisciplinary nature of a semiotic method, I study two paintings in detail and discuss other pictorial works more briefly. These are all pictorial works that would be considered "narrative" in the context of nineteenth-century art criticism inasmuch as their meaning derives not only from their formal arrangement of lines and colors but also from their clearly definable subject matter. Moreover, all of them employ symbols and politicizing strategies similar to those found in the novels of the revolutionary period, and all of them in some sense tell the story of the French Revolution as do novels, although they do so in pictorial form. Studying these works of art can help to fill in many of the details needed to understand the larger picture of the narrative semiotics of the French Revolution. The analyses of key paintings are thick descriptions of art, which supplement the thick descriptions of literature.

The main thesis and principles of organization of this book follow from the basic ideas contained in its title. My thesis is that, although in the aftermath of the French Revolution women were set back in terms of political rights, they were also propelled forward culturally and symbolically as political participants. Even works that denigrate feminine public roles dramatize them so effectively that they paradoxically bring visibility to issues of gender. As Nina Auerbach shows through her probing analyses in *The Woman and the Demon* of how oppression and empowerment intermingle in cultural representations of Victorian women,

> in the nineteenth century the dialectic between womanhood and power was so central and general a concern, one so fundamental to the literature, art, and social thought of the period, that it is misleading to pigeonhole it as "feminist" as though it were the concern of one interest group alone. Legally and socially women composed an oppressed class, but whether she was locked in the home, exiled to the colonies, or haunting the banks of the Thames, woman's very aura of exclusion gave her imaginative centrality in a culture increasingly alienated from itself.[23]

This book will show that in both England and France the very semiotic patterns that often diminish women—allegorization, domestication, sexualization—also strengthen them in unexpected and paradoxical ways. As Landes observes about nineteenth-century culture generally, "Although women failed to achieve political emancipation, the Revolution bequeathed them a moral identity and a political constitution. Gender became a socially relevant category in post-revolutionary life."[24] The present inquiry attempts to develop this important insight of Landes's by applying it to a series of literary and pictorial examples. The literary examples are all drawn from representative French and English novels.

The visibility of gender and women's association with politics in the nineteenth century are admittedly highly ambivalent matters, involving a delicate balance between positive and negative elements. It may indeed be hard at times to keep sight of the positive side in examining the various allegories, deviants, and stereotypes who will parade through the following pages. But I will try to show that behind the disempowering masks women often wear, significant indications of feminine empowerment show through. I will call attention, for example, to the feminine intertextuality whereby such women writers as Mary Shelley and George Sand make literary reference to the heroic example of Staël's Corinne. I will also dwell on the very fact of women writers' concern with politics, which has often been overshadowed by their domestic interests. Describing the account of the French Revolution that she provides in *Desmond*, Charlotte Smith writes, "This excursion into the field of politics, where, for the most part, only thistles can be gathered, and where we, you know, have always been taught that women should never advance a step, may, perhaps, excite your surprise."[25] Although *Desmond* is one of many novels from the revolutionary period that time does not allow me to do more than mention in passing, Smith's remark holds true for the other political narratives by women writers that will be considered in detail here, all of which made a limited but real contribution to feminism. For although these women writers did not write primarily or directly to further the cause of women, they did further that cause indirectly by taking on political issues and playing the active role of proposing solutions, albeit only symbolic and literary ones, to the public issues and conflicts of their times. Emphasizing the political side of women's writing counterbalances the far too prevalent tendency to view that writing only in terms of its surface emphasis on romantic or domestic concerns. When viewed only thus in personal terms, works by women seem to abrogate their role in public life. However, when the personal is placed instead in the larger political context to which it belongs, works by women can be seen to call into question, if not reject, patriarchal control.

This book examines the large semiotic process of politicizing gender by breaking it down in each of the five following chapters into five smaller processes. That each of these chapters highlights only various parts of the process is not to say that the other parts are not applicable. I proceed by using only parts of the process in order to exemplify the method more effectively. Chapter 2 treats allegorizing women; chapter 3, mixing genders; chapter 4, sexualizing family relations; chapter 5, censuring maternity; and chapter 6, politicizing marriage. Although very different in the texts they treat and the narrative problems they confront, these chapters have in common an attention to semiotic detail, systems, and their political implications. All five of these chapters deal in one way or another with the symbolic linking of femininity and revolution, designated here as "politicizing gender," and they all dwell on works that can be read, in some cases directly and in others far less so, as narrative reenactments of the French Revolution. All five of these chapters, moreover, highlight certain semiotic elements—for example, names, clothing, women's writing—that contributed to expressing and shaping the culture of the revolutionary period. A complete list of those elements and the chapters in which they occur is provided in the Appendix. Both the recurrence and the combination of those elements in a variety of nineteenth-century paintings and novels serve to support my claim that a common semiotic code is at work in nineteenth-century representations of the revolutionary story.

The main examples in these chapters are nineteenth-century French and English novels, ranging from those written more or less contemporaneously with the revolution to those written nearly a century later, from Jacobin to counterrevolutionary viewpoints. My other main examples are paintings, one by David and another by his student Anne-Louis Girodet, both of which echo and shed light on the narrative semiotics of politicizing gender. Other closely related novels and pictorial works are also mentioned in passing or discussed briefly. That the works studied here are evenly distributed between works by men and women is significant because it helps me to make the point that women were active participants in elaborating gender positions in the nineteenth century, that they did not passively submit to a process controlled by men. And even for the authors and painters who are men, feminist issues show through. I have arranged the book so that women's contribution, considered in chapters 2 and 6, frames that of their masculine counterparts, who were unquestionably more numerous and influential in the nineteenth century. That frame highlights the importance of women writers and also points up a positive evolution, from women as emblems of revolution with Staël and Shelley near the beginning of the century to women as social or economic beneficiaries of the revolution with Sand and Charlotte Brontë.

My choice of male writers—François-René de Chateaubriand, Balzac, and Charles Dickens—also deserves comment. These novelists, who played a decisive role in the development of nineteenth-century narrative literature, are often regressive in their treatment of gender issues. By regressive I mean relegating women to confining domestic or familial roles and emphasizing such negative semiotic features of women as violence, sexuality, foreign birth, and aristocracy. Balzac stands out as especially inimical to a forward-thinking approach to women. As Schor observes, "If, according to Barthes, the 'Flaubertization' of Literature marks the beginning of our modernity, I would like to suggest that its 'Balzacization' marks the divorce between women and modernity which is only now beginning to be healed."[26] But Balzac too politicized gender by promoting images of women as symbols of social processes and changing power relations, as did Chateaubriand and Dickens, and although their images are typically more regressive than those conjured up by women, there is no strict dichotomy between masculine and feminine along gender lines at the symbolic level. After all, both men and women in the nineteenth century were writing within what Schor aptly designates as "the constraints of a representational system coterminous with patriarchy."[27] The tale about the politicizing of women that I am about to tell has many participants, all of whom can be placed on a continuum in terms of how their work empowers women. There is not here a neat division into the two opposing camps of men and women or of those who empower women and those who do not. There is, however, the foundation for what Hélène Cixous and other modern feminists call "feminine writing," based on the centrality of women's control of language in certain nineteenth-century works, most but not all of which were written by women.[28]

Chapter 2 combines an analysis of Staël's immensely popular *Corinne*, a work that was written in French in 1807 in the immediate aftermath of the revolution, with an analysis of Mary Shelley's little known and rarely appreciated *The Last Man*, an English work dating from 1826. Both are palimpsests, in which the story of the French Revolution is a hidden layer under more recent stories of other political events: the Napoleonic Empire in both works as well as the Greek revolution of the 1820s in *The Last Man*. What links these two works is their similar use of a neoclassical style and allegorization of women in order to make visible that largely hidden layer. Other reasons for combining these works include the fact that Shelley quotes *Corinne* within the pages of *The Last Man* and that the two writers had recourse to such common semiotic elements as the sibyl and opposing nationalities. There also is the admittedly extraneous fact that Shelley wrote a biographical work about Staël.

Chapter 3 brings together two French works, one contemporaneous with the revolutionary events—David's painting *Marat assassiné*—and the other written three decades later—a short work by Balzac entitled *La Fille aux yeux d'or*. The fact that David and Balzac are politically antithetical—the former stands firmly on the Left and the latter on the Right—illuminates through contrast in chapter 3 what the juxtaposition of Staël and Shelley accomplishes largely through similarity in chapter 2. But although David's prorevolutionary and Balzac's counterrevolutionary uses of the process of politicizing gender differ greatly, *Marat assassiné* and *La Fille aux yeux d'or* have recourse to such similar semiotic elements as names, the feminized male body, and women's writing, which function in certain ways to empower women. Among the many features that forge links between these seemingly disparate works, one can note their common focus on violent acts by women and certain curious onomastic similarities among their principal political participants.

Chapter 4 treats the sexualizing of family relations in a group of closely related French works that date from the first decade of the nineteenth century: Chateaubriand's short novels *René* and *Atala* along with Girodet's painting *Atala au tombeau*, based on Chateaubriand's novel. Common to these works, which can again be described as palimpsests that only reluctantly reveal the embedded story of the revolution, is a politicized tale of incest between brother and sister. That tale, which brings to mind details rumored at the time of the revolution about Marie Antoinette's illicit sexual activities and her alleged incestuous involvement with her son, reveals the important extent to which sexuality within the family served as a metaphor for political issues in post-revolutionary society. Moreover, Girodet's painting, by providing an illuminating set of comparisons and contrasts with David's, makes it possible to record significant changes in the process of politicizing gender in the decades following the revolutionary events.

Chapter 5 groups Staël's well-known *Delphine*, published in 1802, with one of Balzac's lesser-known novels, *La Rabouilleuse*, published several decades later. What they share is a common indictment of mothers, who are held responsible in a variety of ways for the political ills besetting contemporary French society. Although similarly forceful in their symbolic censure of maternity as a viable political substitute for traditional patriarchy, these two works differ greatly in the relationship between women and politics that they evoke. Balzac's maternal figures, although empowered in the public sphere, are uniformly negative, whereas Staël's exercise power in conjunction or opposition with other feminine figures who balance or neutralize their pernicious effects.

Chapter 6, like chapter 2, dwells on novels by a French and an English woman novelist: Brontë's *Shirley* and Sand's *Nanon*. In this chapter the novels date, however, from much later in the nineteenth century. Not surprisingly, then, other events—Chartism in England, 1848 and the Commune in France—are interwoven with the story of the French Revolution. *Shirley* is a palimpsest in which the revolution can be deciphered under the direct account of more recent historical events. *Nanon* reverses the process by dealing directly with the revolution and burying the story of current political events at a less visible level. Common also to these two otherwise disparate works is the political implication of marriage. In both works, marriage serves to unite nationalities, classes, or genders in ways that are empowering for women. For both Brontë and Sand, marriage provides ways for women to gain control of property and power in bourgeois society.

The Epilogue takes a look at a classic of world literature, as the beginning of this introduction did somewhat more briefly with *Le Père Goriot*. That classic is *A Tale of Two Cities*, from which many of us derived our first and most lasting symbolic image of the French Revolution. Discovering a broad range of the processes studied in this book through an analysis of Dickens's novel makes it possible to summarize the semiotic, political method proposed here and to emphasize the interrelatedness of all of those processes, which, for the sake of developing my argument, I treat separately in the earlier chapters. Applying that method to one of the most familiar stories of the French Revolution and interpreting that novel as a story of politicizing gender confirm one last time my argument in this book that gender bears a far larger burden in telling the revolutionary tale than we have tended to suspect.

2

Allegorizing Women:
Corinne and *The Last Man*

Germaine de Staël's *Corinne* and Mary Shelley's *The Last Man* have in common a neoclassical style, which consists of the use of heroic figures, artificial language, and an antique setting. Neoclassicism goes hand in hand in both works with allegorizing women characters as symbolic participants in the collective story of the French Revolution. Although neoclassicism was popular in France under republican and imperial forms of government that severely curtailed women's political rights, and although it represented women in allegorical ways that seem to strip them of their individuality, I want to argue that it was not inherently incompatible with a progressive attitude toward women and society. On the contrary, in the hands of women writers, that very style helped to assert women's political role, in a variety of indirect ways to be examined in this chapter.

Staël's novel stands out as an especially significant example of a woman writer's use of neoclassicism to assert woman's role, notably through her heroic presentation of Corinne. *Corinne*, first published in 1807, was avidly consumed in more than forty editions by nineteenth-century readers, many of whom found in it a source of inspiration because of the heroic model of woman as genius that it provided. Sand is one of many women writers who named Corinne within the pages of their novels and celebrated her in one of her well-known neoclassical poses. In *Lélia* she reflects, "Corinne, dying, must have been plunged into mournful attention when she listened to her last poems being spoken at the Capitol by a young girl." [1] Sand's tribute to *Corinne* is not

surprising for, as Ellen Moers explains, "*Corinne* served as a children's book for
a special kind of nineteenth-century child: girls of more than ordinary intelligence or talent, and rising ambition to fame beyond the domestic circle.
Reading *Corinne* made an event of their youth—for some, a catalyst to their
own literary development."[2] Prominent among the women writers identified
by Moers as having acknowledged Staël's influence are Harriet Beecher Stowe,
George Eliot, and Elizabeth Barrett Browning, who establishes obvious parallels with *Corinne* in *Aurora Leigh*.[3] Shelley's biographical sketch of Staël
contains, among other encomiums of her French predecessor, the statement
"No writer of her epoch had left such luminous ideas on her route."[4]

Before examining the works themselves, the importance of the semiotic
processes of allegory and neoclassicism in the nineteenth century needs to be
acknowledged. As noted earlier, allegorical figures, many of them female,
were abundant during the revolutionary period, especially representations of
liberty and the republic as Marianne. Allegory as a political strategy went
hand in hand with neoclassicism, the prevailing artistic style at the time of
the revolution. The widespread popularity of that style in the late eighteenth
and early nineteenth centuries forms part of the necessary backdrop for understanding *Corinne* and *The Last Man*, works that partake of the same stylized
and artificial use of classical Roman figures and settings as the china designed
by Josiah Wedgwood or David's highly popular neoclassical paintings from
the 1780s.[5]

The popularity of such a seemingly cold, uninviting style as neoclassicism
can be explained in sociopolitical terms as a rejection of the frivolous, erotic,
aristocratic style fashionable in the eighteenth century under the ancien régime. Values that would later emerge as distinctive of republicanism—
simplicity, virtue, heroism, patriotism—found cultural expression in works
inspired by antiquity such as David's celebrated *Le Serment des Horaces* (*The
Oath of the Horatii*), exhibited several years before the revolution in 1785, and
Les Licteurs rapportant à Brutus les corps de ses fils suppliciés (*Brutus receiving the
bodies of his sons*), exhibited shortly after the storming of the Bastille in 1789.
Late eighteenth-century audiences reveled in neoclassical representations of
figures who embodied bourgeois virtues of action and achievement, in contrast
with aristocratic privileges of birth and tradition. Figures that for us today
seem academic and rigid—nikes, muses, sibyls—at the time embodied nascent social values and thus evoked strong feelings. In addition to its rejection
of aristocratic values, neoclassicism bespoke the spirit of secularization that
marked the revolutionary period, in which goddesses of reason or allegories of
freedom replaced the Virgin Mary in public ceremonies and festivals.

In a culture thus permeated by allegorical processes and neoclassical style, it is not surprising that real women—those who participated in revolutionary events or art—came themselves to be allegorized. As a result, strong symbolic links that transformed women into symbols of revolution were forged; a familiar case in point is Dickens's depiction of the *tricoteuses*—women knitting during the revolution—in *A Tale of Two Cities*. The popular identification of women with revolution was rooted in the notoriety of French feminists and activists such as Olympe de Gouges and Théroigne de Méricourt, women's attendance at revolutionary political clubs, their creation of their own clubs and publications, their participation in marches and bread riots. Other women—Manon Roland, Corday, Mary Wollstonecraft—were similarly allegorized, their personal lives or individual political commitments serving as stereotypical representations of women's revolutionary involvement.

Brutus illustrates some of the typical political strategies and issues of gender involved in neoclassical style and thus can serve as a useful counterexample in examining Staël's and Shelley's far different uses of that style. By choosing the subject of Brutus, the consul of the Roman Republic who condemned his sons to death for having plotted to restore the monarchy, David followed the example of Voltaire and others in the eighteenth century, who used this and other classical subjects to hint at the political issues surrounding absolutism and rebellion, well before the onset of the revolution. What is new with David, however, is the special role that women play. In *Brutus*, as in the *Horaces* and other neoclassical paintings, masculine and feminine groups are sharply divided, and although weaknesses and strengths mark both groups, David politicizes gender by associating masculinity with the positive values of patriotism and republican virtue. Although the figure of Brutus on the left is obscured by shadow and expresses a sense of moral and emotional defeat, he and the other masculine figures display courage and physical strength, as suggested by their rigid poses and the emphasis on their feet, vehicles for movement and action. A sharply different treatment marks the group of women figures on the right. It is true that light falls on them and that David's attention to the still life on the table—the basket, scissors, ball of wool, and embroidered fabric—constitutes "a silent tribute to the world of women" in which "modest and persistent energies work to preserve life and repair it."[6] David's women are primarily associated, however, with feeling and emotional weakness, as suggested by their soft, curving bodies and clothing, and the emphasis on their arms to convey such stereotypically feminine gestures as imploring, shirking, fainting, and weeping.

Another form of politicizing gender is apparent in the statue of the goddess

1   Jacques-Louis David, *Les Licteurs rapportant à Brutus les corps de ses fils suppliciés*, 1789. Courtesy of the Musée du Louvre, Paris.

Roma in the shade behind Brutus. This feminine allegory of the republic, whose rigid pose echoes that of Brutus as the defender of the republic, legitimizes him by adding public, mythical meaning to his actions. The base of the statue, moreover, features the wolf that, according to tradition, nurtured the founders of Rome. And if it is true, as Norman Bryson observes, that the association with the wolf diminishes Brutus by placing him and the origins of Roman power "outside the human family, in feral nature,"[7] it is also true that the association suggests the vitality and endurance of his masculine values and lineage. The pose of the wolf, suckling two male children, is echoed in that of Brutus's wife, clasping to her body two female children. But whereas the wolf gives nourishment to the living—the male line of future republicans—

Brutus's wife, whose matrilineal line conspired against Brutus and the republic, can only cry for the dead, and thus her line seems doomed.[8] Bryson
observes that the fleur-de-lys pattern of the women's embroidery (visible in
the painting although lost in most reproductions) reveals Brutus's wife as
"a source of death" who, during her sons' execution, "has been busy em-
broidering monarchist emblems."[9] Portraying women as weak, using them
to legitimize masculine acts of heroism, associating them symbolically with
motherhood, and promoting the notion of a male, patrilineal legacy: these
politicizing strategies apparent in David's use of the neoclassical style differ
dramatically from Staël's and Shelley's progressive use of that style to assert
women's political role.

For those who are unfamiliar with *Corinne*, a brief summary of the plot may
prove helpful. A young British aristocrat, Oswald Lord Nelvil, travels to Italy
in the winter of 1794–1795, despondent and guilt-ridden about the death of
his father, whom he neglected while embroiled in a love affair in France. On
his arrival in Rome, he hears an oral improvisation that the celebrated poet
known as Corinne presents to an adulating crowd of Italian spectators on the
occasion of her being crowned for her artistic achievements. Corinne's perfection in both the English and Italian languages intrigues Oswald; the two
meet, fall in love, and conduct the numerous visits to ancient monuments and
the Italian countryside that are described in such great length in the novel.
Oswald learns eventually that Corinne had lived in the British Isles and met
his father, who strongly disapproved of her as a potential spouse for his son
because of her excessively independent, artistic ways. Torn between love on
the one hand and respect for paternal authority, convention, and tradition on
the other, Oswald chooses the latter and marries Corinne's half-sister Lucile.
Corinne dies, despondent and incapable of reviving her artistic powers. But
because before her death she succeeds in exercising a strong influence on
Oswald's and Lucile's daughter Juliette, the novel closes on the positive note
of a feminine intellectual and creative legacy: the very legacy that Staël herself
passed on to her female successors like Shelley. Whereas David's *Brutus*

represents heroic men and allegorized mothers' passing social values on to sons, Staël represents heroic women and artists' passing those values on to daughters.

Critics have acknowledged, but not fully explored, the political elements in *Corinne*, which Simone Balayé characterizes as "quite clearly evoked in the novel."[10] Similarly, they have observed, but not sufficiently delved into, the focus in that novel on the facts and symbols of the French Revolution. Henri Coulet warns us not to forget, in reading Staël, "to what extent revolutionary events were crucial to her thinking, with the hopes they aroused in her and the disappointment their outcome caused her, and how, without appearing in the forefront of her works of fiction, the revolution inspired the creation of her characters, their relationships, and the structure of her plots."[11]

The focus on the politics of the French Revolution in *Corinne* is, however, only indirect, a fact that is consistent with the role of politics generally in the works and lives of women writers in the late eighteenth and nineteenth centuries. Staël's strong political views found other such indirect means of expression through the influence she exerted in her salon or on the careers of her husband and her lover Narbonne. As Carla Peterson remarks, "Exiled by Napoleon, relegated to the sidelines of history, condemned to watch helplessly as power-wielding men determined the direction of French history, Mme. de Staël had only the recourse of writing her own female epic."[12] And Charlotte Hogsett notes, in a related vein, that whereas Staël's model Jean-Jacques Rousseau or her contemporaries Benjamin Constant and Chateaubriand wrote both confessionally and politically, following the rhetorical rules of accepted literary genres, such writing was considered inappropriate for women. That critic concludes, "Perhaps one reason why the writing of many women has not been adequately appreciated, why not as many works by women find their way into those canonized as the great classics, is that in many cases women writers do not work according to that kind of rhetorical rule."[13] Efforts currently being made by feminist critics to restore women writers to their rightful place in the canon will perhaps be furthered by the recognition that their "female epics" and "rhetorical rule" were distinctly, albeit indirectly, political in nature.

We can turn now to the first of three narrative strategies through which political issues are indirectly raised in *Corinne*, the treatment of Corinne as an allegory of the republic. What is at issue is not only woman as liberty and the republic but woman as representative of a new, nonroyal, nonaristocratic class. In Staël's novel, Corinne embodies certain of the new values of that emerging class, in sharp opposition to the fixed, traditional values of her aristocratic lover Oswald Lord Nelvil. In the nascent system of bourgeois values with which she can often be identified, superiority is based on talent and merit, not on genealogy and tradition, as in his older system of aristocratic values.

One key scene in *Corinne* presents a salient illustration of that character's allegorical presentation as a figure of the republic and the newer system of nonaristocratic values. In chapter 2, Corinne appears before the adoring eyes of Nelvil and the Italian people as what Madelyn Gutwirth has identified as sibyl and nike,[14] seated on a "chariot built in the ancient style,"[15] ascending the stairs of the capitol, to the sound of music and canons. In addition to personifying talent and merit, she emerges in this scene as a figure of liberty and the republic, not only by the repeated emphasis on the adulation of her by the people, with whom she shares the virtues of simplicity and spontaneity but also by the tricolor setting in which she appears: white and blue in her clothing ("She wore a white tunic with a blue drapery fastened beneath her breast") and red in the background ("Everyone came forward to see her from their windows which were decorated with potted plants and scarlet hangings") (21). Corinne's clothing in this scene recalls the "imagined simplicity of classical republican dress" designed by David, which Warner describes as follows: "The style was patriotically termed 'en gaule', and was created by muslin-like shifts, usually white to connote purity" with a sash under the bust, to emphasize woman as nurturer.[16]

Corinne's appearance can also be linked to the use of living allegories during the revolutionary period, that is, the employment of live female models as participants in revolutionary festivals. Through that practice, the revolutionary governments attempted, with only partial success, to replace traditional religious symbolism. Of the pietà-like pose of David's painting of Marat's death, to be discussed in the next chapter, Anita Brookner observes, "The gradual elision of the boundaries between sacred and profane is one of the most fascinating stylistic accomplishments of the Revolution."[17] Not surprisingly, then, one notes that, although appearing as an allegorical representation of freedom, Corinne also appears constantly in a religious, divine guise: "She is a goddess among the clouds" (21), "a priestess of Apollo" (21); "No longer a fearful woman, she was an inspired priestess" (32). The text also identifies her as sibyl ("She was dressed like Domenichino's Sibyl, an Indian turban wound round her head," [21]), a symbol of feminine genius.

Whether as a divinity, nike, sibyl, personification of liberty, or object of adulation by the people, the triumphant Corinne at the beginning of the novel is clearly associated with the positive, moderate, non-Jacobin side of revolution and with the lofty goals and aspirations that Staël conceived after 1793 for a republic controlled by the emerging middle class. Corinne's symbolism points to the first stage of the revolution, before the Terror, when hopes for genuine and lasting freedom were possible and when an ideal synthesis of the best in aristocratic and bourgeois values seemed feasible. Gutwirth sums up Corinne's revolutionary significance when she designates her as "a goddess of excess who, like the revolution, was guilty of having expected too much from mankind." [18]

The second narrative strategy to be considered here is closely associated with the first: the treatment of Corinne as an analogue of Italy. The close association between the two strategies stems from the fact that, like the revolution in its positive phase and like Corinne as a representative of non-aristocratic values, Italy represents freedom, liberation from oppressive traditions, enlightenment through artistic achievement, and classical simplicity and humility. [19] With respect specifically to tradition, Italy stands in sharp contrast to England, which is depicted in *Corinne* as embodying an aristocratic commitment to the past, family lines, and property. This is not the England of liberalism and constitutionalism that Staël strongly admired at other points in her writing career, but rather the England at war with France after 1793, harboring French émigrés and menacing France with the restoration of the ancien régime through force.

The symbolic value of Italy in contrast to aristocratic England is enhanced by the novel's further identification of Italy with the feminine, which has already been seen to have privileged links with the newer, nonaristocratic class. Italy is tied to the maternal in the novel by virtue of Corinne's mother's being Italian. Moreover, there are repeated references to the feminine nature of Italy and to Rome as a female ruler of the world: "Liberty made her queen"; "queen, too, by her scepter of thought"; and so on (27), and to Italy as the country of artistic rather than military power. Marie-Claire Vallois notes in this regard the appropriateness of the full title *Corinne ou l'Italie* for a work in which Italy and woman are intimately related. [20]

The nonaristocratic significance of Italy is also enhanced by the values and aspirations of its people. If the Italian people worship Corinne it is because as the embodiment of the republic she is the ideal of a country whose people hark back to the republic of ancient times. Common to Italy, the people, and Corinne as the feminine embodiment of the republic are such qualities as simplicity, spontaneity, and imagination. Moreover, the people, Italy, women, and the republic are presented in the novel as similarly lacking in power and autonomy, and accordingly as subject in like fashion to oppression. Italy in *Corinne* is a mere shadow of its former glory, and its interest in the arts reflects its political and military impotence. Thus it is unable to resist such nefarious forces of power as Napoleon, whose oppression of women like Staël and whose destruction of the republic constitute, as Vallois reminds us, the true "unsaid" of *Corinne*.[21]

The close association of the people, Italy, and women marks the treatment of narrative voice throughout the novel. Corinne's specialty is oral improvisation, an essentially female art form that is shown to be highly valued in Italy and is identified as especially appropriate for the people: "It lends something poetic to the lowest orders of society" (44). More generally, orality marks Corinne's role as narrator. Her monologues on the arts, travelogues on Italy, improvisations, descriptions of nature, and the like, provide the novel's chief narrative components. In this distinctly feminine novel, close ties are also established among femininity, orality, and the return to maternal origins in Italy. Peterson remarks, "Mme. de Staël is clearly subscribing to the myth of spoken language as unmediated presence, plenitude, a return to nature, and recovery of origins." And that myth of spoken language is sustained throughout the novel, if not by Corinne herself, whose voice is less distinct near the end, then by the female narrator who stands with her throughout the text and who "gradually comes to displace Corinne as the center of the novel."[22] Staël's allegorization of Italy thus has the important function of valorizing the feminine literary voice and, by implication, a pre-Oedipal, mother-centered language. For, as Julia Kristeva observes, one of the only ways to reject paternal authority is through oral forms (music, rhythm, prosody, paragrams), which permit the reunion with the mother's body. Underlying Kristeva's observation is the Lacanian contention that we accede to the patriarchal law represented by the father's name—the "non/nom du père"—by acceding to highly structured, symbolic uses of language. Only through other, more poetic forms of language, then, can we escape from the father's authority.[23] It is this escape that the oral, feminine literary voice in *Corinne* strives to achieve.

Further evidence that Italy is far more than a geographical and cultural entity in *Corinne* can be seen in the decline of its narrative importance during the course of the novel. That decline reflects and reinforces the popular nineteenth-century notion of degeneration, which closely associated political, physical, and moral factors and which typically linked women, illness, and society.[24] Italy shows its most resplendent, enlightening side at the beginning of the novel, as did the revolution in its early phase. The novel then depicts the gradual period during which the wonders of Italy are exhausted by Corinne, a period analogous to the decline of the revolution after 1791. That decline is expressed thematically through the consistent emphasis in the novel on the bad air in Italy. Revealingly, the nefarious effects of that bad air are most pronounced in Rome, the site of the ancient republic, and are experienced in the form of contagious disease by Corinne, the embodiment of the republic. Finally, the novel suggests the triumph of England over Italy, as toward the end Oswald assumes full control of the novel and asserts English male virility by assuming the role of war hero. At the close, Italy, like Corinne and the positive early side of the revolution, has been largely eclipsed and silenced although, as noted earlier, Corinne's influence on her niece Juliette suggests the promise of an enduring feminine legacy.

The third narrative strategy to be considered here is the treatment of Corinne as a substitute and alternative king and father. That the patriarchal roles of king and father have been inextricably linked throughout history is well known and is stressed within the pages of the novel itself, when, in an aristocratic spirit of allegiance to family and king, Oswald designates paternity as a "noble image of a supremely good master" (182). Although not referred to as such within the pages of the novel, the national loss of the king Louis XVI during the Terror can be seen as underlying and explaining the kind of obsessive sense of guilt and loss that Oswald, more than Corinne, is portrayed as feeling, although both characters are depicted in the novel as having lost their fathers, whom they loved very much. As the narrator observes near the beginning of the novel, "Indeed, how is it ever possible to replace that affection born with us, the natural empathy of blood relations, the friendship that heaven compounds to unite a child and his father?" (17).

Corinne does attempt, however, both to replace the father and the king and to propose meaningful alternatives to traditional patriarchal and aristocratic figures of power. In the public domain, Corinne first emerges as an alternative king in the key scene of her crowning as a poet, with its unmistakable overtones of the crowning of Staël's archenemy Napoleon. Like this ruler, Corinne has aspirations to heroic stature and glory and is adulated by the people. Such aspirations strike a remarkably modern note. For in her role as substitute king, Corinne not only promotes the value of women; she also acts to grant women, if only symbolically and indirectly, the political powers of men. One is reminded of a contemporary example, Monique Wittig's "guérillères," who are not content merely to be lovers and nurturers but strive to perform as rulers and fighters as well.[25] The importance of Corinne's role in this regard as an alternative to patriarchal power cannot be overemphasized. For although Staël ultimately fails to valorize the notion of a female alternative to male power in society or even within the family *politically*, she does promote that notion *symbolically*, an important consideration in a period when the political and the symbolic were inextricably linked. In the final analysis, Corinne proposes a far more meaningful alternative to traditional power than do other, male figures depicted or evoked in the novel. Unlike her absolutist, aristocratic lover Oswald, she values cultural diversity and liberation from mere tradition. Although she is Italian and Catholic, she points out to Oswald: "Our principles are liberal, our dogmas are absolute; and yet in practice, our despotic orthodoxy comes to terms with individual circumstances, and your religious freedom requires that its laws be followed without exception" (181). Moreover, she is presented in the novel as an antithesis rather than the female equivalent of Napoleon. She is a peace-loving ruler whose crown is earned for merit not traditional privilege, whose glory is aesthetic not military, whose freedom is gained through the powers of the mind and the pen rather than brute force and the sword. She stands as an alternative to Napoleon's absolutist aspirations to royalty and aristocracy as emperor.

In the private domain, Corinne plays an equally significant and modern role as substitute father, for both herself and Oswald. For herself, she replaces the father by assuming, on his death, the control that a father traditionally exercised over his daughter's life. She succeeds thereby in escaping the rigid patterns that his English upper-class society sought to impose on her. Her rejection of her father's name is symptomatic in this regard of her larger rejection of patriarchal authority, which in *Corinne* marks the aristocracy most visibly, although in reality it similarly characterized the nascent bourgeoisie as well. It is true that she ultimately fails in her attempt to replace the father: revealingly, she adopts the traditional Catholic form of address to a confessor at the end, stating "Father now that you know my sad destiny, judge me" (418). It is nonetheless her valiant if only transitory success prior to the end that gives her heroic stature.

For Oswald, Corinne replaces the father by assuaging his feelings of filial guilt and loss. In one crucial scene during his illness, she even assumes a male voice by reading aloud to him from his father's spiritual reflections. But whereas she succeeds to some extent in her own life in breaking out of the aristocratic patterns represented by paternal influence, Oswald remains a prisoner of and reactionary adherent to them. It is significant to note in this regard that he, not Corinne, is the chief figure of conflict in the novel, the character who is torn between the competing demands of the old and the new, between allegiance to the aristocratic patriarchal father and the bourgeois substitute father. Revealingly, the novel begins with him in the winter of 1794–1795, at the moment when the Terror had reached its end, when the fate of the republic, torn between the forces of reaction and revolution, was at issue. And it is he who, by rejecting the alternative to patriarchal authority that she proposes, symbolically kills both her and the republic, as did the similarly male, absolutist figures of the ancien régime, the Terror, and the empire. His role as a figurative assassin is underlined in the text. Maija Lehtonen notes, "Corinne feels as though she has been sentenced to death," and she calls attention to the revealing existence of scaffold images in Staël's novel. She concludes, "All these images make Oswald seem like a murderer." [26] If men have killed the republic in the past, Staël suggests, they should in their future efforts to restore it give serious consideration to the alternative models that women like Corinne have to offer.

In short, it is possible to cast Staël in a more positive feminist role than she has typically been credited with playing. On the basis of the thoroughgoing political nature of *Corinne*, I would urge that politics along with love provide the keys to interpreting that novel. Corinne must be betrayed because the revolution was, and not just because Oswald preferred Lucile. She must die because the early dreams for the revolution did, and not just because she was the hopeless romantic that some readers might take her to be. Such an interpretation highlights the political significance of a novel whose feminist importance has often been questioned. When viewed romantically, that novel seems to glorify submission to male control. When the romantic is placed in the larger political context to which it belongs, *Corinne* can be seen to call into question, if not openly reject, paternal models of authority. Through her indirect presentation of key political and class issues surrounding the French Revolution, Staël can today be seen as having promoted a new system of nonaristocratic values in which women had a highly significant, if still largely symbolic, role to play.

Mary Shelley's lesser-known work *The Last Man*, published in 1826, is a novel preceded by a narrative frame, which consists of a short "author's introduction." Since that introduction is part of the novel, I will resist the temptation to take the author as Shelley herself and will instead treat the "frame author" as a fictional entity and narrative participant. The frame author is presented as traveling with a companion to Italy in 1818. There they find the pages of a book containing a story that the narrator Lionel Verney, the "last man," supposedly wrote, surprisingly, in the year 2099. The point of the frame is to explain and give credence to the truth of this account of the future. The explanation that the frame author presents of how a work written in the future could be found in the present is that a visionary sibyl served as Lionel's intermediary, transcribing his story at some unspecified moment before 1818 through her ability to read the future. The frame author then retranscribed the sibyl's pages.

Having passed through the narrative frame, the reader enters Lionel's first-person narration of how he alone survived the worldwide annihilation from the plague that occurred in the twenty-first century. His tale begins, as we have come to expect, first with the death of the father, who leaves Lionel and his beloved sister, Perdita, as penurious orphans, and then with the loss of the king, who abdicates in favor of a republican form of government in the year 2073, several years before his death. The king's enlightened son Adrian befriends the two children, thereby acquitting himself of an unpaid debt of gratitude that the king owed to Lionel's father, banished from the court on the spiteful order of the queen. With the death of the king, various factions arise that provide transitory alternatives to the republican principles to which Adrian and Lionel remain faithful. Political complications are doubled by romantic ones. Although Lionel is happy in his marriage to Adrian's sister, the former English princess Idris, Perdita is less fortunate with her ambitious and unfaithful husband Lord Raymond, who is lured away from her by the seductive Greek princess Evadne. Personal and social problems are gradually eclipsed in importance, however, by the menace of a deadly plague, whose presence is first noticed in Constantinople during the Greek uprising against Turkish oppression. The futile attempts made collectively to arrest the deadly disease constitute the main events of the last half of the novel.

As this summary of the plot reveals, *The Last Man* is a diffuse work, which not surprisingly has remained unpopular with general readers and critics alike since the time of its publication. It is also a work that has been considered difficult to classify because although it does not conform neatly to definitions of science fiction, the fantastic, or the gothic novel, it nevertheless has some affinity with each of these genres. To highlight its allegorization of women and its neoclassical style may not provide a ready-made generic category but will shed new light on its political and feminine meaning.

Allegorization affects the treatment of narrative voice, which in *The Last Man* is distributed among three narrative participants, whom I want to read as three faces of the feminine, prophetic sibyl. They are the fictional "author"

of the frame, the sibyl or "Cumaean damsel," and the embedded narrator
Lionel Verney. Although the first two disappear after the author's introduction, the strangeness of Lionel's position in the twenty-first century implicitly
reminds the reader throughout the novel that his narration, far from standing
alone, derives from other narrative sources. What unites the three figures
moreover as a single three-sided narrative entity is their ability to capture and
recreate each other's innermost thoughts. The allegorical figure of the sibyl
demonstrates this ability by portending the future, conjuring up the futuristic
tale of the last man. Similarly the author has gained entry into the thoughts
of the sibyl by not only transcribing her written words but imaginatively
reconstructing them: "Sometimes I have thought that, obscure and chaotic as
they are, they owe their present form to me, their decipherer. . . . Doubtless
the leaves of the Cumaean Sibyl have suffered distortion and diminution of
interest and excellence in my hands." [27]

The existence of close ties among the narrative participants in *The Last Man*
leads me to hypothesize that the feminine gender of the neoclassical sibyl can
be read as extending indirectly to the frame author and the narrator Lionel.
Extratextual evidence supports this idea. The frame author's travels with a
companion to Italy in 1818 mirror those of the female author Mary Shelley's,
with Percy Shelley, to Naples in that year. The novel has frequently been
viewed as a roman à clef in which Adrian represents Percy Shelley; Lord
Raymond, Lord Byron; and Lionel, Mary Shelley herself. One nineteenth-
century reviewer even asked why the author did not simply acknowledge
having written a novel about "the last Woman." [28] In a further intertextual
mode, the novel hints at Lionel's identification with Corinne, who is identified
as the sibyl in Staël's novel. Among those hints are the fact that Lionel ends
his days in Rome visiting monuments, one of Corinne's favorite occupations,
and that he actually evokes her in the text: "I called to mind Corinna ascending
the Capitol to be crowned, and, passing from the heroine to the author,
reflected how the Enchantress Spirit of Rome held sovereign sway over the
minds of the imaginative" (336). Feminine gender will also be seen later to
characterize the addressee of Lionel's narration. The novel thus suggests the
possibility of a feminine legacy, of a feminized narrator's passing on truths to
subsequent generations of women.

The fact that femininity thus surrounds the narrative voice in *The Last Man*
through association with the sibyl, Corinne, and Mary Shelley sheds new light
on the narrator Lionel, who can too easily be dismissed as merely a "passive
observer of political and natural disasters." [29] It should be remembered that

this highly political work was written by a woman, and one who directly incorporated femininity into the narrative process through the allegory of the sibyl, which promotes a heroic, visionary image of the woman writer. True, Lionel is gendered as male, as are most of the major political positions represented in the novel. Like Staël, Shelley could conceive only indirect expressions of her political views. But her novel is obviously not meant to be free of political considerations of feminine gender. Nor does it represent women in the exclusively nurturing and emotional roles discovered earlier in David's *Brutus*.

In addition to the tripartite narrative voice, the allegorization of women also plays an important role in the reenactment of the French Revolution that *The Last Man* presents. That reenactment can be accounted for in terms of three political phases: the ancien régime, the empire, and the republic. With respect to all three, women are allegorized, although not always in positive terms; *The Last Man* also has recourse to negative stereotypes of women as foreign and sexual. An overridingly positive image can be detected in the novel as a whole, however, through the portrait of Idris, who, like Staël's Corinne, embodies the republic, with the emphasis placed in Shelley's case on its egalitarian principles.

The Last Man begins as did *Corinne* with the loss of absolute patriarchal power. In Staël's work, that loss was represented symbolically as the death of Corinne's and Oswald's fathers. In Shelley's novel, it is represented both symbolically as the death of Lionel's father and directly as the abdication and death of the king. The diminution and eventual disappearance of the king's power, which precipitate the end of the ancien régime in *The Last Man*, are attributed by some characters to the king's weakness in abdicating, as many people have singled out Louis XVI's weakness in failing to control the revolutionary events. The king was frequently mocked for his weakness, as in the satiric drawing of him by the British caricaturist James Gillray in March 1793 entitled *Louis XVI Taking Leave of His Wife and Family*. It bears the inscription "The above is an exact copy of an infamous French print, which has lately appeared in Paris, among numberless others, intended to bring the conduct of their late monarch in his last moments into contempt & ridicule." The issue of the king's weakness in Shelley's novel is echoed moreover in that of his closest adviser, Lionel's father, whose flawed handling of money (gambling) parallels that of Jacques Necker, Staël's father and the chief economic adviser to Louis XVI, by failing to deal squarely with the nation's budgetary crisis. The theme of the weakness of patriarchal aristocrats is echoed repeatedly in

2   James Gilray, *Louis XVI Taking Leave of His Wife and Family*, 1793.

The Last Man, for example, in the case of another father who, "though of high rank, had in the end dissipated his fortune and even destroyed his reputation and influence through a course of dissolute indulgence" (79).

Politically and economically then men from the ancien régime show weakness in *The Last Man*. But symbolically it is the feminine and foreign characters who serve to allegorize the chief defects of the old order. Following a semiotic pattern that recurs frequently in late eighteenth- and nineteenth-century culture, the aristocratic woman is singled out to represent the ills of autocratic government, and in this case aristocracy is coupled with the otherness of the outsider. Consider the queen, who is clearly fashioned after the historical model of Marie Antoinette. Like her historical counterpart, Shelley's twenty-first-century queen is Austrian, fashionable, married to a weak king, mother of a girl and a boy, and excessively haughty. Semiotically her most important quality, however, is her aristocracy, which Shelley follows Staël in denigrating in order to promote the primacy of middle-class values. Foremost among the major characters, the queen refuses to renounce her class privileges and resists sympathizing with the plight of objects of injustice.

A related but somewhat different semiotic process affects the Greek princess Evadne Ziami. Evadne duplicates the devalorization of the foreign, aristocratic woman found also in the queen, with a particular accent placed here on the duplicity of language and form, what one could call the deceptive signifier. An insidious letter first indicates her duplicitous nature. That letter, an elegant but insincere message of love (23), is symptomatic of Evadne's false behavior toward Adrian, which will reduce him to mental and physical incapacity. Evadne also makes use of the deceptive signifier in her drawing, which "was new but faulty . . . Raymond contemplated it with delight; the more he gazed, the more pleased he was; and yet the errors multiplied under inspection" (77). What is at issue semiotically in Evadne's case is the linguistic threat associated at the time with aristocratic women at the court and in salons. Their use of language conformed to a stereotype reinforced during the revolutionary period in France according to which aristocratic women used language in artificial, stylized, emasculating ways. [30]

That for Shelley these allegorized aristocratic, foreign women are as much victims as agents of social ills is a point that becomes even more evident in the second phase of the revolutionary drama in *The Last Man*, that phase bearing on imperial government. The key male player in this case is Lord Raymond, whose French model is acknowledged directly as Napoleon: "I intend to be a warrior, a conqueror; Napoleon's name shall vail to mine" (40). Like that emperor, whom Shelley following Staël denounces, Raymond is bellicose, ambitious, and monarchist. Although he leaves England to fight and die for the freedom of the Greeks against their Turkish oppressors, the motives for his foreign entanglements are largely imperialistic. Significantly, a woman functions in the novel to allegorize his excessive ambition and militarism. Deserting Adrian, whose mild republican nature fails to excite her passion, Evadne follows Raymond to Greece and engages in battle as a revolutionary fighter. Her bellicose role is doubly stigmatized in the novel. Evadne is presented as sexually and unfemininely threatening in her relationship with Raymond and her amazonlike role as a revolutionary participant: "The dress of this person was that of a soldier, but the bared neck and arms, and the continued shrieks discovered a female thus disguised" (131). At one point in the novel she is compared to a Grecian statue (78), and at the moment of her death she is designated as a "monument of human passion and human misery," before being buried in "her warrior shroud" (132).

Shelley's treatment of Evadne conforms to a semiotic and political pattern that is common in nineteenth-century literature. In the postrevolutionary period, as Warner observes, "The women who call to mind revolutionary Liberté are often seen as sexual beings, driven by passion, not political consideration."[31] To a significant extent, the sexualization of revolutionary women derives from Burke, as mentioned earlier. W.J.T. Mitchell observes,

> Burke is especially concerned to stress the sexual, and particularly the feminine character of the violence, alluding perhaps to the popular notion that men in women's clothing participated in the march to Versailles. . . . This is unnatural, feminine violence, a reversal of the natural order of strength and weakness; perhaps even worse, the "abused shape" of a transvestite mob.[32]

Evadne's allegorical presentation in *The Last Man* owes much to this characterization of revolutionary violence as feminine, sexual, and deviant. Later in the century, as Armstrong explains, that same characterization lives on in writers who express hostility toward the working class through the figure of the prostitute, or who describe class conflict as "sexual misconduct and family scandal."[33]

The contrast between Raymond and Evadne with respect to gender and nationality sheds important light on Shelley's allegorization of women. Although born and buried in Greece, Raymond is a prototypically French and Napoleonic figure, whose excessive ambitions correspond to the same masculine search for power that Shelley decries in the figure of Victor Frankenstein. Not surprisingly Raymond proclaims near the time of his death, "I thought that the title of Victor of Constantinople would be written on my tomb" (141). In Victor Frankenstein too, as I have recorded elsewhere, the male drive to power coincides with symbolic French nationality.[34] Sterrenburg perceptively observes of both of these male characters that for Shelley, "Projects for the improvement of mankind produce demonic results." He continues, "*The Last Man* contains far more references to actual history and politics than *Frankenstein*, yet in both novels a previous age of revolution gives way to isolation, demonism, and death. . . . As in *Frankenstein*, the world becomes haunted with phantoms and monsters that are a fatal nemesis."[35]

Raymond's masculine gender and symbolic French nationality stand in sharp contrast with Evadne's allegorization as a feminine victim, like the Greek nation. True, she is a monstrous, sexual hybrid, like Balzac's "others," an androgynous pariah like Frankenstein's monster. But like the monster and

Greece in its war with Turkey, on which the novel dwells at length, she is the victim, not the oppressor. Greece is symbolized by Evadne in much the same way that Italy is by Corinne. Greece in *The Last Man* suffers as the object of a masculine, militaristic drive for power that parallels the conquest of Italy, for which Staël denounced Napoleon. Both countries, significantly, represent culture as opposed to war, and both connect with the classical heritage that Shelley and Staël seek to preserve through their adoption of a neoclassical style. Not surprisingly Shelley gives names with classical overtones to all three of her major feminine characters: Idris, Evadne, and Perdita. Like women, Greece and Italy are victims, and their oppressors are the patriarchal figures who have replaced those of the ancien régime under the Napoleonic empire.

To turn now to the third phase of Shelley's enactment of the French Revolution in *The Last Man* is to consider the opposition between England in the first half of the novel and the world beset by the plague in the second half. England illustrates the virtues of republican government devoted to the principle of equality, whereas the plague-ridden world provides a symbolic depiction of the Terror. Shelley's plague arises significantly in 2092. That date and the many others supplied in the novel correspond exactly, by subtracting 300, to the key events prior to and during that violent reign. Although the plague affects all countries, the penultimate decimation of humankind—the reduction of the remaining survivors from thousands to merely fifty, prior to the ultimate reduction to merely one—occurs in the novel in France, following violent internecine feuds clearly drawn from the historical model of French politics after 1793.

The allegorization of women again plays a key role here. England at the beginning of the novel, like Switzerland in *Frankenstein* before the creation of the monster, is marked by femininity, domesticity, simplicity, and humility, all of which are associated with the egalitarian, nonaristocratic values of the republic. Lionel and Perdita, members of the oppressed lower classes, whose lot the republic strove to better, are joined in their humble, rural existence by the compassionate, egalitarian nobles Adrian and Idris. Together the four characters figure in the neoclassical poses of "Arcadian shepherds" (94, 110), forming the same kind of utopian union between peasants and nobility that Sand will be seen later to conjure up symbolically in *Nanon*. England in *The Last Man* is a feminine allegory, personified most saliently by the English princess Idris, whose divine nature resembles Corinne's: "her gait, goddess-like, was as that of a winged angel new alit from heaven's high floor" (35); "that form is the temple of a residing deity" (248). She is born, dies, and is buried in the England she personifies, as do Corinne in Italy and Evadne in Greece. Her embodiment of "the admired type of feminine perfection" (262) is designated as deriving from "patience, forbearance, and sweetness," qualities that are named "peculiarly feminine virtues" and "particularly English" (301).

English, republican, domestic, egalitarian, feminine: this cluster marks the positive values allegorized in *The Last Man* by Idris and duplicated in the persons of her husband Lionel and brother Adrian, both embodiments of feminine rather than typically masculine values. With Lionel, the links with feminine gender are narrative, as noted earlier. With Adrian, they are physical and moral; he is described as slight, weak, and gentle: he says about himself, "From my childhood aspiring thoughts and high desires have warred with inherent disease and overstrained sensitiveness" (289). The feminine functions here, as in *Corinne*, as an allegory of liberty and the republic, of woman as representative of a new, nonroyal, nonaristocratic class. In both, however, the feminine principle declines in importance during the course of the novel. So too did the positive, moderate, non-Jacobin side of revolution decline and yield to the masculine, violent principles embodied in the Terror. The two novels are remarkably similar in their depiction of that decline as an intertwined process of physical and social degeneration that links femininity and illness. *The Last Man* echoes *Corinne* notably in its similar emphasis on the theme of bad air: "As it was an epidemic, its chief force was derived from pernicious qualities in the air" (178). At the close, both feminine allegories of the republic, Corinne and Idris, have been similarly eclipsed and silenced by forces unleashed by masculine figures of power, violence, and destruction.

Curiously, the plague itself figures as a feminine allegorical figure, which shares with Evadne and the queen the negative connotations of aristocracy, although ultimately the plague is shown to be a by-product of maleficent masculine forces. Near the end Lionel declares, "I saw plague no more. She abdicated her throne, and despoiled herself of her imperial sceptre among the ice rocks that surrounded us. She left solitude and silence co-heirs of her kingdom" (310). As this image suggests, the plague has strong thematic links with the monster in *Frankenstein*, who is similarly portrayed in arctic and alpine settings. Both are forces set in motion, like the Terror, as a result of masculine ambitions that were revolutionary, overambitious, and lacking in moderation, foresight, or feeling. The cause of the plague is not merely fate, blind nature, something external to humanity. The cause is human, not cosmic, as is clear from the emphasis the novel places on internal dissension that exacerbates and symbolically replicates the conditions that have produced the plague. The cause lies in *man*kind. If women have a political role to play,

Shelley suggests following Staël, it is to remind men of the gentler principles
on which postrevolutionary society can be built, once power-seeking men like
Raymond and Frankenstein, who produce feminine menaces like the plague
and the monster, have been controlled. Shelley's highly critical representation
of Raymond contrasts sharply with David's largely admiring representation
of Brutus, who similarly stands for masculine violence in the name of patriotism
and republican virtue.

The fate of humanity in *The Last Man* is represented allegorically and
narratively at the close of the novel as lying in the hands of women, a feminine
empowerment that has significant class implications. The novel closes with
images of Italy, which, like women in both novels, embodies classical simplicity, equality, and freedom. The lower classes are also evoked as Lionel
makes his triumphal if solitary entry into Rome through the Porta del Popula
(335) as a representative of the people: he stresses that his lowly origins enable
him to survive in a new world in which class privileges have been rendered
meaningless (338). Traditional patriarchal figures of authority have passed
away: first the king, then Raymond, then Lionel's sons—legitimate heirs to
the traditional patriarchal monarchy—then Adrian. Lionel survives the
plague, as Corinne survived the illness brought on by the bad air of Rome;
Lionel, the sibyl, and the author live on to bear a feminine political message
of moderation and compassion. If Lionel does not die it is because that message, for Shelley, is timeless.

Like *Corinne, The Last Man* also places great hope in the notion of a feminine
legacy, of truths being transmitted to subsequent generations of women. That
legacy is passed down among Lionel, the author, and the sibyl through the
tripartite narrative act, and it is also passed on to Lionel's niece Clara, whom
he raises as his own child. Significantly, she and Adrian are the last characters
to die, and their death by drowning is a result not of the plague but of Clara's
heroic determination to revisit the classical setting in Greece where her mother
and father were buried. A similar pattern can then be discerned in both *Corinne*
and *The Last Man*: the narrator's sister marries a patriarchal figure, but their
daughter is symbolically handed over to the female or symbolically feminized
narrator to raise or influence, and thus to inculcate with feminine rather than
masculine values. What the mother lacked as a product of patriarchal society
will be rectified in the daughter; thus Corinne instills Juliette with feminine
genius and Lionel develops Clara's sense of moral fortitude. (It will be seen
later that Staël's *Delphine* also depicts the adoption of a weaker woman's daughter by a stronger, more liberated one.) There are signs, moreover, that Lionel
conceives his reader, to whom he passes on his story, as a young woman like

Clara. He speaks of his harrowing tale, "whose minutest word would curdle the blood in thy young veins," of his story as a monument "for thy instruction." And he elaborates: "Patience, oh reader! whoever thou art . . . thou wilt here read of the acts of the extinct race, and wilt ask wonderingly, if they, who suffered what thou findest recorded, were of frail flesh and soft organization like thyself. Most true, they were—weep therefore; for surely, solitary being, thou wilt be of gentle disposition" (291).

Although the participants, the countries, and the explicit gender of the narrators differ, *Corinne* and *The Last Man* thus provide remarkably similar illustrations of the narrative use of allegory and neoclassicism at the beginning of the nineteenth century to express feminine political values and to propose meaningful alternatives to traditional patriarchal and aristocratic figures of power. The existence of those alternatives has too often been overlooked, especially in Shelley's case. Thus, for example, one critic states, "She gives us the decay and fall without the renovation and progression" and "Mary Shelley could find no . . . formula for rebirth, either on a personal or a collective level."[36] True, she proposes no specific political system as providing a remedy against evils like the plague and the larger process of physical, political, and social degeneration that it reflects. But symbolically she does propose political principles—moderation, equality, freedom, simplicity—that she associates with a feminine commitment to life and culture and that, like Staël, she views as the basis of republican government and the positive revolutionary legacy. And although it is true, as Mary Poovey observes, that "successful symbolic resolutions do not by themselves materially affect the social inconsistencies that made such resolutions necessary in the first place," it is also true, as Poovey goes on to explain, that "imaginative responses to social experience *can* actively contribute to the evolution of ideology" inasmuch as "the mere representation of ideology (whether conscious or not) can sometimes expose its implicit contradictions and thus lay the groundwork for outrage and eventual change."[37] Staël's and Shelley's symbolic representations of the revolutionary legacy need to be viewed as laying such a groundwork for change.

3

Mixing Genders in *Marat assassiné* and *La Fille aux yeux d'or*

DAVID'S *Marat assassiné* depicts a key moment during the French Revolution when in 1793 Marat, a Jacobin defender of the lower classes, was killed by Corday, a Girondin descendant of the provincial aristocracy. Echoes of that act, which some have claimed actually precipitated the Terror, and echoes of its pictorial representation by David shortly after the event occurred resound in the nineteenth-century novel, as can be illustrated by Balzac's *La Fille aux yeux d'or* (*The Girl with the Golden Eyes*), a short novel included in the three-part *Histoire des Treize* (*History of the Thirteen*). The similar focus in these two works on a variety of semiotic elements—most notably, women's writing, the feminized male body, mixed categories of the masculine and feminine, names—along with the contrasting relation of those elements to social class in David's and Balzac's works are the subjects of this chapter.

Both David's painting and Balzac's short novel focus on the key moment in the now familiar story of the French Revolution when the king is replaced by an illegitimate substitute. Marat, the subject of David's painting, served as a substitute for the king inasmuch as he had come to embody the republic in the popular mind after the death of the monarch.[1] It is around the time of Louis XVI's execution that Lord Dudley, a shadowy presence on the sidelines of Balzac's novel, seeks a substitute for himself, who will marry his French mistress and act as a father for his illegitimate son, Henri de Marsay.[2] Both the painting and the novel show how these acts of substitution result in violence committed by women assassins. In David's painting, Corday is not actually depicted committing the violent act, although it will be seen shortly that her feminine presence is included in subtle but highly significant ways. In *La Fille aux yeux d'or*, de Marsay's half-sister Margarita-Euphémia Porra-béril, the marquise of San Réal, is described performing a bloodthirsty murder, and the lurid details of that description have much to say about the role of both women and politics for Balzac.

Not surprisingly, in the light of David's position on the Left and Balzac's on the Right, the versions of the common story of the French Revolution that are told in *Marat assassiné* and *La Fille aux yeux d'or* cast women in dramatically different political roles. But both versions, by focusing on violent acts by women assassins, dramatize women's role as active participants, as figures—albeit misguided or degraded—of power in the public realm. Corday and Margarita, like Wittig's "guérillères" mentioned earlier, provide militant images that go beyond the chiefly peace-loving roles that Staël and Shelley assign to women. This is not to say that David or Balzac presents a positive image of women; on the contrary, they often portray femininity as threatening, sexual, aristocratic, or foreign, and in some cases such as Margarita, all of these. They do conceive a feminine empowerment of sorts, however, by portraying women of action, and their similar ways of doing so merit critical attention. But first, two semiotic elements require a few preliminary comments: first, names; and second, the relationship between masculine and feminine genders, the central focus of this chapter.

Although names constitute only one small element, they play a privileged role in Balzac's narrative semiotics and provide a link between the two works joined together in this chapter. That link is based on the echo of *Marat* in *Marsay* and his sister *Margarita* (the "marquise"). As onomastic critics have explained, the nineteenth century subscribed widely to the notion of "mimologism," whereby sounds are linked to meanings, to the subjectivity of the producer, or to historical patterns of signification. Martine Saint-Pierre points out that for Balzac, names recall history, generate stories, link characters to their predecessors, predict their futures, and express the duality of their natures; she adds, "The determinism of names often acts at a distance, as if, almost like a genetic program, the signifier contained the seeds of the later development of the subject's activity."[3] All of these observations can lend support to the hypothesis of a hidden relation among Marat, Marsay, and Margarita. It is interesting to speculate mimologically that in Balzac's semiotic system /mar/ is a signifier whose signified is impurity; that de Marsay's and Margarita's names provide a narrative program for the moral decay and the violent events that lie ahead for them in the story; and that those names hint at Marat as a historical predecessor and personification of the Terror's legacy.

Another preliminary comment concerns the relationship between masculine and feminine genders in *Marat assassiné* and *La Fille aux yeux d'or*, the chief subject of this chapter. I want to argue that these works function paradoxically to mix the two genders and yet to retain them as separate. With David I will speak in terms of inclusion and exclusion, positing that the two processes function together, inextricably, in his treatment of femininity. With Balzac I will use the figure of the hybrid in an attempt to explain the relevance of mixed gender relationships to various phases of the revolution. What needs to be described and explained in the two works, of course, differs greatly, and thus the two parts of this chapter will follow divergent paths. One of the many threads that brings them together, however, is their common concern with the semiotic issue of how relations between genders are established.

I might add that I have learned much from Dorothy Kelly's recent exploration of similar issues in *Fictional Genders*, which shares the present inquiry's concern with the process in nineteenth-century novels of establishing relationships between genders and with the ideologies that underlie that process. A significant difference lies, however, in the fact that Kelly describes an essentially psychological process, which occurs in time during "two structural moments: the first is that of aporia and ambiguity when the two genders cannot be distinguished from each other; the second is a repositioning of the genders into their original, traditional definitions."[4] Kelly's concern is the formation of psychological subjects, who can never totally escape distinctions of gender. My concern, in contrast, is the formation of a political unconscious, which can defy biology symbolically by combining the two genders. Yet sometimes she too draws the sort of political solution that interests me, as in the case of Stendhal's *Le Rouge et le noir*, where Kelly concludes, "Julien's link to women, and the relation of gender and class that emerges in this novel, remain to haunt us and evoke a startling comparison with what has been called the emergence of the new feminine 'underclass' and feminization of poverty in our century."[5] A very similar case of politicizing gender occurs in David's *Marat assassiné*.

Cultural critics today concur that certain works not only represent history but actually participate in producing its meaning by determining how events are perceived and even perhaps the events themselves, as Burke's right-wing prophecies of violence have been said to have contributed to the sanguinary phase of the French Revolution.[6] David may well stand as Burke's counterpart on the Left. Along with his active role in organizing revolutionary festivals, opposing the academy and art establishment of his times, and participating in Jacobin politics, David painted patriotic, revolutionary works that profoundly affected the meaning of the French Revolution for all classes, including the masses. His paintings stemmed from the revolutionary conviction that the people could best be reached and attached to the revolution not through reason but through the kind of vivid visual impressions produced by depicting violence perpetrated against revolutionary martyrs. Enlisting the support of the people became especially crucial as the revolution encountered such obstacles as counterrevolutionary movements in Vendée, negative developments in the war with Austria and England, financial crises, food shortages, and attacks by the radical left-wing Enragés against the Convention.[7]

An illustration of how David's painting contributed to producing the meaning of the French Revolution can be provided through an analysis of his celebrated and, as we shall see, curiously ambiguous and feminized *Marat assassiné*,[8] commissioned by the National Convention immediately after Corday's assassination of Marat on July 13, 1793. Now, it may seem strange to characterize as "feminized" a painting that at first seems to exclude femininity altogether. For David avoids a direct representation of Corday, unlike other treatments of this subject at the time that depicted her with knife in hand such as the anonymous *La Mort du patriote Jean Paul Marat député à la convention nationale* and *La Mort de Jean Paul Marat* by Nicolas Schiavonetti. After all, why "honor" by representation the doer of a deed that you find evil or abhorrent? What better memorial to Marat than to avoid the assassin and represent her only indirectly? As French women were excluded from politics in 1793, David thus excludes Corday from his painting.[9]

I want to argue, however, that Corday's femininity, although excluded in the obvious sense of her nonrepresentation, is included and used to produce class consciousness in *Marat* through the painting's two most salient pictorial features, visual representations of the written word and the body of Marat. Although David diminished the direct significance of Corday in the act, he opened the door for connotations of femininity to arise at an indirect level, where they serve to intensify David's appeal on Marat's behalf to the people.

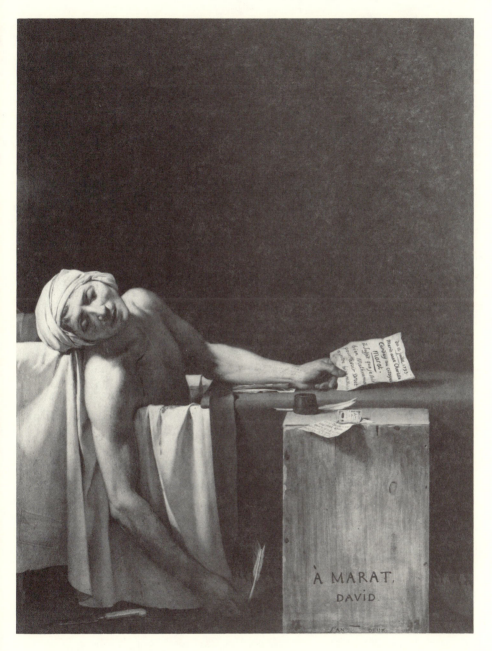

3   Jacques-Louis David, *Marat assassiné*, 1793. Courtesy of the Musées Royaux, Brussels.

LA MORT DU PATRIOTE JEAN PAUL MARAT DÉPUTÉ A LA CONVENTION NATION.ᴸᵉ en 1792; *NÉ À GENÈVE;*
Assassiné le 13 Juillet 1793, étant dans son bain, par Marie Anne Charlotte Corday ci-dev.ᵗ de Sᵗ Amans, native de Sᵗ Saturnin des Lignerets, Départem.ᵗ du Calvados.
Peuple, Marat est mort; l'amant de la Patrie   *Est tombé sous les coups d'une horde flétrie,*
Ton ami, ton soutien, l'espoir de l'affligé;   *Pleure, mais souviens-toi qu'il doit être vengé.*
(Paris, chez Basset, M.ᵈ d'Estampes, rue Sᵗ Jacques, au coin de celle des Mathurins.)

4   Anonymous, *La Mort du patriote Jean Paul Marat député à la convention nationale.*
Photo courtesy of the Bibliothèque nationale, Paris.

That appeal is developed through analogy with the suffering, vulnerability, victimization, and purity of women.

First, however, an issue that looms large on my interpretive horizon needs to be acknowledged: the problematic nature of the terms *exclusion* and *inclusion,* whose meanings vary according to their psychological, political, cultural, or other application. More is involved here than simply the exclusion and inclusion of Corday from the painting, where much depends on the expectations and historical knowledge of the viewer: a modern viewer who is only vaguely familiar with the story of Marat's assassination may not think of her in viewing the painting in the same way that David's contemporaries did. General issues are also involved, however, concerning the exclusion and inclusion of women in art and politics, as several examples showing the highly relative and often ambiguous nature of these dichotomous terms will illustrate.

5 Nicolas Schiavonetti, *La Mort de Jean Paul Marat*. Photo courtesy of the
Bibliothèque nationale, Paris.

The ambivalence underlying the psychological inclusion of women by male writers in the postrevolutionary period is Neil Hertz's subject in "Medusa's Head: Male Hysteria under Political Pressure." Hertz provides a psychoanalytic explanation of the recurrent use of highly sexualized discourse when French writers of the mid- and late nineteenth century describe revolutionary incidents. Relying on Freud's insight that a boy's fear of castration may be reenacted in later life under threatening conditions, Hertz argues that revolutionary women provoked that fear: "At the barricades, the women's—or the revolutionaries'—lack of 'property' betokens the soldiers'—or society's—risk." [10] The political and sexual threat then finds expression in such phallic revolutionary symbols as the Medusa's snakelike hair or the drooping Phrygian cap. He shows that the ambivalent psychological inclusion of women in postrevolutionary France also points to a political exclusion, and that diverse writers such as Hugo, Du Camp, and Toqueville all had recourse to similarly phallic, Medusan anecdotes in recounting contemporary political events because they were all similarly both obsessed and threatened by the inextricably linked phenomena of castration and revolution. According to Hertz, they returned compulsively to images of threatening women and thus included them psychologically while holding them at bay or excluding them politically. Hertz shows then that political exclusion was tantamount to cultural inclusion by demonstrating how vital women were, if only negatively, for articulating representations of revolution. [11]

Another example of the relative nature of the terms *inclusion* and *exclusion* can be drawn from the historical record concerning Marat and David. With Marat, political exclusion must, of course, be stressed: along with Robespierre and other republicans, he opposed women's suffrage and thus set back the political rights of women in 1793. Women played a greater role, however, in the Cordelier Club in which Marat was active than in the Jacobin Club to which Robespierre belonged and whose exclusion of women from any civic activity Marat actively challenged. Moreover, Marat's writings—his *Plan de législation criminelle* as well as *L'Ami du peuple*—provide evidence of an enlightened concern for the injustice of women's conditions, as wives, daughters, unwed mothers, or prostitutes. Not surprisingly an organization led by two women, his sister and his common-law wife, was formed during his lifetime and existed up until the middle of the nineteenth century. The organization's purpose was to promote public awareness of Marat's contributions to women and the poor. Surely it would be one-sided to cast him solely in the role of supporting the general republican exclusion of women from public life in 1793. Trying to achieve a meaningful inclusion of women in society can also be attributed to him, and, not surprisingly, several critics do speak of Marat's "feminism." [12]

The record is similarly mixed regarding David. Like Marat, he adhered to an essentially male conception of the republic that excluded women. But as an artist and teacher, he was known for his support for women artists and students. [13] And in his artistic career, he moved away from the division of masculine and feminine figures into two separate worlds that has been seen to characterize *Le Serment des Horaces* and *Brutus*, paintings in which men embodying masculine resolution and violence stand far apart from women embodying feminine suffering. A transition occurs in 1789 with *Paris et Helen* and *M et Mme Lavoisier*, in which masculine and feminine figures appear together at the center of the painting, closely linked both emotionally and pictorially. Another step occurs in the three paintings from the period of 1793–1794—*Lepelletier de Saint-Fargeau*, *Marat assassiné*, and *Joseph Bara*— all of which depict partially or totally nude revolutionary heroes, whose bodies display similarly feminized or androgynous features. [14] And a further step, to be considered in chapter 6, occurs in 1799 with *Les Sabines*, where women of action figure at the center of the painting.

If the lesson to be learned is that there are inextricable links between the exclusion and the inclusion of femininity in the revolutionary period, it does not follow that the distinction should be abandoned but rather that the distinction must be properly historicized so that the relative, contextual meaning of the painting and the larger issues of competing class interests that it raises can emerge.

In David's painting, a woman acts as either sender or indirect receiver of a letter in two acts of writing. The first instance is the letter from Corday that Marat is holding in his left hand: "July 13, 1793, Marie-Anne Charlotte Corday to citizen Marat: My great unhappiness gives me a right to your kindness." The second is another letter positioned in the foreground: "You will give this assignat to that mother of five children whose husband died in the defense of his country." [15] Clearly this is a letter written by Marat and intended for a soldier's widow.

The special legitimizing role of writing during the French Revolution helps us to understand why these representations of writing to and from women are important. The revolutionary period produced a proliferation of acts of writing—public discourses, proclamations of law, images combined with writing—by which revolutionary leaders attempted to lend authority to their actions and theories. At issue, as Marie-Hélène Huet explains, was an attempt to imbue the citizens of the nation with the authority and legitimacy that had formerly been situated in the very person of the king; accordingly, "the Assembly passed no law that was not immediately the subject of a public proclamation. . . . The written object must be proclaimed and, conversely, the proclaimed object must be put in writing, thus attesting the Assembly's constant concern for the legitimacy of its acts." And Huet also notes that acts of writing were conceived as providing access to truth: "The judicial system established by the National Constituent Assembly was conceived as a kind of anti–*lettre de cachet*. . . . Its antithesis and antidote were the public proclamation and the transcription of that proclamation, which in turn would be distributed and read aloud." [16]

Viewed in this larger context of a search for legitimacy, the existence of women as author and intended recipient of writings in *Marat* reveals David's purpose of including women in his larger goal of legitimizing that still amorphous formation known at the time as the "people." It was common at the time, as in Marat's use of that term, to blur the distinction between the urban and the rural, between the proletariat and the peasants. Milton Brown observes that in the eighteenth century, even the distinction between bourgeois and peasant "was not a conscious part of the ideology of the bourgeoisie" and that at the time of the revolution, "the consciousness of class divisions within society was limited to the distinction between aristocrat and republican." [17] In order to present Marat as the true "ami du peuple," David needed to supply material, pictorial support for the very existence of the people as a class, in this case portraying Marat as reading and responding to appeals from suffering women: we see the letter from Corday and the letter to the widow. Writing is so important to the meaning of the painting that David depicts Marat's symbolically holding a pen in his right hand, even though he is no longer writing the letter to the widow. Thus David represents Marat as legitimizing through writing the people, whose suffering is symbolized by women's suffering. David also used the feminine for purposes of legitimization when, in his speech to present the commissioned painting to the Convention, he included women among the "people" receiving the painting: "Come hither all of you! mothers, widows, orphans, down-trodden soldiers, all of you whom he defended at the risk of his life, draw near! and behold your friend; he who watched over you lives no longer. . . . O despair! our tireless defender has died. He has died, your friend, giving you his last piece of bread."[18] David thus had recourse to women in order to affirm his commitment to the people. In contrast, women's writing is reduced to a mere scribble in *La Mort du patriote* and eliminated altogether in *La Mort de Marat*. This perhaps explains why they are far less politically potent representations of the revolutionary story than David's.

A certain degree of ambiguity surrounds David's presentation of Corday's writing, however, if one identifies the viewer of the painting as visually positioned with Marat, that is, seeing the letter from his "point of view" at the moment of his death. Regarding point of view, it is important to give serious consideration to Michael Fried's theory in *Absorption and Theatricality: Painting and Beholder in the Age of Diderot* that painters in David's time, and David notably among them, sought to replace traditional *externalized* events, in which the viewer focuses on historical, dramatic actions, with highly *internalized*, "absorptive" states, in which the viewer entertains the illusion of being "with" the pictorial subject and psychologically participating in his or her internalized world. According to Fried's theory, Marat could be viewed as the subject of David's painting, absorbed in reading Corday's letter at the precise moment of his death and in the sleeplike state of dying. For as Brookner reminds us, "Marat as painted is not dead but dying; his hand can still hold the pen and the letter."[19] (An interesting contrast is formed by *La Mort du patriote*, which highlights the point of view of a masculine observer, and by *La Mort de Marat*, which highlights Corday's point of view.)

Interpreting Corday's writing as the focal point of Marat's point of view brings out David's ambiguous inclusion and exclusion of women. True, a woman's text is highlighted by the painting's point of view and thus acknowledged as important. Her textual "body"—represented by the letter—is thereby cast, however, in the disempowered role of object of the traditional "male gaze," in which the viewer (the implicit source of power) is active and masculine, whereas the object of vision (the implicit object of domination) is passive and feminine. Woman's presence in David's painting in the positive role of writer is thus counterbalanced by her relegation to the role of image, a mere object of vision.

A similar ambiguity arises with respect to the notion of subjectivity. At first one is struck by the positive, modern side of this painting, which rejects a stereotypical depiction of masculine subjectivity. For the strict gender positions presupposed by the notion of the male gaze do not necessarily pertain to David's painting, whose subject will be seen shortly to be as much feminine as masculine. To talk of Marat's or the viewer's male gaze is to posit a naively unitary represented and viewing subject; talk of the male gaze overlooks the multivalent gender positions that in fact characterized not only Marat but also Corday, who will be discussed later in connection with Balzac's novel as a hybrid. But the painting does highlight a masculine subject and was destined at the time of its viewing for a predominantly masculine viewing public. The extent to which David's painting conveys women's subjectivity is at best very limited.

Ambiguity also marks the presentation of Corday's writing. True her letter is pictorially central to the viewing of the painting, but at the same time, her authority as a writer is undermined by the deceptive nature of the letter, a falsified report of her suffering, contrived to appeal to Marat's sympathy and thus gain her entry into his home. The deceptive use of language by Corday, as a member, albeit impoverished, of the provincial aristocracy, conformed to the popular stereotype noted in the last chapter according to which artificial, aristocratic women like Corday used language to lie, whereas sincere, republican men like Marat used language "naturally," to tell the truth to the people.

The same ambiguity that surrounds Corday's writing affects the letter to the widow in the foreground. The situation in the painting makes it clear that Marat is the author; the recipient of the letter is not identified other than as an intermediary who will transmit the money attached to the letter to the soldier's widow ("you will give this assignat to that mother of five children . . ."). On the one hand, this letter, which conjures up a presumably simple woman, provides a way of mitigating the negative effect of Corday's deceptive letter. Significantly, the historical record provides no support for the existence of such a letter, which David presumably added to supply a contrast with Corday's.[20] That it serves only to suggest the simplicity of its ultimate recipient and the contrast with Corday perhaps explains its minimal legibility (and illegibility in reproduced copies): its contents per se count for little. On the other hand, however, the widow is presented as merely a recipient once removed, not a writer or even herself the direct recipient of the letter. She is the passive, submissive counterpart of the active, revolutionary Corday, whose threatening political and linguistic presence David carefully controls and confines.

As a final point about the ambiguity that surrounds women's writing in *Marat*, it is perhaps necessary to state the obvious, that the masculine painter David exercises the ultimate control and has the last word: his hand rewrites Corday's letter. More importantly, his written inscription on the wooden box—À MARAT DAVID—provides the work's final authority and source of legitimacy. The last word is not the same, however, as the only word. Admittedly the masculine ranks higher on the republican pecking order than the feminine. But it has perhaps not been sufficiently observed that the feminine does appear there too. At a time when women were being banished *politically* from the public sphere, women were being included *culturally*, although only in a limited and ambiguous way.

There is further inclusion of the feminine with respect to Marat's body, although it is only indirect; for although remaining clearly recognizable as masculine, his body displays a variety of features that trigger associations—admittedly perhaps clichéd—with the feminine. Prominent among them are the limpness and vulnerability of his body, features that David has been seen to attribute to his women subjects in earlier works such as *Brutus*. Marat's body seems limp largely because of his turbaned head and his passive, exposed, vulnerable nudity. And if the two engravings of Corday's assassination differ so profoundly from *Marat assassiné*, one important reason is surely the fact that both present Marat as fully dressed. As Margaret Walters observes, "The nude offers a touching glimpse into the sexual uncertainties underlying David's confident classicizing"; she goes on to say, "David's greatest painting—the one that comes closest to confronting his contradictory attitudes toward the nude, toward revolutionary heroism—is the *Marat Assassinated*."[21]

Marat's submersion in water further reinforces his feminization because of the traditional association between women and water whereby the female nude appears as a bather, endowed with erotic overtones, whereas the male nude assumes an active public role in civic or religious settings. It is significant then that David chose to present Marat's nudity in the personal, private, and vaguely erotic position of a bather in a bathtub—and in a coffinlike bathtub at that. Marat's vulnerability and victimization are thus enhanced in David's painting, as is Marat's appeal to the similarly vulnerable and victimized people. Neither of the two engravings feminizes Marat or represents him as a bather—*La Mort de Marat* indeed eliminates the bathtub altogether—and thus neither achieves the political effect of David's painting.

A number of peripheral facts from the historical record of Marat's assassination remind us of how firmly implanted the association between women and bathing was in the collective mental outlook of David's society. Consider the fact that Corday's execution, which took place in the rain, was described in terms of the erotic tradition of the female bather. Lamartine, for example, presents the scene as follows: "The rain made her clothes cling to her figure and under the wet cloth outlined the shapely contours of her body, like those of a woman stepping out of her bath."[22] Thus through a curious twist of history, the victim and his assassin are united through the common symbolism of water and the feminine vulnerability it connotes. Consider also the fact that women were the ones who carried the bathtub in the procession for Marat's funeral.[23] Both historical facts suggest that there exists a special bond between women and water, which David sought to exploit through the curiously feminine, liquid symbolism that he attributed to Marat's body, thus enhancing the emotional impact of his martyrdom.

The white drapery that surrounds and envelops Marat's nude body and androgynous face also acts indirectly to femininize him. The sheets forming that drapery functioned in reality to protect Marat's diseased skin from contact with the copper lining of the bathtub.[24] In the painting, however, they seem to serve the function of draping Marat's body, and their whiteness, echoed in the draped, white fabric of the turban, triggers associations with a pure, virginal femininity that provides a convenient metaphor for the purity of republican ideals. The white, classically draped fabric also invites association with feminine allegorical figures popular at the time such as Marianne, linking Marat to the republican ideal of liberty, and this at a time, in 1793, when a tension existed in the cultural arena between competing masculine and feminine symbols of the republic, between Hercules and Marianne.[25] As a "male Marianne," Marat serves to evoke both of these competing symbols. Since, as noted earlier, Marat had come to embody the republic in the popular mind after the death of the king, whose body traditionally represented the body politic, the inclusion of femininity in Marat's body is thus tantamount to the inclusion of women in the body of the republic.

Many pictorial and political ambiguities surround David's presentation of Marat's body, however, and thus the inclusion of femininity is often an exclusion as well. On the one hand, for example, this work cannot be completely dissociated from the historical, heroic style of David's painting generally and from his masculine concept of republicanism, with its reliance on antiquity's notion of a masculine public sphere. On the other hand, however, David chose after all to immortalize Marat's assassination precisely where it in fact occurred, in the kind of private, indoor setting that is traditionally associated with women and domestic activity in such pictorial traditions as still life and genre painting and that could trigger such positive republican connotations as the simplicity and virtue of domestic life. Thus David highlighted the simplicity of Marat's apartment, and in a period when, as Norman Bryson points out, "one could be denounced by one's servant for wearing clean linen," he included such discrete indications of Marat's frugality as the paint stain on the wooden packing box and the patch on the sheet.[26] Signs of simplicity function in conjunction with signs of feminine domesticity to connote republican virtue.

Ambiguity similarly surrounds conflicting interpretations of Marat as a Christian martyr. True, a Christian interpretation of *Marat* can be supported and linked with an inclusion of femininity based on the painting's similarity with such pictorial representations of the dead Christ as Michelangelo's *Pietà*; common to the two works are the limpness of the arm, the turn of the head, and the bleeding wounds or stigmata. Walters links David's feminization of Marat's body to traditional portrayals of the body of Christ: "Christianity retreated from the phallic pride and assertiveness of the ancient world. In Christian iconography the male nude is in a sense feminized—it is shown as passive and submissive."[27] David thus used Christian feminization to produce an emotional effect on the people by enhancing Marat's image as a martyr.

It is also true, however, that the painting can be interpreted in terms of an exclusion of both religion and women. As Frank Bowman has demonstrated, it would be wrong to attribute more than superficial Christian symbolism to representations of Marat at the time of the revolution.[28] A close look at the painting itself supports such an interpretation. What becomes apparent is the strongly materialist, antitranscendent nature of David's work: not surprisingly, Stendhal claimed, "David's school can only paint the body; they are clearly unequal to painting the soul."[29]

The dark, greenish, unbroken background of the painting again merits attention in this regard. Green was Corday's color, the color of her hat and ribbons, which "was banished from clothing, by the Commune of Paris, for its significance as a sign of rallying."[30] David tinges the background with the forbidden female color to hint at without directly representing the murderess and thereby to exclude symbolically not only Corday but women and the kind of religious or spiritual transcendence with which they have been associated, notably in the Marian tradition. The exclusion of any opening onto the world beyond the interior scene of the assassination is palpable. The contrast with *La Mort du patriote*, with its glaring light of daylight, is striking. Indeed, the extensive blank upper half of David's painting suggests that what occurs in the lower half—the masculine, fraternal acts of writing, helping others, suffering and dying for the poor—constitutes the only real or meaningful dimension of the human experience. As Michael Marrinan observes, David formally highlights Marat's importance in that lower half by creating an indeterminate space—a "great hovering void"—in which Marat seems suspended.[31] Whatever transcendence may be suggested in that lower half through the vertical lines of the sheets, Marat's right arm, one of his pens, and the packing box is still relegated to the lower human realm, not a lofty religious domain. Too, those vertical lines are carefully balanced by the horizontal ones formed by the letters, the knife, the second pen, the bathtub, Marat's head and his left arm, and David's writing on the packing box. If the horizontal represents here the values of masculine fraternity in this world, and the vertical the values of feminine transcendence in the world beyond, then at best David suggests a tension between the two, clearly not the victory of the latter.

It has been possible to see, in short, that femininity is not merely excluded from David's *Marat assassiné*, as one might think at first glance. Nor is it ever fully included or unconditionally endorsed, however. In selective ways—for example, through the letter to the widow or through Marat's feminized body—femininity is used to evoke suffering, poverty, vulnerability, and the like. But as Hertz was quoted earlier as observing, it also remains tied to notions of all that is socially and psychologically threatening in society. Corday embodies that threatening presence for David, as will Margarita, her violent counterpart, for Balzac. Not surprisingly, then, David's painting is never able, nor does it even try, to synthesize masculinity and femininity, either in Marat's body or in women's writing. The two genders mix together but retain their separate if overlapping roles in the revolution.

Balzac's *La Fille aux yeux d'or* also illustrates the process of mixing genders, but through a special structure that I refer to as the hybrid. The notion of the hybrid falls under the broad nineteenth-century notion of degeneration, which was seen earlier to encompass the related notions of illness and epidemics. All of these closely related notions stem from the threat posed by "others" in the nineteenth century. As Nancy Stepan observes, "There was a deep social aversion to 'bad breeding,' and to 'impurity of blood.' There was a worry that the incorrect mingling of classes, or ethnic groups, would produce a social chaos that would break down the traditional boundaries between groups." The hybrid, as Stepan goes on to explain, became "a metaphor of the kinds of degenerations threatening society, and the kinds of separations needed to contain classes and individuals in their proper social and physical spaces."[32]

Hybrids and other nineteenth-century manifestations of degeneration invariably have inextricable links with femininity.

Preliminary examples of hybrids in *La Fille aux yeux d'or* can help to introduce the cast of characters in the novel while giving an idea of what is special about that structure. Consider the protagonist de Marsay and his half-sister Margarita, who only learn of each other's existence in the closing scene of the novel. Each is the illegitimate offspring of the English bisexual aristocrat Lord Dudley and a foreign mistress; de Marsay's mother was French and Margarita's, Spanish. In addition to their mixed nationality, both of these characters also appear in the novel as possessing a mixture of feminine and masculine characteristics. Margarita is a strikingly feminine and beautiful woman, but because she loves a woman, her enslaved lover Paquita Valdès, and plays a dominant, masculine role in their relationship, the text implies that she acts like a man. Paquita, too, is a hybrid, "linked through her mother with the houris of Asia, belonging to Europe by virtue of her upbringing and to the tropics by the incident of birth."[33] As for Margarita's half-brother de Marsay, his hybrid nature too is shown to contain a mixture of genders in a variety of ways, to be examined shortly, that often bring to mind David's similar depiction of Marat.

Mixtures of gender and other semiotic elements such as mixed nationalities in *La Fille aux yeux d'or* provide illustrations of the hybrid, which can be defined as the presence of heterogeneous parts, an uneasy cohabitation in one living organism of different and incongruous elements. Those elements mix but do not combine in the hybrid; as a result, elimination of difference is only partially achieved. De Marsay, for example, is manifestly both French and English, an individual in whom a seamless, harmonious blend of the nationalities of his two parents has not occurred. To borrow an analogy from chemistry, one could compare de Marsay to a mixture, as of oil and water, as opposed to a compound, as of sodium and chlorine in salt. Whereas the parts in the compound lose their individual identity and a new identity results, the parts in the mixture retain their original identity to a large extent and can be separated out easily.

De Marsay and Margarita do not then merely combine diverse characteristics. Because their heterogeneous elements fail to blend, they as hybrids seem nonharmonious, unnatural, in short impure. In contrast with David, who integrates feminine characteristics into Marat's very person, Balzac keeps femininity separate and emphasizes the impure effect of all admixtures. Highlighting the impurity of his hybrid characters helps Balzac to make the evaluative political claim that class differences have been obscured and undermined as a result of the revolution, but not wholly obliterated. Thus for Balzac there have arisen new impure individuals standing in the place of legitimate aristocracy, which has allowed itself to be relegated to a position of marginality. Deviant sexuality together with mixed nationality—the hybrid—constitutes this impure, deviant presence in society.

Paradoxically, however, the structure of the hybrid results in a representation that is both disempowering and empowering for women, as was similarly the case with the interplay of inclusion and exclusion of femininity in David's *Marat*. The feminine in *La Fille aux yeux d'or* is marked by impurity and violence, but it also connotes strength: women have power and control that men like de Marsay mirror and even usurp. In order to describe how the hybrid functions to represent the impurity, strength, and violence of femininity and French society in the aftermath of the revolution according to Balzac, I want to focus on de Marsay and his sister as representatives of the three social classes that played central roles in the successive phases of the revolution: the aristocracy, the bourgeoisie, and the proletariat. Those phases are duplicated in the novel. It begins with a description of Paris's and de Marsay's parallel aristocratic manner and behavior and then dwells in the next and main part of the novel on his bourgeois acquisition of the aristocracy's property: "la fille aux yeux d'or" (the girl with the *golden* eyes). In the last phase of the novel, which corresponds to the historical phase when the revolution moved toward violence and control by the people during the Terror, the links among Marat, Marsay, and Margarita noted earlier with respect to names will be seen to take on special relevance.

La Fille aux yeux d'or begins, in the prologue, by associating the city of Paris with a particular kind of impurity, which will then be linked after the prologue to the protagonist, Henri de Marsay.[34] That impurity is identified with the feminized, morally bankrupt aristocracy, whose impure power prevails in Paris, according to Balzac. At the start of the novel, then, he emphasizes the first phase in the revolutionary drama, in which the existence of a weakened, defective aristocracy precipitated the onset of the revolution. The following description of Paris reveals the nature of its impurity: "There impotence reigns; there ideas are non-existent: like vigour of character they have been contorted into boudoir affectations and feminine mannerisms" (323). Another description is similarly telling because it sets side by side Paris's sexualized, aristocratic, feminine side with its intellectual, progressive, masculine side: "This city with a diadem is a queen who, always with child, is vexed with the irresistible desires of a pregnant woman. Paris is the intellectual centre of the globe, a brain teeming with genius which marches in the van of civilization; a great man, a ceaselessly creative artist" (324). With hybrids like Paris, the prologue shows, the two sides fail to combine, resulting in an impure mixture.

The description of de Marsay's physical appearance in the pages immediately following the prologue illustrates how, as with the inhabitants of Paris, mixed genders and other semiotic elements fail to form a coherent whole and result in figures like de Marsay, effeminate hybridized versions of the true aristocracy: "From his father Lord Dudley he had inherited the most amorously bewitching blue eyes, from his mother an abundance of black hair, from both of them pure blood, a girlish complexion, a gentle and modest air, a slender, aristocratic figure, and exceptionally beautiful hands" (330). In mixing features from his English father and French mother, de Marsay appears as an impure hybrid characterized by such feminine charms as "a girlish complexion, a gentle and modest air, a slender aristocratic figure." His role as a hybrid is further emphasized in this initial description through reference to him as the half-human and half-animal figure of the centaur (330).

Just as disparate elements fail to integrate semiotically in the description of de Marsay's appearance, the masculine and the feminine remain separate in his sexual identity. Although he is a seductive male aristocrat, who possesses women like Paquita as if exercising his feudal droit du seigneur, his masculinity stands side by side, nonharmoniously, with the femininity of the female aristocrat, as a variety of semiotic details can serve to demonstrate. One such detail is his more than two-hour-long toilette, which demonstrates an extreme shallowness, materialism, and egotism modeled according to him after those of women (347). Like the castrato in *Sarrasine* according to Roland Barthes,[35] de Marsay is sapped from within and made to embody an internal void. Another telling detail involves his attire. In his first amorous encounter with Paquita, she dresses him in his sister's clothes, a mode of attire that he himself subsequently chooses to adopt: "'Put my velvet gown on me,' said Henri coaxingly" (380). He thus impersonates a woman and a female aristocrat too.

De Marsay's impure essence as a feminized aristocratic hybrid is summed up onomastically; as noted earlier, names assume crucial importance in Balzac's semiotics. De Marsay receives a feminine name when Paquita cries out his sister's name during an intimate moment. She thereby relegates him to the roles of a mere stand-in for a woman and a mere sex object in her quest to discover the nature of heterosexuality. De Marsay also shares in the essence of a woman because his name phonetically echoes the name Margarita and the feminine aristocratic title, marquise. Moreover, Margarita is often referred to in the novel by the nickname "Mariquita," which as Shoshana Felman observes, is not just a woman's name; it also means, in Spanish, an effeminate man. Furthermore, the name "Mariquita" can be read as a composite, either of "*mar*quise" and "Paq*uita*" or of *Mar*say (Hen*ri*) and Pa*quita*; as a signifier, the word "Mariquita" thus names both Paquita's ambiguity, as part of two different couples, and the linkage of de Marsay and Paquita in Mariquita.[36]

In short, names reveal de Marsay's true identity as the marquise's hybrid double, and one of the key functions of the hybrid thus becomes apparent. De Marsay is an aristocratic male of "pure blood," but his effeminate ways and impure feminized appearance, behavior, dress, and name reveal the erosion of the true aristocracy for Balzac and its failure to form harmonious combinations of gender, class, or nationality.

It is interesting here to interject an anecdote from literary history that brings the story of Balzac's ambiguously gendered "marquise" and "Marsay" full circle. Paul Valéry at the beginning of the twentieth century mocked such descriptive predecessors as Balzac and challenged novelists to attribute true narrative significance to the sentence "The marquise went out at 5 : 00." The new novelist Claude Mauriac later in the century accepted the challenge by constructing the plot of his *La Marquise sortit à cinq heures* around the fact, only gradually disclosed through subtle narrative effects, that his central character, called the marquise, is a man whose gender identification is problematic. Ironically, more than a century before Mauriac and more than a half century before Valéry, Balzac had himself accepted the challenge.

It is time now to turn a page in the novel, as in history, and move from that phase that provoked the revolution, in which the weaknesses of a feminized aristocracy were central, to the phase in which the bourgeoisie took control of property and power in society. This second phase is enacted symbolically in the main part of the novel, in which de Marsay takes possession of his aristocratic sister's "gold." He does so, significantly, because the marquise has absented herself from France, as emigrating aristocrats did at the time of the revolution. De Marsay is thus presented in a new phase, which shows a side of him that differs from his role as merely a feminized aristocrat. Mixing features of the aristocracy with those of the bourgeoisie, he symbolically plays the role of a hybrid with respect to class, as he similarly does with respect to gender and nationality.

De Marsay fails, however, to mediate the diverse features of class and gender in postrevolutionary society. As a result, his bourgeois power is as flawed, as unfaithful to the true spirit of republican government, as was the bourgeois phase of the revolution itself according to Balzac. The following description of de Marsay's power reveals it as an impure, hybrid mixture of the new and the old.

> His period of growth had coincided with a conjuncture of secret circumstances which invested him with an immeasurable occult power. This young man held a mightier sceptre than that wielded by modern kings, almost all of whom are bridled by the law in their slightest whims. De Marsay exerted the autocratic power of an Oriental despot. But this power . . . was increased tenfold by its combination with European intelligence and *l'esprit français*, which is the keenest and sharpest of all instruments serving the intellect. (362)

Allusions at the beginning and end of the work to the Thirteen, a clandestine group involved in illicit private and public affairs, are significant not only because de Marsay is shown to have powerful friends but because he is said to share their physical and psychological strengths. Not surprisingly, the reader learns at one point that de Marsay became "one of the shrewdest politicians of his age" (376). But the Thirteen are also criminals, who mix together bourgeois energy and strength with aristocratic secrecy and privilege. De Marsay and the Thirteen are presented as illegitimate substitutes for legitimate aristocracy, which has allowed itself to be relegated to a position of marginality within French society or through emigration.

De Marsay's mixing of class interests in the bourgeois phase of the revolution parallels his mixing of genders as a hybrid, who mixes the masculine strength of the Thirteen with "the power that a woman may yield" (*le pouvoir féminin*) (380) of women's sexual desire. In order to acquire his strength, de Marsay must turn to women, as does Eugène de Rastignac in *Le Père Goriot* and so many other of Balzac's aristocratic characters, who derive their social and economic position from women and from the bourgeois wealth to which they have access. For de Marsay, as for Marat, acquiring that power is represented symbolically as gaining control of women's "language," with that term used both broadly, to designate women's looks, movements, silences, and so forth, and narrowly, to designate texts written by women.

De Marsay acquires the "girl with the golden eyes"—the woman as economic resource—by treating her as a language, as a series of signifiers that he has the ability to "read." He can thus interpret Paquita's physical features, for example, as a message of love and desire addressed to him: "Judging by the expression on her face, she seemed to be saying, 'What! you are here, my ideal, the being I have thought of, dreamed of night and morning! How come you here? Why this morning? Why not yesterday? Take me, I am yours. . ."

(338). Her way of walking signifies voluptuousness (339); her eyes convey desire (351); her silence means acquiescence (351). Love, as he observes, "finds a meaning in everything, and everything is of good or evil augury" (357). Love is thus a semiotic system, and women are signifiers to be read so that their secrets—their energy, passion, desire, in short their power—can be drawn out and possessed by men. De Marsay's skill at reading the language of women parallels that which he will demonstrate later in understanding and manipulating the language of politics. He comments revealingly at one point that a woman will always be jealous of "glory, ambition, politics or art, those public wantons [*ces grandes filles publiques*] whom she reckons to be her rivals" (348). As this remark suggests, de Marsay's ability to read Paquita's prostituted body duplicates and prefigures his ability later to read the prostituted body of modern politics in bourgeois society. But at the same time as that ability shows de Marsay's cleverness and adaptability, it bespeaks his impure ties with prostitution and thus his inability to bring together femininity and masculinity, aristocracy and bourgeoisie, into a pure, harmonious social formation.

La Fille aux yeux d'or again illustrates symbolically how de Marsay's new, impure, bourgeois breed of successful, hybrid men acquire power, money, and property in society by representing de Marsay's appropriation of women's language, in this case in the narrow sense of messages and letters sent by women. His first step in usurping the "gold" of the girl with the golden eyes consists, significantly, in bribing the mailman who delivers letters from the marquise, which reveal Paquita's name to him. By gaining access to the aristocratic woman's writing, the bourgeois takes possession of her sexual/textual property: possession of the name on the letter leads to possession of the person who is named. De Marsay's next move consists of duplicating his sister's paper, ink, and seal in order to counterfeit her writing and communicate with Paquita. The linguistic duplicity associated with aristocratic women noted earlier in connection with Corday again surrounds writing. In this case it attaches to de Marsay in his feminine mode as a result of having usurped the writing of an aristocratic woman.

De Marsay's defective need as a hybrid to draw on the strength that, along with impurity, women represent for Balzac is illustrated vividly in the moving description of the emotional letters that Margarita sends to her lover Paquita: "strange figures similar to those of a rebus, traced in blood and expressing the most passionate sentiments" (380). Women, for Balzac, are capable of almost superhuman expenditures of energy and feeling. De Marsay, in contrast, is marked at the start of the novel by a sexual indifference bordering on impotence: "Diving into the very depths of pleasures, he brought back more gravel than pearls. . . ; passion itself had almost no attraction for him. Constant satiety had weakened the faculty for love in his heart" (346). Only by imitating and usurping Margarita's passion, which he does symbolically by appropriating her letters, can de Marsay derive the strength he needs to exercise power in postrevolutionary society. Like David, Balzac uses letters from or to women in order to endow the male protagonist with the advantages to be derived from another class: the energy of the bourgeoisie in de Marsay's case, the sympathy due to the people in Marat's. In both cases, a paradoxical movement occurs in which women's political significance is both acknowledged and co-opted at the same time. But whereas David endorses Marat's appeal to women and the people as legitimate and uplifting, Balzac denigrates that appeal as illegitimate and degrading.

Having passed through the successive phases represented in the novel by the aristocracy and the bourgeoisie, *La Fille aux yeux d'or* focuses at the end on the proletariat, whose importance in the revolution was similarly evoked in *Marat assassiné*. The proletariat is represented in this case by Paquita, who is killed by Margarita in the closing scene. The structure of the hybrid comes into play here because both de Marsay and his sister display excessive, violent behavior toward Paquita that is discordant with their gender and class. De Marsay is like Marat, not as David depicts him, but as Balzac and others thought of him: as the ultimate in impurity, a bloodthirsty executioner, the personification of violence. Margarita resembles Corday and Marat, as will be seen shortly. Margarita is a hybrid in failing to integrate masculine strength and feminine vulnerability, upper-class power and lower-class disorder. Both de Marsay and Margarita, in short, serve as impure symbols of a failed revolution, of the inherent weaknesses in the revolution that were so visible during the Terror.

Although impurity marks both de Marsay and Margarita as representatives of revolutionary excess, the impurity is far more egregious in her case than in his. Because Margarita plays the more prominent role with respect to violence and the proletariat, her strength as a woman is highlighted, as it is through the novel's treatment of feminine language and desire, but it is also stigmatized. The respective roles that David assigns to Marat and Corday come to mind. De Marsay, like Marat, is violent, but he pales in comparison with Margarita since she is the one, like Corday, who raises the knife and commits the assassination. In Margarita's case, the violence is accentuated because she is actually depicted committing the act. As with the militant couple Raymond and Evadne in *The Last Man*, it is the woman who ultimately symbolizes the revolutionary excess that during the revolution came to be associated with women and the masses.

A careful look at the text reveals that the two violent hybrids, the brother and the sister, are indeed presented differently. De Marsay is described as Marat was by many during and after the revolution as an executioner (359, 377, 384), as an implacable judge (363, 382), as one who provokes terror (368), and as an individual characterized by ferocity (377, 385); in short,

> De Marsay coldly condemned to death any man or woman who had seriously affronted him. Although such a sentence was often lightly pronounced, the verdict was irrevocable. . . . Women are prodigiously fond of such men, who promote themselves to the rank of pasha and seem to go about with an escort of lions and executioners and all the paraphernalia of intimidation [*un appareil de terreur*]. (363)

His hybridization here consists of mixing the light and the irrevocable, of appearing seductive while eliciting terror. Hers, however, is far more threatening and profoundly linked to the menace of the disorderly masses. As I noted in chapter 1, the link between women and revolution begins far back in history.

Margarita's portrayal as an assassin carries feminine impurity, strength, and violence to graphic and affecting limits. Going far beyond Shelley's portrait of Evadne in battle, Balzac's depiction of Margarita opens the door for the kind of horrific image of bloodthirsty violence by women that Dickens creates in *A Tale of Two Cities*. Her allegorized presentation in the following passage as a Medusa-like monster merits close attention:

> The marquise was still holding her blood-stained dagger, her hair had been torn out in handfuls, she was covered with bites, several of which were still bleeding, and her tattered robe revealed her half-naked form and her lacerated breasts. She was a tragic picture.
>
> She had the face of a fury avid for and redolent of blood. . . . She did not see Henri . . . she was too intoxicated with warm blood, too fighting mad, too beyond herself to have noticed even the whole of Paris had it been formed in a ring around her. (389)

The fact that this lurid depiction of feminine violence brings to mind both feminine and masculine representations of revolutionary terror accentuates its hybrid nature. One thinks of Corday's holding the lethal dagger in *La Mort du patriote* and *La Mort de Marat*. One also thinks of the possibility of representing

Corday as a hybrid—a possibility that David did not develop in his painting but that others at the time of the assassination did envision. (The severe lines of the dress and masculine hat in *La Mort du patriote* are perhaps intended to masculinize Corday in that engraving.) The marquis de Sade, for example, wrote, "Marat's barbaric assassin resembles those mixed creatures who do not belong to any sex, who, regurgitated from hell for the torment of both sexes, belong directly to neither one," [37] and as mentioned earlier, Chénier spoke of the revolution as a generalized inversion of the sexes, citing Corday as a prime example. One also thinks of other feminine figures in the story of revolutionary terror. Burke made much, as noted earlier, of the mob's similarly forcing the queen to reveal her "half-naked form." At the same time, however, this passage evokes Marat, the celebrated "drinker of blood" (*buveur de sang*) who was associated with events such as the bloody September massacres in 1792. Her "bites, several of which were still bleeding" evoke Marat's wounds, which as noted earlier were compared to stigmata. And her obliviousness to "the whole of Paris," represented here by de Marsay, which forms a ring around her while reveling in an orgy of cruelty, corresponds to how Marat was commonly viewed, especially among counterrevolutionaries.

Balzac's novel thus succeeds in establishing a close association between Margarita as a hybrid woman and the excessive behavior that occurred during the Terror. Paradoxically the text manages to link Margarita's violence with the acts committed *against* as well as *by* the proletariat. On the one hand, as Leyla Perrone-Moisés observes, the novel records the repression of that class by dwelling on the lurid details of Margarita's murder of Paquita: "The story shows us that the social body is fatally ill. The 'fantasies' of the aristocracy turn out to be completely dependent on the proletariat and the colonized, whose silence and bodies must be bought." [38] On the other hand, Nicole Mozet points out that as a result of being a lesbian, Margarita also assumes somehow the sins of the unruly masses:

Margarita kills IN THE PLACE OF the workers. Margarita, despite her noble birth, her luxurious tastes, and her aristocratic scorn for others, finds herself therefore, like the workers, outside of society. . . . Since her being illegiti-mate certainly does not act alone to lower her social class, although it is surely much harder for a woman to be illegitimate than for a man, we must conclude that her social exclusion is a direct consequence of her homo-sexuality. . . . Of course, *La Fille aux yeux d'or* condemns neither workers nor lesbians, but the novel encloses them both (or rather, it states that they are enclosed) in a circle of violence, which only creates in order to destroy. [39]

As a final item in the inventory of stigmatized roles that devolve on Balzac's characters in association with the revolution, I would like to mention the role of partner in incest. Because that role will be highlighted in the next chapter, it is important to contrast it with that of the hybrid. Impurity affects both hybridization and incest, and it does so in ways that have distinct political overtones. But in *La Fille aux yeux d'or*, the threshold separating the impurity of the hybrid from the societally forbidden practice of incest is never crossed. The case of Lord Dudley is illustrative. At the beginning of the novel, struck by de Marsay's beauty, he exclaims, "Ah! He's my son. What a pity!" (331), thereby expressing but immediately controlling his incestuous homosexual impulses. It is enough, Balzac suggests, that he partake of the impure structure of the hybrid, as do his illegitimate children; he need not also be guilty of incest. The revolutionary events were brought about by impure aristocrats like Lord Dudley, who undermined a stable monarchical patriarchy. Violence such as the murder of Paquita originates in a weakening of the twin social institutions of the monarchy and the family. But the hybrid keeps the impurity within acceptable societal limits. Incest, for Balzac, lies beyond those limits and marks the point at which total collapse occurs.

The subject of incest arises again in the closing scene when Margarita declares that she intends to seek exile in a convent. "'You are too young and too beautiful for that' said Henri, taking her in his arms and kissing her" (391). Not surprisingly the text is quick to exile her to Spain and to note that the siblings would never meet again. Balzac suggests that incest symbolizes forces that threaten the very existence of postrevolutionary society. The impurity of the hybrid, in contrast, is a fact of life for Balzac, as the persistent inclusion in his novels of male and female deviants attests. But he seems to suggest that impurity, which manifests itself most egregiously for him in women and the lower classes, can be mitigated. Not surprisingly, then, women and the proletariat are virtually eliminated at the end of the novel, whereas de Marsay and Lord Dudley, having avoided the ultimate contamination of incest, survive and flourish. As a politically conservative pragmatist, Balzac realized that the day of the hybrid had arrived in modern French society. All he could do was to minimize the losses by keeping the unbridled impurity and threatening presence of women and the proletariat at bay.

Balzac on the Right and David on the Left both produced stories of the French Revolution, then, involving mixed genders, stories that are *politically* very different but *semiotically* quite similar; and it is in order to stress their semiotic similarity that I have chosen to consider them together. Although Balzac's work is a short novel and David's is a painting, the two works share key elements: the representation of women's writing, feminized men, substitute fathers, violence, militant women, and the like. Thick descriptions of works of literature and art can thus yield remarkably similar and enlightening illustrations of how the process of politicizing gender occurred in the aftermath of the French Revolution. Discovering echoes of David's painting in Balzac's short novel also makes it possible to uncover certain key recurrent elements in the nineteenth-century political unconscious, notably Corday as a hybrid and Marat as a semiotic element connoting impurity.

4

Sexualizing Family Relations in *René, Atala*, and *Atala au tombeau*

Aɴ ᴇxᴀᴍɪɴᴀᴛɪᴏɴ ᴏꜰ Cʜᴀᴛᴇᴀᴜʙʀɪᴀɴᴅ'ꜱ short novels *René* and *Atala* along with Girodet's painting *Atala au tombeau* reveals the extent to which similar politicizing strategies were used in the literature and art of the first decade of the nineteenth century. *Atala*'s publication in 1801 was followed by its inclusion with *René*, the following year, in Chateaubriand's celebrated apology for the restoration of religion in France, *Le Génie du christianisme*; the two works were then reissued together in 1805 and published side by side in numerous subsequent editions. Three years later Girodet rode the crest of *Atala*'s popularity, as did a number of other artists, and exposed *Atala au tombeau* at the Salon of 1808.

Since in addition to the three works' close proximity in time *René* and *Atala* are bound together by their joint publication, and *Atala* and *Atala au tombeau* by their common subject matter, it is inevitable that meaning circulates around these three works for the many readers who read the two novels together and viewers of the painting who have read or known about the literary text from which its subject is drawn. There is also textual and pictorial evidence, to be considered later, that supports the circulation of meaning around the two novels and the painting. To show how the circulation of meaning affects all three works, I will depart somewhat in this chapter from standard chronological and thematic patterns. Thus although *Atala* was published first, I consider it after *René*, which makes the stronger, more direct statement about sexualizing family relations and thus needs to be highlighted at the outset. And although Girodet's painting draws on *Atala* alone for its subject, I consider that painting in relation to *Atala* and *René*, both of which share many common semiotic elements with it.

My topic in this chapter and the key element circulating around the three works is symbolic incest, which in a variety of indirect ways assumes both sexual and political meaning. In *René*, as Pierre Barbéris rightly observes, sexualized family relations symbolize historical processes: he observes that the "sexual taboo is clearly revealed in the story, but it is not presented as a simple personal anecdote in the life of a hero" and adds that "what happens to René symbolizes a historical lack." Barbéris identifies that lack as the loss of the patriarchal anchor and resulting social disorder at the time of the revolution: "For Chateaubriand, the nobility no longer exists, and the revolution has occurred."[1] Symbolic incest in both the sexual and the political sense that Barbéris identifies is central to all three works examined in this chapter. Whereas incest is hinted at quite obviously in *René*, it is interestingly implicit in *Atala* and *Atala au tombeau*. In all three works, however, it functions similarly to sexualize family relations and thus to politicize gender, as have the other related processes examined in the previous chapters.

That incest could have political significance was already evident at the very time of the revolution. As noted earlier, allegations were made of incest between the queen, Marie Antoinette, and her eight-year old son, Louis Charles—allegations that were made, significantly, directly after the execution of the king.[2] When the royal family—the king, the queen, their daughter, and her younger brother Louis Charles—were imprisoned, they were handed over to various guards, among whom figured Chaumette and Hébert (also known as Père Duschesne, the extremist and often obscene left-wing journalist). It is the group of the royal family with their guards that Gillray represents satirically in *Louis XVI Taking Leave of His Wife and Family*. Having learned of Louis Charles's engaging in certain sexual practices, these guards had the idea for a story of incest between the son and the mother. At the trial of the queen, after the boy had been separated from his mother and cared for only by these guards for some time, he testified that in the past he had slept between his mother and aunt and that sexual activity had occurred among them. The boy signed a statement to that effect, which Hébert wanted to use as evidence against the queen. We learn further, "Robespierre . . . called Hébert an imbecile for concocting such a thing—and the Committee of Public Safety ordered it suppressed at the trial. But a juror insisted, and the matter had to be brought up. The Queen simply appealed 'to every mother' present in the court room, and the episode came near saving her. But in the end Hébert had his verdict." [3]

It is hard to know whether this story influenced Chateaubriand's political treatment of incest, although later I will examine some textual evidence from *René* that lends support to my intuition that the queen's story was an active component of the political unconscious in Chateaubriand's time. More important than influence, however, are the similarity between the "historical story" and the strictly "fictional story" and the fact that in both kinds of stories the issue of incest arises after the decline or loss of patriarchal control. I do not mean to imply, of course, that the subject of incest first arose at the time of the French Revolution; indeed, as E. Daniel Wilson has amply demonstrated, it was widely debated and often treated in literature throughout the eighteenth century. For a nineteenth-century example by a woman writer, one can cite Shelley's short novel *Mathilda*. Like gender, incest existed at the time and thus provided a convenient symbolic vehicle for articulating political issues. [4]

With Chateaubriand and Girodet, symbolic incest serves the function of reconciling the central opposition between monarchy and the revolution. Monarchy is represented not only through kings but also through a variety of other patriarchal figures such as biological or adoptive fathers, older brothers, priests, or warriors. The loss of patriarchal control by these figures leads to revolution, which is equated with the unruly feminine sexuality of queens, biological or substitute mothers, sisters, and daughters. Although their sexuality represents a force of disorder, it also has a positive side, as revolution does for Chateaubriand. As one critic has observed, although Chateaubriand was "violently opposed to all revolutionary activity," he was at the same time "incapable of hiding a certain enthusiasm for the results that could come out of it." Indeed, if Chateaubriand viewed the republic that resulted from revolution with ambivalence, he also viewed it with sympathy, as is clear from his memoirs, "A gentleman and a writer, I was a Bourbonist by honor, a royalist by reason, and a republican by taste." [5]

Sibling incest is the chief vehicle for bringing together and reconciling symbolically the familial and political oppositions between the patriarchal and monarchical, on one hand, and the feminine and republican solutions on the other. Brothers and sisters represented in literary or artistic relationships of symbolic incest stand in a middle ground between patriarchy and revolution, where as individuals and as couples they embody the heterogeneous forces of masculinity and femininity. That sisters appear on this important middle ground where political conflicts are resolved constitutes a symbolic empowerment of women. Interestingly, as Wilson points out, it was not unusual for enlightened writers in Chateaubriand's time to defend incest between brothers and sisters: "Thinkers like Bolingbroke and Diderot repeated the point of Pufendorf and others that Adam and Eve's children must have committed incest," a point that Chateaubriand also makes in *René*, as I will show later. Wilson notes further that in 1796, very shortly before the time that Chateaubriand wrote his novels, Goethe did not hesitate to call incest natural, "Look at the lilies: don't the mates shoot forth on the same stalk? Aren't they united by the flower that bore them, and isn't the lily the very image of innocence, and isn't its sibling union fertile?"[6] To treat incest, especially sibling incest, positively as well as negatively was thus far from unique at the time. And although neither Chateaubriand nor Girodet, both working in a Christian mode, endorses incest, I would argue that, at a deep-seated level, it has a number of positive functions for both of them. Most notably, incest between brother and sister enables them to reconcile republican and Christian principles of liberty, fraternity, and equality with monarchical and patriarchal principles of order and control. Since women are key participants in the process, they receive a politicization and empowerment of sorts, as they did during the same period from Staël.

Chateaubriand's indirect feminine empowerment through incest parallels the indirect masculine empowerment through male feminization that, according to Margaret Waller in a recent article, applies to René and other romantic heroes. I agree with Waller's claim that the treatment of these heroes as feminized is a hidden way of representing their power by bringing out their sensitivity, sincerity, profundity, and the like. But by failing to consider women's empowering role in sibling incest, Waller concludes wrongly, to my mind, that Chateaubriand fails to "experiment with sex-role reversal for both genders" and limits himself to presenting "a feminized hero but not a virilized heroine," an example of which, Waller claims, is only supplied later in the century by Sand's Lélia.[7] Admittedly Lélia stands far down the road from Amélie and Atala, neither of whom could perhaps be truly described as a "virilized heroine." But there are other ways of empowering women, and I think that by failing to consider them, Waller casts Chateaubriand in an unduly regressive role. Although it may seem strange to speak of symbolic incest as empowerment, I will try to show that in the nineteenth-century political unconscious that Chateaubriand drew on and contributed to forming, sexualizing family relations was one available way of representing the power of women.

Symbolic incest, as a way of reconciling political conflict, involves a variety of relationships and semiotic elements, to be considered in this chapter. Since incest results from the fall of monarchy and patriarchy, a central role in the treatment of incest is played by such elements as the father's disappearance or substitution, as well as by scenes of execution and liberation. The social disorder that incest attempts to mediate affects a variety of familial and social patterns: relationships between mothers and sons along with matters of patrilineal or matrilineal descent and social class. The representation of incest itself entails a number of semiotic elements considered elsewhere in this book, such as feminine language, dress, Christ-like and feminized bodies. It is through these common elements that gender is once again politicized in nineteenth-century literature and art.

Few works discussed in this book depict the semiotic element of the loss of the father, the first step toward incest, as strikingly as *René*, whose articulation of that element at the very beginning of the nineteenth century serves appropriately as its *locus classicus*. The role of the father in setting the processes of incest and revolution in motion is highlighted from the start of the novel. Acceding to the demands of two substitute fathers, the Natchez warrior Chactas and the Christian missionary Father Souël, René agrees to tell the story of his life, recognizing that he will have to reveal the secret that has tormented him and that he had thought until then "must forever be buried in oblivion."[8] His awful secret, to which he alludes obliquely at this point in the text, will turn out later to be incest. The fact that he alludes to it when he is physically and emotionally surrounded by fathers, as he is at the moment of the storytelling, suggests an association between incest and responsibility to fathers. René Galand explains that association as follows:

> The text tells us . . . that René only frequents Chactas, his adopted father, and Father Souël. Now Chactas is the one who, after Atala's death, renounced love. He is old, and he is blind, which for some analysts would be a symbolic equivalent of castration. Father Souël, who is a priest, has also made a vow of sexual abstinence. The figure of the father, for René, is thus not that of the *paterfamilias*.[9]

The first sentence of the novel stresses indeed both social authority and denial of sexuality: "On arriving among the Natchez René was obliged to take a wife in order to conform to the Indian customs; but he did not live with her" (85). To obey the father and society in *René* is thus to adhere to a patriarchal system that is depleted and incapable of regeneration. As Galand comments further, "The refusal of sexuality is a refusal to give life, to participate in the perpetuation not only of the species but even of a certain social order, of civil society." [10] That desexualized paternal system is at the antipodes of the disorderly passion that sexualized women introduce into the family and society.

René's story of his life reinforces the notion of a nonregenerative patriarchal system, the demise of which will later result in incest. He dwells on his father's death, which for René is sacred and unforgettable: "The impression was profound, it is vivid still"; we are told that his father passed away in his arms, that his father's "features had taken on a sublime quality in his coffin," and that "in my religious sorrow, close akin to joy, I hoped one day to join the spirit of my father" (88). Significantly, René's older brother, the family's legitimate heir, fails to attend his father's funeral, to acknowledge his younger siblings' existence, or to retain the ancestral estate, thereby causing René to be brought up, as he says, "far from my father's roof" (87).

There are a number of interesting references to kings in *René*, which suggest a close link between the demise of patriarchy and monarchy. For example, directly after the death of his father, René visits Greece and Rome, and he wanders, like the Last Man, "where palaces are buried in the dust and royal mausoleums hidden beneath the brambles," feeling the pain of having often "stirred up . . . the dust of a crime-ridden past" (90). Another example occurs later in the novel when, having stripped leaves from a willow branch and watched them carried off by the stream, he reflects, "A king in fear of losing his crown in a sudden revolution does not feel sharper pangs of anguish than did I, as I watched each peril threatening the remains of my bough" (97).

To understand these disguised allusions to the demise of the monarchy, one needs to recognize, as Barbéris explains, that Chateaubriand wrote *René* at the end of the revolutionary period when he was torn between his pragmatic inclination to return to Napoleonic France and his nostalgic desire to continue his allegiance to legitimate monarchy. Thus although he transposed events from the 1790s to the 1720s and rewrote the political revolution as the cultural one that took place in France during the Enlightenment, the shadow of the revolution hovers over *René*. Barbéris observes in this regard, "At the beginning of *René* (and already at the beginning of *Atala*) there is a malaise. The world is disturbed. Something abnormal is happening"; he notes further,

"What René confronts here, before any personal catastrophe, is an historical catastrophe, still muted but real." [11]

The various ways in which *René* represents the demise of patriarchy and monarchy have now been observed, and it is time to turn to the ways in which, in a process leading to incest, women are both sexualized and politicized after that demise. The basic fact developed in the novel is René's strong affection for his sister, whose affinity of character and mood with him derives, significantly, from their maternal side: "we both had a strain of sadness, given us by God or our mother" (88). Amélie is in fact everything to him—sister, mother, and wife—as his passionate expression of their mutual feelings reveals: "I welcomed Amelia with a kind of ecstasy in my heart. . . . As she uttered these words, Amelia looked at me compassionately, tenderly, covering my brow with kisses; she was almost a mother, she was something more tender. . . . Like a child, I had only to be consoled, and I quickly surrendered to Amelia's influence" (100). In turn, when writing to him, she intermingles fantasies about being his wife, as at the beginning of the following passage, with recollections of having been his mother, as at the end: "Ah, how joyfully she would clasp you in her arms and press you to her heart! . . . In your presence she would become all love and innocence; you would feel that you had found a sister again. . . . Though hardly older than you, I once rocked you in your cradle. Many times we used to sleep together. Ah, if we might one day be together again in the same tomb!" (102–103). And just as she serves as his mother at times, she asks that he play the role of her father for the profession of her vows: "Be pleased to serve as my father" (106).

Several features of the allusions to incest in *René* indicate its political significance. One is the close association between René's and Amélie's mutual affection and their shared attachment to home, nature, family, and nation. Thus Michèle Respaut concludes that for René, "in the end his 'native land' turns out to be his sister." [12] Now, if the native land was monarchical historically, it was republican in Chateaubriand's times, as he himself observed: "The republicans held their principles within themselves, in their midst, whereas the principles of the royalists resided outside of France." [13] It is not surprising then that although Amélie is noble, she does not receive the stigmatization attached elsewhere in the nineteenth-century novel to the race of feminized aristocrats. She is an aristocrat, but at the same time she is devoid of the negative connotations of the ancien régime. Indeed, she partakes of many of the positive features that Chateaubriand and others identified with revolution and the republic. One such feature is allegiance to the native land for, as Jean-

Pierre Richard observes, "Despite its desire to be emancipated and to break with the past, the revolution remained, because of its ties to the native land, attached to its national roots."[14] Another feature is compassion for the less fortunate: far from being one of the haughty and egotistical aristocratic women encountered elsewhere in these pages, Amélie dies—yes, from the "bad air" of an epidemic—while helping others, "a victim of her zeal and charity, while caring for companions stricken by a contagious disease" (112).

To understand further the political significance of incest in *René*, it is necessary to look carefully at the key scene of Amélie's profession of vows, when she unwittingly confesses her incestuous passion in the presence of her brother. This scene provides a number of semiotic elements that are echoed in Girodet's painting, as will be noted later. The scene begins with an emphasis on the religious ceremony as a symbolic death or execution: "Amelia took her place beneath a canopy, and the sacrifice began by the light of torches amid flowers and aromas which lent their charm to this great renunciation [*l'holocauste*]" (106). Next, in a symbolic act of disrobing that Amélie will soon duplicate, "The priest put off all his ornaments, keeping only a linen tunic" (106–107). Then the ceremony begins:

> Sustained by two young sisters Amelia knelt down on the bottom step of the altar. Then someone came to get me in order that I might fulfill my role as a father. At the sound of my faltering steps in the sanctuary Amelia was about to collapse [*défaillir*]. I was placed beside the priest for I was to offer him the scissors. At that moment once again I suddenly felt my passion flame up within me. . . . Taking advantage of my confusion, Amelia boldly brought her head forward; under the holy blades her magnificent tresses fell in every direction. Her worldly ornaments were replaced by a long muslin robe, which sacrificed none of her appeal. . . . However, Amelia had not yet pronounced her vows, and in order to die for the world she had to pass through the tomb. She therefore lay down on the marble slab, and over her was spread a pall, while a torch burned at each of the four corners. With his stole round his neck and his book in his hand, the priest began the service for the dead . . . I was obliged to kneel beside this mournful sight. (107–108)

It is at this point that Amélie speaks the incestuous words, which affect René dramatically:

> Suddenly a confused murmur emerged from under the shroud, and as I leaned over, my ears were struck by these dreadful words, audible only to

myself: "Merciful God, let me never again rise from this deathbed, and may Thy blessings be lavished on my brother, who has never shared my forbidden passion" [*ma criminelle passion*].

With these words escaping from the bier the horrible truth suddenly grew clear, and I lost control of my senses. Falling across the death sheet I pressed my sister in my arms and cried out: "Chaste spouse of Christ, receive this last embrace." (108)

After this René is carried away unconscious, only to learn when revived that "the sacrifice had been consummated."

This scene can be read symbolically at two levels, which are interwoven in the text. The first is as a consummation of the incestuous union between René and Amélie. It serves, in other words, as the culmination of the kinds of sexualized semiotic elements mentioned earlier: expressions such as ecstasy, tenderness, kisses; clasping in the arms, pressing to the heart, rocking, sleeping together, and so on. Amélie is about to *défaillir* or swoon. René feels passion flame up within him. Amélie is clothed in thin muslin, suggesting in a very subtle way an eroticism that Girodet's painting will be seen later to make explicit. Finally they are united, embracing, on her deathbed, and the consummation is proclaimed. This deathlike scene fulfills Amélie's earlier wish when she said: "Many times we used to sleep together. Ah, if we might one day be together again in the same tomb!"

The text suggests, I would argue, that Amélie is a victim of incest, not its cause. She bears the weight on her shoulders of private disorders, just as she and other feminine figures who fill the gap left by the disappearance of patriarchal authority bear the symbolic burden of public disorders such as revolution. But Chateaubriand's sexualized women are heroic figures too, who, unlike Balzac's, are marked more by their courage than by their impurity. It is true, as Diana Knight perceptively remarks, that the reader can never fully assess Amélie's and René's respective guilt or responsibility—"whether René's affection for his sister was always incestuous or simply 'caught' from her"—and thus we remain with "the problem of whether René's 'incest' is to be regarded as a fact, a retrospective projection of his own, a projection on the basis of Father Souël's suggestion, or simply an interpretation made by the post-Freudian reader." [15] And it may also be true, as Respaut convincingly argues, that Amélie is a psychological scapegoat of sorts for René: "René's behavior actually looks like the symptomatic behavior of people suffering from a double. That is to say that it is the double that the sick person or in this case the hero heaps with his faults, blames for his desires." [16] But one should not

conclude, and neither Knight nor Respaut does, that the text as a whole
endorses René's behavior or holds Amélie single-handedly responsible for
either the sexualizing of family relations or disorder in society.

The second level of symbolic meaning that I want to pursue relates to the
execution of Marie Antoinette, whose strange involvement in a story of incest
was noted earlier. Whereas Amélie, tainted by her private thoughts about her
brother and symbolic son, condemns herself to a death of sorts, her "sacrifice"
or "holocauste" for her "criminelle passion," Marie Antoinette, similarly
tainted—in her case by public rumors about her nefarious influence on her
son—was condemned to a real death for various real or alleged crimes. The
parallel between Amélie and Marie Antoinette is supported by many elements
in the scene under consideration that evoke an execution. Amélie kneels while
an official prepares the "holy blades"; she then "boldly brought her head
forward" for the dramatic, ritualistic cutting off of her hair, a symbolic act of
decapitation. Her simple attire in this scene recalls that which Marie Antoinette wore, as captured in the celebrated sketch, to be discussed later, that
David made of her shortly before her execution.

Amélie's association with the queen reinforces the point made earlier that
she is the victim, not the cause, of social disorder. As a royalist, Chateaubriand
undoubtedly held the view that the queen's execution was a travesty of justice
and that it was the disappearance of patriarchy, not her behavior, that precipitated the tragic fate of her family. So too with Amélie, the novel suggests that
dangers and upheavals beyond her control surround her. Near the end of the
novel René sees her behind the bars of the convent window, as the queen was
similarly imprisoned, seeking shelter from the chaotic world that surrounds
her. Amélie writes to René that in the convent she hears "the storms raging"
and that she has found there "a shelter from the tempest" (110). Had she not
entered the convent, she writes, "everywhere my steps would be harried by
storms" (111). And observing the convent from outside, he too is struck by
"the wailing of the winds" and "the roar of the surf"; what he senses around
that secluded, sheltered spot is a "storm on the waves," "men shattered on the
reefs," "the uncertain lot of the seaman" (111). Like the queen who, far from
causing the revolution, bravely endured its consequences according to counterrevolutionary interpretations, so too Amélie seeks shelter from the disorder
that surrounds her. But she does not merely seek shelter. She meets her death
in actively helping her sisters in the convent. In the final analysis she is a
blameless symbol of courage in the face of the upheaval represented symbolically as incest.

It is possible now to take a comprehensive look at incest in *René* as a symbolic resolution of the opposing political alternatives of monarchy and patriarchy versus revolution. The patriarchal alternative is summed up at the very end of the novel when, after hearing René's story, Father Souël judges him harshly and articulates the strict moral and social standards of the church. On the other side of the political opposition stands the feminine and revolutionary alternative to patriarchy, which also is evoked in the closing pages, but this time through Chactas. In Chateaubriand's symbolic system of family relations his gentle response is closer to a mother's or sister's than a father's; in this connection, one will recall the symbolic role of his blindness as castration. In addition, numerous details place Chactas in the nonpaternalistic camp: "Throwing himself into the arms of Chactas and stifling his sobs, he waited as the missionary read through the letter"; "Chactas clasped René in his arms; the old man was weeping"; "René raised his head from the bosom of Chactas. The blind sachem began to smile, and this smile . . . seemed to possess some mysterious, heavenly quality" (112–113). That heavenly quality points up Chactas's nonauthoritarian, natural quality, in sharp contrast with Father Souël's institutional, patriarchal power.

Torn between Father Souël and Chactas at the end of the novel, René clings to the idealized memory of Amélie. This is not the Amélie whose sexual passion disrupted the profession of vows but her purified self who, through religious seclusion and saintly vows, becomes a positive figure of incest and force of mediation in the novel. She, like Marat for David, is a Christ-like figure for Chateaubriand. René observes that after the ceremony, "she went courageously forward as a heroine in the face of affliction; bent under the cross she saw in her struggles the certainty of triumph and overwhelming glory in her overwhelming woe" (109). This presentation of Amélie supplies the semiotic element of the dying woman as Christ, which Girodet will be seen later to develop. Amélie serves as a force of mediation in *René* because she symbolically brings together opposing social, political, and sexual forces. She submits to patriarchy, but she also affirms fraternal, egalitarian, and nonpaternalistic alternatives. As Richard explains, Chateaubriand always yearned for a solution of "and . . . and," in which he could be both a republican and a royalist, an aspiration that Lamartine scorned: "Chateaubriand, 'a knight for the royalists,' 'a leader of the future for the republicans,' is in reality 'a fake on both sides.' "[17] Whether misguided, insincere, or utopian, his political desire arose from the same source as incest in *René*. If René was never able to forget Amélie's confession and never able to "look a little farther"

(113), as Father Souël admonished him to do in order to resolve his conflicts in Natchez society, the reason is perhaps that his incestuous relationship with his sister already enabled him to reconcile symbolically the diverse personal and political oppositions of his times.

In *Atala,* as in *René,* the loss of the father plays the symbolic role of representing the loss of a patriarchal, monarchical, and religious system. In both novels, the results of that loss, the social disorder of revolution and the new alternative of the republic, are also represented as feminine sexuality unleashed within the family. And in both works, moreover, incest serves to reconcile religious and republican ideals with traditional, patriarchal principles.

Atala differs to a small but noteworthy extent from *René,* however, in focusing more on women than on men. Indeed like Staël's *Delphine,* to be considered in the next chapter, it could be called the novel of mothers, and *René,* like *Corinne,* designated as the novel of fathers.[18] Highlighting *Atala*'s importance in this regard is necessary, as Schor observes, for making "subtle displacements within the canon," notably making a place for *Atala* "as the founding text of nineteenth-century French literature." Surely, the boy's loss of his father in *René* is no more important than the girl's loss of her independence in *Atala.* Schor explains that loss in terms of "the enchaining of the female protagonist," the transformation of the heroine from "the mobile liberatrix of the male captive" to a victim of social and sexual repression furthered by her mother.[19] Although my political interpretation of Atala may differ somewhat from Schor's, I wholeheartedly concur with her that the importance of *Atala* in raising key issues related to the role of women and mothers in society has been seriously undervalued.

Atala like *René* begins with the telling of a life story, and the two novels contain two of the same characters, Chactas and René. But here the symbolic father, Chactas, recounts his story to his adopted son, René, and accordingly there is none of the submission to a paternal authority that characterizes the opening of *René.* On the contrary, at the moment when he tells his story, Chactas, who is termed "the patriarch of the wilderness" (19), is weakened with age and blindness. And what is more, even his simplest physical movements are dependent on a young girl, who assists him, "just as Antigone once guided the steps of Oedipus" (20).

Chactas's weakness in old age, when he tells his story, is echoed in that of the patriarchal figures who appear in his retrospective account of his past life. The reader learns that at age seventeen he lost his father, Outalissi, in a battle against an enemy tribe. Fleeing to Saint Augustine with the remnants of the allied Spanish army, he is adopted by a Castilian named Philip Lopez, who, despite the connotation of Spanish royalty supplied by his first name, proves to be remarkably unpatriarchal; indeed he is more like a nurturing mother to Chactas than a traditional father. Rather than exercising control over his adopted son, or harshly judging him, as Father Souël judged René, Lopez lovingly agrees to release Chactas, who misses his "terre natale," and Lopez even tacitly agrees that the most important thing is to return to maternal origins when he says, "If I were younger myself, I would accompany you into the wilderness—for I too have sweet memories of it!—and I would restore you to your mother's arms" (23).

Matters are not much different for Atala. Her biological father is the very same Lopez who adopted Chactas. And although he passes his Christian religion on to his Muskogee mistress, he disappears from his daughter's life altogether. As for her adoptive Muskogee father Simaghan, although he is "like a king" (45), he accepts Lopez's daughter as his own and refrains from punishing or judging either mother or daughter. Nor does his opinion seem to matter much to Atala. Even though Simaghan captured Chactas on his return from Saint Augustine and is holding him prisoner, Atala does not hesitate to fall in love with him—not knowing him to be her adopted brother—and to effect his liberation.

Patriarchs are also depicted as weakened and lacking in authority in the political palimpsest of the French Revolution that shows through directly on a few occasions in *Atala*. Consider Chactas's depiction in the following passage of weeping European kings:

> What would you have thought had you witnessed the evils of society, had your ears been assailed, as you set foot on Europe's shores, by the long cry of woe rising out of that ancient land? The hut dweller and the palace lord both suffer alike, and all lament together in this world. Queens have been seen weeping like simple women, and men have stood aghast at the volume of tears in the eyes of kings! (64–65)

On another occasion, Chactas blames himself for having still neglected to convert to Christianity, and he asks, "What petty motives of politics and patriotism have kept me in the errors of my fathers?" (70). This comment can be read as a disguised reference to contemporary events. Like the allusions that, as noted earlier, Barbéris has discovered in *René*, this comment suggests Chateaubriand's break with an absolute allegiance to legitimate monarchy by rallying to Napoleon. This comment can also be read as another indication of the weakened allegiance to patriarchy and monarchy in *Atala* as a whole.

The first phase of the revolution constituted by the symbolic loss of the father is followed in *Atala*, as in *René* and indeed the other nineteenth-century novels considered so far, by a second phase in which women's sexuality, in this case Atala's and her mother's, is associated with the revolution and the republic. The disorder of Atala's sexuality, which corresponds to that of revolution, is evoked as Amélie's was in *René*, through images of the upheaval of nature in a storm. In the key scene in the forest after Chactas's liberation, nature is described in symbolically tempestuous terms:

> Meanwhile it grew much darker, and the lowering clouds moved in among the dense woods. Suddenly the heavens burst open, and a fiery shaft of lightning flashed through the sky. A fierce wind sprang out of the west, rolling up cloud over cloud. The whole forest bent, the sky split apart again and again, and through its rifts appeared new heavens and blazing vistas. Frightful, magnificent spectacle! The thunderbolt set fire to the woods, and the burning expanse spread like a flaming mass of hair. (44)

The presentation of the forest fire as hair, which in its abundant "mass" seems like a woman's, is significant. So too is the fact that the height of this storm corresponds to the height of the lovers' sexual passion.

This is the precise moment when Chactas learns that he is Atala's "half-brother," that is, that his adoptive father is the same as her real father. Although such a tenuous, largely symbolic sibling relationship between the two lovers may seem to be unimportant, the novel treats it with the utmost seriousness. Chactas's reaction to Atala's revelation of the nature of their relationship recalls René's in the parallel scene of Amélie's revelation of incestuous desires during her profession of vows. Chactas describes the scene as follows: "Clasping Atala to my heart I cried out between my sobs: 'O my sister! O daughter of Lopez!'" (46). And from this point on in the text, not only do the protagonists treat each other as siblings but the text treats them in the same way. Atala gives her cross to Chactas at the moment of her death—"Lopez, your father and mine, sent it to my mother a few days after my birth. Take this heritage from me, O my brother"—and like Amélie she reveals that she expects to be united with him in heaven (69). In burying her, Chactas cries out, "Lopez . . . behold your son interring your daughter!" (74). Aubry says, "Listen now to your sister" (60), and one reads that "the old priest, with marvelous tenderness, hurried between brother and sister" (63). Like Amélie's desire for René, then, Atala's desire for Chactas is implicitly incestuous, suggesting a symbolic disruption of order within the family and society.

Atala's desire not only connotes disorder, however; it also suggests freedom and liberation, and thus the republic. Schor was quoted earlier as observing the significance of Atala's role as the female liberator of the male captive in this novel; and I would add that this is a role Atala shares with other active heroines identified in earlier chapters, who similarly constitute empowered forces in the public sphere. Acknowledging her power, Chactas states, "Atala's influence [*empire*] over a man could never be weak; she was as irresistible as she was passionate [*pleine de passions, elle était pleine de puissance*]; and she had to be worshipped or hated" (41). Her first appearance before Chactas brings to mind an allegorical representation of Liberté: "I made out a large white figure leaning over me, silently untying my bonds" (37). He then refers to her twice as his "deliverer" [*ma libératrice*] (38).

Mention needs to be made of one special semiotic element in the representation of Atala as an allegory of freedom and revolution, an element that will also have special significance in the later discussion of Girodet's painting. It is the bare breast of the revolutionary woman, so well known from Delacroix's celebrated *La Liberté guidant le peuple*. This element is highlighted in Chactas's first vision of his "libératrice," who, in order to bandage his wound, tears away "one of the coverings of her breast [*un des voiles de son sein*]" (39). When she is prepared for burial, the reader learns that her "feet, her head, and shoulders, and part of her breast were uncovered" (72); when she is finally placed in the earth, again, "her breast rose above the black soil, as a white lily rises out of dark earth" (74).

The symbolic significance of the bare breast in the allegorical representation of the female body is explained by Warner as follows:

> Liberty's exposed breast stands for freedom because thereby a primary erotic zone is liberated from eroticism. As eroticism is a condition of the depicted female body, a semi-naked figure, who is no longer constrained by it, becomes free. . . . The allegorical female body . . . proclaims its virtues by abandoning protective coverings, to announce it has no need of them.[20]

This concept of freedom clearly applies to Chateaubriand's Atala, as it does with some differences, to be examined shortly, to Girodet's Atala as well.

One further aspect of Atala's close association with revolution and the republic needs to be noted. As in *René*, Chateaubriand associates the republic with the native land, which he in turn associates with women—Amélie and the queen in that novel, American Indian women in *Atala*. Thus one sees, for example, a Natchez mother who "moistened the ground with her milk" to nourish her deceased child, and scenes such as these prompt Chactas to say that in observing the customs of Natchez women, he and Atala "were . . . overwhelmed by these images of love and motherhood" (31). Atala herself is, of course, the best example of the American Indian woman's dual devotion to mother and land, as the following scene depicts: "Throwing herself upon the ground, she breathed a fervent prayer to her mother and to the Queen of Virgins" (31). Elsewhere, Chactas says that to console him, "she spoke to me of my mother and my native land" (67). And at the end, after Atala's death, Father Aubry chastises Chactas to return to his mother (74), in order to make the point that he must accept the responsibilities that he owes to his native land. As an ultimate tribute to Atala's virtue and courage, Aubry chooses to bury her "in a piece of European linen, which had been spun by his mother; it was the only possession he still had from his native land" (72).

The social stability of allegiance to the native land is celebrated at the very end of the novel, which presents "the daughter of the daughter of René" (80), an appellation that strongly suggests the matrilineal character of Natchez society. But at the same time, that matrilineal side combines with masculine, patriarchal authority to produce the structure of social mediation with which the novel closes, a procession of the departing Natchez: "The young warriors led the march and their wives brought up the rear. Those in front were laden with the holy remains, while those in back carried their newborn infants. In the middle, trudging their slow way, came the elders, placed between their ancestors and their posterity, between their memories and their hope, between the lost homeland and the homeland to come" (82). Fathers, of course, come first, and the "holy remains" of the patriarchal line are not forgotten. But at the same time, that line connotes "the lost homeland," whereas the matrilineal line represents "the homeland to come."

It is possible to view sibling incest in *Atala* as a mediating structure similar to the procession of the departing Natchez people. The symbolic union of Atala and Chactas blends femininity and masculinity, Christianity and Native American culture, into an idealized union that is fraternal, in both patriarchal, religious and nonpatriarchal, republican senses. When Father Aubry first rescues Atala and Chactas, he explains to them that, in all men, Christ "saw only brothers and sufferers" (48). Christian brotherhood and republican fraternity can thus be seen as closely related concepts. Later Aubry speaks of "those marriages of the first-born of men, those unutterable unions [*ces unions ineffables*] when the sister was wife to the brother, when love and brotherly affection [*l'amitié fraternelle*] were blended in the same heart and the purity of one swelled the delight of the other" (65). This statement is complex because although it seems to hold up *l'amitié fraternelle* as a republican, Christian ideal, it also expresses ambivalence regarding "those marriages of the first-born of men." Translating *ces unions ineffables* as "unutterable unions" is too negative, I believe, since *ineffable* in French has very positive meaning, as in *joies ineffables,* happiness so great that it cannot be expressed. What incest represents ultimately in *Atala*, as in *René*, is also something that cannot be expressed. It is the resolution of political and sexual oppositions, which in Chateaubriand's times could only be discovered in symbolic, "ineffable" form.

Girodet's *Atala au tombeau* foregrounds a triad of fully or partially clothed figures—Father Aubry, Chactas, and Atala—poised between the physical realm of the open grave and the spiritual realm of the distant cross, all three transported in the key moment of Atala's apotheosis as an object of human and divine love. The painting does not only depict the burial of a beloved and pious native American maiden, however. Beneath the surface of its romantic and religious story, one can discover traces of the revolutionary story, in which patriarchal control declined and sexual relationships arose within society and the family. Like Chateaubriand, Girodet does not cast that story in an exclusively negative light, however, as, for example, Balzac has been seen to do. Instead, Girodet follows Chateaubriand in conceiving it ideally as a mediating union between patriarchal, Christian and nonpatriarchal, republican principles, a union that he, like the author of his literary model *Atala*, represents symbolically as incest.

I want to look closely at the sexual and political meaning of a painting that has too often been labeled and then dismissed as merely an example of preromanticism. And I also want to give serious consideration to the limited but

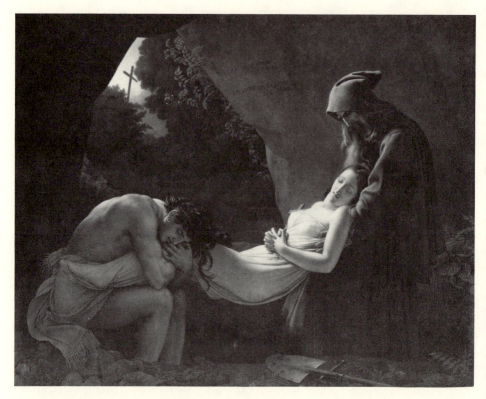

6   Anne-Louis Girodet de Roucy-Trioson, *Atala au tombeau*, 1808. Courtesy of the Musée du Louvre, Paris.

significant empowering of women that can be discovered in a painting that, ever since its first exhibition in the Salon of 1808, has been denigrated as "too sensual" and even dubbed "a masterpiece of bad taste."[21] Girodet's Atala is not merely an erotic object, however, as even a cursory observation of the painting reveals. Atala's body forms a "natural bridge"—the place of her burial in the novel—between two forces, one situated symbolically on the left, the other on the right. Placed on the left, like the revolution, is the disruptive passion of Atala's "brother"; on the right, like the church and other patriarchal institutions, is the possessive authority of her "father." Situated in the center, Atala reconciles the two opposing forces. Her beatific look and pietà-like pose endow her with strong religious significance. But at the same time, she displays certain features connoting both femininity and republican- ism, notably her draped white clothing and partially exposed breasts. Her feminine sexuality thus transcends mere eroticism and participates symbolically in the painting's larger political meaning. To understand fully that meaning, it is important to turn now to examining in detail each of the three figures depicted in *Atala au tombeau*.

Father Aubry stands to the right of the triad of figures, and that position reveals an important facet of his role in the painting and in the story it enacts. As a priest, he represents the paternal authority of the church, to which the political Right adhered. His authority is reinforced by his standing position and by the physical control he exercises as father over Atala's dead body, relegating Chactas, the lover and brother, to the same position of inferiority to which René was assigned during Amélie's profession of vows. That position, one will recall, was described as follows in *René*: "With his stole round his neck and his book in his hand, the priest began the service for the dead. . . . I was obliged to kneel beside this mournful sight" (107–108). Aubry also derives authority and power from his clothing, which contrasts with the partial nudity of the other figures. Because he is fully dressed in the attire of a member of the church, and because he is standing directly over Atala, he seems, despite his closed eyes, to be gazing down at and visually possessing her scantily clad body. His fingers grasping and sinking into her flesh, he also seems physically to exercise power over her body.

A similar treatment of Aubry's authority occurs through Girodet's use of another semiotic element, women's writing. That writing appears on the right wall of the grotto, which bears the following two lines, attributed to the "ancient poet named Job" in *Atala*: "I have passed away like a flower" and "I am withered as the grass of the fields" (73). In the context of the painting, as in the novel, these lines are feminine inasmuch as the *I,* who passes away and is withered like the grass, refers to Atala. But they are also written by a man: Aubry has inscribed them on stone as a memorial to Atala, who presumably would not have been literate enough to write them herself, even had she been so inclined. The effect of Aubry's inscription, which amounts to a masculine co-opting of feminine writing, is thus mixed, as was the similar use of women's writing in *Marat assassiné*. It is true that Aubry takes possession of Atala's voice, as he does symbolically of her body. But it is also true that Aubry's representation as the friend of the native Americans and as a Christian hero is reinforced by his use of women's writing, just as Marat's representation as "the friend of the people" was seen earlier to rely on the representation of written appeals to him from suffering women. Masculine figures of power "have the last word" in both paintings—Girodet rewrites Aubry who rewrote Job, just as David rewrote Corday and placed his name prominently in the

painting—but the voice of women is acknowledged, albeit ambivalently, as
providing a privileged means of access to the suffering masses, whose interests
Christianity and republican government purport to represent.

To turn now to Chactas, who sits at the left of the painting, is to turn to
another side of the symbolic story of incest and revolution that lies beneath
the surface of Girodet's work. Chactas appears in an intensely erotic state, his
body largely uncovered, his lips parted, his arms clasping his beloved "sister,"
in much the same way that René clasped Amélie in his arms during the final
moment of their symbolic, incestuous union during the holocauste of her
profession of vows. His thick black hair, a wild mass of curls and braids, falls
with abandon on Atala's thighs, as if reaching out to take possession of her
outstretched virginal body; his scanty garment carelessly entwines his lower
body, like the vines that surround him in the natural setting; his feet reach
down into the earth, with which he seems to have a natural affinity. Unlike
Atala and Aubry, who share certain elements of his dress and physical position—Atala too is scantily dressed; Aubry also has flowing hair and stands in
the excavated tomb—no spiritual elements counterbalance Chactas's intensely
physical and sensual presence in the painting. Readers of the novel may
remember that only much later in his life does he fulfill the promise made to
Atala before her death to convert to Christianity.

The strong emphasis placed on Chactas's sensuality in Girodet's painting
parallels that which was placed on women in *René* and *Atala*. Standing,
significantly, on the left, he serves the function that women do in the novels
of suggesting sexual and revolutionary disorder. Not surprisingly, his sensuality bears the mark of both femininity and revolutionary symbolism. His
garment is red, the revolutionary color, and it is draped and fringed in a
feminine manner. His earring, braids, curls, long eyelashes, delicate features,
and hands all act to feminize him, to the point that his face and dress seem in
many ways more feminine than Atala's.

His hair deserves still further comment. As noted in the last chapter, Hertz
has used Freud's analysis of the Medusa's head to explain the recurrence of
Medusa-like images in literature of the revolutionary and postrevolutionary
period; he attributes those images to the obsessive fear at the time of the
castrating results of revolutionary violence. As his analysis makes clear, Freud
identified the Medusa's head, through association with hair and blood, with
the mother's genitals and thus with the boy's fears of castration and decapitation while also identifying the snakelike hair as a comforting phallic symbol,
which reassures the child that the missing penis has been restored. Freud's
notion of the combined masculine and feminine sexual symbolism of the

Medusa's head, and Hertz's insight that Medusan images connote revolution-ary violence, receive graphic illustrations in Chactas's snakelike hair. That hair functions both as a symbol of Chactas's disruptive sexuality, which is feminine and masculine at the same time, and as a symbol of castration, decapitation, and violence. It is not surprising, then, that Chactas, although included in the triad, is relegated to the lowest position, holding Atala's feet, whereas the more conservative figure of Aubry holds her head. Girodet retains him and the revolutionary legacy he represents, but the painter also acknowledges the need to control carefully the symbolically incestuous, revolutionary, dis-orderly passion that his body and especially his hair evoke.

Atala's central position in the triad of figures—and her centrality to the sexual and political meaning of the painting—needs to be considered now. It was noted earlier that Girodet's painting mirrors *René* in depicting the young heroine as the object of symbolically incestuous desire, and it is worth adding that the representations in the painting and the novel of the high point of that desire are remarkably similar. Consider again the description of Amélie's profession of vows in *René*:

> I was placed beside the priest for I was to offer him the scissors. At that moment once again I suddenly felt my passion flame up within me. . . . Taking advantage of my confusion, Amelia boldly brought her head forward; under the holy blades her magnificent tresses fell in every direction. Her worldly ornaments were replaced by a long muslin robe, which sacrificed none of her appeal. (107)

Atala's body in the center of the painting and Amélie's in this scene provide the focus for the numerous erotic elements that the painting and the novel share: physical proximity of father, brother, and sister; flaming up of passion; disorderly hair; thin muslin fabric.

Atala also provides the focus of the painting's political significance. Like Chateaubriand's Muskogee maiden, Girodet's appears in white, like a femi-nine, republican allegory of freedom. In keeping with her allegorical presen-tation, she displays bare, or nearly bare, breasts, although only in a modified form. For according to artistic tradition, as noted earlier, it is the single breast that connotes freedom. The republican significance of Atala's barely covered breasts is also attenuated by their strongly erotic nature. Ann Hollander has noted that clothing with nakedness underneath is more erotically potent than nakedness itself, and she further observes that a preoccupation with the bosom was characteristic of Empire style: "Among the fashionable French, who had first invented the acutely neo-Greco-Roman female costume of this period, no corsets were worn, and a truly revolutionary nudity was permitted for a short time to show through thin muslin. . . . Nineteenth-century Romantic notions of female sexuality eventually produced a still more intense eroticization of the breasts."[22] By following the popular Empire style that Hollander describes, Girodet attenuated but did not obviate the allegorical representation of the feminine body as an emblem of social forces and the republic.

Femininity constitutes one side of Atala's emblematic role in Girodet's painting, but there is another side and there are other semiotic elements at work as well. Significantly, a cross appears behind Atala's right breast, serving to counterbalance or neutralize the erotic effect of the visible nipple of her left breast. The cross behind her breast is also echoed in the crosslike shape of the shovel in the foreground and the cross of the cemetery in the background. Atala's Christian side can be discovered moreover in her pietà-like position in the painting, a position that was similarly assigned to Amélie in *René* ("In order to die for the world she had to pass through the tomb. She therefore lay down on the marble slab") and, as discussed in detail in the last chapter, to David's Marat.[23] That Girodet's white-clad, seminude feminine figure plays the role of Christ—and that she plays it, significantly, in the center of the painting—points to the mediating political role that she is called on to play as a combination of feminine, republican and patriarchal, religious principles. The key to her playing that role is her virginity, which is suggested pictorially by her white clothes, traditionally reserved in mourning for children and the unmarried.[24] Her virginity indeed serves to masculinize her otherwise feminine body. For as Warner notes, according to traditions dating back to early Christianity, chaste women are "honorary males, for virginity's principal attraction is its ability to cancel woman's womanliness. The Christian soul, who achieves a true resemblance to Christ, also changes gender: 'The enlightened spiritually receive the features and image and manliness of Christ.' "[25]

The similarity between David's and Girodet's pietà-like figures is thus striking: nude or seminude upper bodies, draped white clothing evocative of Liberté, bent head, closed eyes, parted lips. He is a feminized man and she a masculinized woman; he is a "male Marianne" and she a republican Christ. In those roles, both Marat and Atala are called on to reconcile divergent social and political forces. His head, significantly, is to the left, whereas hers is to the right, and it is certainly true that different political outlooks underlie the two paintings, one produced at the height of the Terror and the other a decade later, when fervent, unquestioning commitment to the revolution was impossible to uphold. Despite their differences, however, the two paintings function

7   Anne-Louis Girodet de Roucy-Trioson, *Le sommeil d'Endymion*, 1793. Courtesy of the Musée du Louvre, Paris.

similarly to politicize gender and to seek political solutions through combinations of masculinity and femininity. For Girodet, as for Chateaubriand, that
combination was represented through the symbolically incestuous union between the forces of fraternity to the left and patriarchy to the right.

Girodet's use of the illuminating effect of the distant sun can provide a final
illustration of Atala's role as a figure of mediation, and it can also furnish a
concluding example of how incest and revolution combine in representations
of Atala. It is helpful to consider in this context Barthes's analysis in *S/Z* of
one of Girodet's other celebrated paintings, *Le Sommeil d'Endymion*. That
painting is illuminated internally by the moon, as *Atala au tombeau* is by the
sun. And the effect of the illumination within both paintings, as Barthes's
analysis makes it possible to see, is a reversal of gender. Barthes points out
that the recumbent male figure of Endymion is feminized by Séléné, the moon:

"In love with Endymion, Selena visits him; her active light caresses the
sleeping and unprotected shepherd and steals into him; although feminine,
the Moon is active; although masculine, the boy is passive . . . the moon-
light possesses Endymion, in a kind of insinuating bath."[26]

Following Barthes's analysis, one can say that structurally, although the
genders are reversed, the situation is the same in *Atala au tombeau*. The divine
light emanating from the distant cross of the Christian God directs its beam
at Atala and at the half-hidden crucifix behind her. As a masculine and active
force, that light thus functions symbolically, as Aubry does within the painting, as a figure of patriarchal power. However, that distant light—which
admittedly is represented as the true source of illumination in the painting—
seems less potent than that which, reflected off Atala's symbolically masculinized, Christ-like body, illuminates the inside of the grotto and the wall on
which the writing is inscribed. The viewer's eye follows a trajectory from
Atala's upper body to the writing, in order to reach the distant cross and light.
In terms of Christian symbolism, this trajectory is not surprising, for according to that symbolism one must pass through Christ to reach God. In terms
of relationships of gender and their political significance, however, the painting does hold surprises. As in *Le Sommeil d'Endymion* according to Barthes's
interpretation, strict boundaries of gender are transgressed in *Atala au tombeau*. With Endymion, feminization occurs, which, as Waller was quoted
earlier as noting, permeates the culture of the early nineteenth century and
amounts in the final analysis to a covert empowerment of men. What needs to
be added is that the masculinization that occurs with Atala similarly functions
as an empowerment, since Atala symbolically takes on powers normally reserved for masculine forces. As in her roles as Liberté and Christ, Atala as giver
of light is an idealized figure, like her literary avatars Chateaubriand's Atala
and Amélie. In all three of these feminine figures, as in the structure of incest
itself for Girodet and Chateaubriand, an ideal synthesis is possible, a combination of masculinity and femininity, fraternal and paternal love, religion and
revolution, monarchy and republicanism.

5

Censuring Maternity:
Delphine and *La Rabouilleuse*

Staël's *Delphine* and Balzac's *La Rabouilleuse* (*The Black Sheep*) put the spotlight on mothers in their retelling of the now-familiar revolutionary story of the demise of patriarchs, the rise of feminine substitutes, and the appearance of disorder in the family and society. They supply, then, a feature that has been strangely lacking in the other versions of the revolutionary story considered thus far, all of which—with the exception of *The Last Man*—virtually pass over mothers altogether. As one might expect, however, Staël the liberal and Balzac the conservative interpret mothers differently, if both in a largely negative vein. *Delphine* is a love story set against the historical background of the revolution, from 1790 to 1792. It leaves off before the Terror, stopping with the September Massacre of 1792, which Staël attributes as much to royalist intractability as to republican excess. By deemphasizing violence, Staël thus confines her indictment of mothers to an early stage in the revolutionary drama, in which mothers figure chiefly as faulty or inadequate substitutes for patriarchy. In *Delphine*, mothers are guilty of the sins of deception and rigid allegiance to aristocratic traditions, both of which are inimical to the success of the revolution, but maternity does not threaten the stability of the family or society.

Matters are quite different with Balzac in *La Rabouilleuse*. The main events, in which mothers are called on to play a central role, occur several decades after the revolution, and thus, like many other works considered in this book, this novel constitutes a palimpsest, in which the story of the revolution is inscribed beneath later historical events. But the revolutionary story that can be uncovered in *La Rabouilleuse* picks up in 1792, where *Delphine* leaves off. The story in which mothers are called on to play a role in *La Rabouilleuse* is a story of revolutionary violence, which is committed directly by the disorderly masses but which is also laid in many ways at the feet of mothers. Indeed, the intention of the novel, as stated in the dedication, is to provide "important lessons for the Family and Motherhood"; to avert the consequences of the erosion of paternal authority by demonstrating "how great are the misfortunes resulting from feminine weakness." [1] And at the end of *La Rabouilleuse*, a priest condemns Agathe Bridau, the mother and main character of the novel: "Your life, my daughter, has been one long act of wrongdoing [*une longue faute*]" (325). Although Agathe's personal story occupies center stage in the plot of *La Rabouilleuse*, the threat of social disorder that she represents is in many ways the profound subject of this novel, which Jameson quite rightly describes as essentially "a meditation on the nature, origins and proper uses of that antisocial energy called 'violence.'" [2]

Other significant differences between Staël and Balzac can be noticed in the semiotic elements that their novels highlight. Special importance in *Delphine* devolves on women's language, both written and oral. Although Staël's mothers too are censured, the narrative expression of the censure is feminized: that is to say, women's voices do the censuring, and thus their voices are empowered not only to deceive, as they often are in nineteenth-century novels, but also to propose alternatives to such deception. Staël's women articulate political positions both for and against the revolution, and they tell stories of patriarchal injustice, within the family and society. Another significant semiotic element is matrilineal descent, which enables Staël's mothers to succeed symbolically in passing on to their daughters such positive values associated with the revolution as freedom and reason. *Delphine* thus foregrounds elements that give significant empowerment to mothers.

Matters are different, again, with *La Rabouilleuse*. Several prominent semiotic features, which have been discussed earlier—dress, hybrid men, images of Marianne—emphasize the defects of mothers. With Balzac, then, mothers' empowerment is largely negative, merely a function of the fact of their prominence in the novel, although, as noted in earlier chapters, such empowerment does constitute a real, if admittedly only limited, way in which women acquired cultural significance in the nineteenth century. Other semiotic elements also discussed earlier such as images of Christ belong to politicizing strategies in which masculine characters obtain control or superiority over mothers, whom they judge and condemn. And regarding the issue of matrilineal versus patrilineal descent, as one might expect, not only do Balzac's mothers fail but their real or substitute daughters are eclipsed and thus also made to fail. Only through the paternal legacy represented in *La Rabouilleuse* by the masculine artist can society find the promise of political strength and renewal in the future.

A pictorial example can help to emphasize the difference between masculine and feminine judgments of mothers that will be studied in this chapter. The example concerns the most famous mother of the revolutionary period, Marie Antoinette, whose public humiliation on charges of incest was mentioned earlier. A further humiliation can be discovered in David's celebrated sketch of the queen on the way to the scaffold. Proud, glamorous, powerful, and young only a few short years earlier, the Marie Antoinette in David's work is humble, plain, pathetic, and aging. J. M. Thompson describes the sketch as showing her "defying death and a hostile mob, with Habsburg disdain" and rightly calls David's treatment of her cruel.[3] Thus the Jacobin painter took revenge on aristocratic women, whose stigmatization has been noted in so many nineteenth-century works. Warren Roberts elaborates on how David took his revenge in this deceptively simple pictorial work:

> Having signed the former queen's death warrant, he now sketched her with her hands tied behind her back, capturing with rapid strokes of his pen her downcast eyes and proud, resolute mouth and chin. Defiant as she was, she was dressed as any other victim of the Revolution, and it was that tension that David caught in his superb sketch. The bonnet on the head of Marie Antoinette and the unkempt hair symbolize the fall of a social and political order. Objective and dispassionate as the sketch may appear, it was, in fact, a vehicle for David's own feelings: it is as if he were again sitting in judgment of the former queen and the world to which she had once belonged.[4]

David renders Marie Antoinette guilty of the kind of royalist intractability that Staël blames for the failure of the revolution in *Delphine* and that Shelley has been seen to subject to similarly harsh criticism in *The Last Man*.

Important differences can be noted between masculine and feminine representations, however. Shelley's queen is represented at least partially as a victim. She even comes around eventually to a somewhat enlightened attitude toward the social changes in her time. Similarly, Staël retained a sense of compassion for aristocratic women, even the ones whom she will be seen to criticize most harshly in *Delphine*. Significantly, in the year 1793, when David sketched the queen, Staël turned to the same subject in a short prose work entitled *Réflexions sur le procès de la reine* (*Reflections on the Queen's Trial*), in which

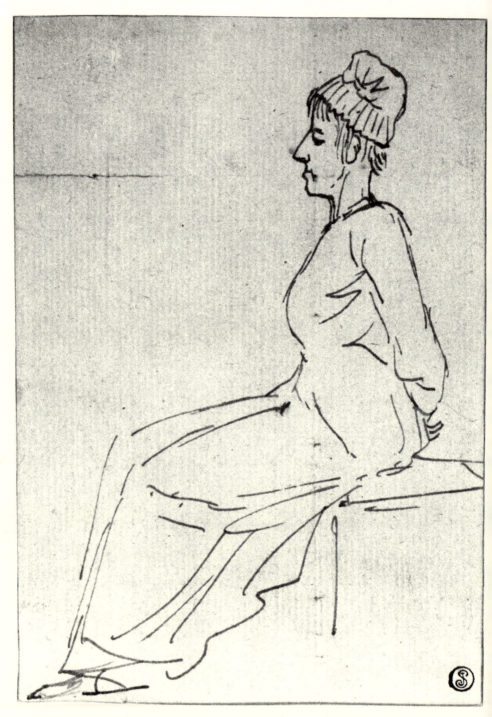

8   Jacques-Louis David, *Marie-Antoinette allant à l'échafaud*, 1793. Courtesy of the Musée du Louvre, Paris.

she defends the queen against charges of excessive spending. Arguing that any abuses the queen may have committed were made through love of the people, Staël appeals to feminine readers for compassion on the queen's behalf: "Women of all countries, of all classes in society, listen to me with the emotion that I feel! . . . You whom she helped, you who today belong to the all powerful people, say whether, in the name of your self-interest, you will stand for them punishing the queen for the generous effects of the pity she felt for you!"[5]

David, in contrast, had no more mercy for the queen than the guillotine was to have. His *Marie Antoinette* strips her of all dignity. It also seems to strip her, in a curious pictorial way, of her ability to speak inasmuch as her mouth seems tragically sealed and disabled. That Staël's mothers in *Delphine*, good or bad, never lose their voice is significant and empowering. They bring to mind Mme Roland, whom Dickens will be seen later to evoke in the closing scene of *A Tale of Two Cities*. Dickens celebrates Mme Roland on the scaffold, giving meaning, as a woman, both to her death and to the revolutionary experience. Not only, then, did history reserve very different deaths for Marie Antoinette and Mme Roland: Writers and painters compounded the differences by representing these women in very different ways. David's strikingly disempowering portrayal of Marie Antoinette comes close to Balzac's representation of mothers in *La Rabouilleuse*, whereas Dickens's more empowering evocation of Mme Roland has significant similarities with the far different representation of mothers that Staël will now be seen to make in *Delphine*.

Although Staël claimed that her lengthy epistolary novel *Delphine* contained not "a single word about politics, even though it takes place in the last years of the Revolution,"[6] the existence of its political meaning is unavoidable, as several important critics of the novel have acknowledged. Balayé emphasizes *Delphine*'s central focus on the demise of the aristocracy: "It is the novel of that class which contributed greatly to the initial reforms before being submerged. With all its ambiguities, it is also perhaps the novel of a class which lost all hope of realizing its ideal."[7] And Gutwirth calls attention to *Delphine*'s interwoven threads of feminist and revolutionary meaning: "*Delphine*'s fervor for

the individual freedom of women . . . represents an authentically revolutionary and individualistic fervor"; "this feminist inspiration gives the work an
essentially political significance, at a much deeper level than its explicit arguments for divorce or against the superstitions of the Church."[8]

Delphine's complex symbolic relation to the French Revolution has not,
however, been thoroughly explored,[9] and this, undoubtedly, because personal, not collective, matters ostensibly occupy center stage. Unlike *Corinne*,
whose neoclassical style and frequently impersonal subject matter signal to
the reader that love is not its only or even main subject, *Delphine* seems to
dwell exclusively on the obstacles that block the union of two star-crossed
lovers, Delphine d'Albémar and Léonce de Mondoville. Two obstacles are the
most notable: in the first half of the novel, Léonce's marriage to Matilde,
Delphine's fanatically religious cousin; and in the second half, at the time of
Matilde's death, Delphine's profession of religious vows. But there are many
indications that *Delphine* should also be read as a story of the revolution. As
even Staël noted in her perhaps disingenuous disavowal of political content,
the novel is set in revolutionary times, between April 1790 and September
1792. Moreover, a crucial role is played by such revolutionary episodes as
emigration, confiscation of emigrants' property, the flight of the king, repri-
sals against aristocrats involved in that flight, the alliance between royalists
and foreign powers to combat the revolutionaries, and the September Massacre
of 1792. Unless the love story between Delphine and Léonce is read politically,
those revolutionary events seem to form little more than a historical backdrop.
A key to bringing together the romantic and the revolutionary stories in
Delphine lies with mothers, whose representation in the novel can be described
in terms of the two crucial moments in the revolution that Staël highlights.
The first is the liberation from monarchical tyranny; the second, the destruction of the dreams that Staël and others held for an ideal union of two opposing
but not necessarily incompatible political ideals: revolutionary freedom and
aristocratic tradition.

Before turning to mothers, who actively determine the course of events in
Delphine, it is necessary to look briefly at Delphine and Léonce, who figure
more passively as symbolic representatives of political ideals. Delphine, no
less than Corinne, is a representative of liberty. An orphan, she was raised by
the elderly M d'Albémar, who married her (but did not consummate the
marriage) in order to pass on his fortune to her on his death. Far more
important to her than the financial legacy, however, were his Enlightenment
principles and his commitment to freedom, which he affirmed by fighting in
the American Revolution and which she reaffirms by rejecting religion, strip-

ping herself willingly of her aristocratic land, favoring the revolution in France, disregarding aristocratic rank and conventions, and governing herself in the absence of patriarchal authority. Like Corinne, she is compared on several occasions to a divinity,[10] referred to as carried on a chariot (I, 191) and draped in white (I, 183; II, 170); throughout the novel she is presented as the model of such revolutionary ideals as sincerity, simplicity, virtue, truth, reason, natural religion, and hope for the future. Most importantly, she reveres freedom, as she states on numerous occasions: "Of all feelings, love of liberty seems to me the most worthy of a generous character" (I, 118); "It would be as impossible for me not to love liberty, not to serve it, as to close my heart to generosity, to friendship, to all the truest and purest feelings" (I, 470). And although less urgently felt than the commitment to freedom, the demands for equality are also acknowledged as important to her: "In all relations in life, in all countries in the world, it is with the oppressed that one must live" (II, 101–102).

Léonce, in contrast, is depicted as deeply committed to aristocratic principles. The son of a French father, whose role is unmentioned, and a Spanish mother—whom Léonce credits with his very existence ("the existence that you gave me" [I, 173])—Léonce is a product, as Delphine observes critically, of the ultraconservative, feudal customs of Spain, with its "military and chivalrous ideas" (I, 421). Along with his many virtues—youth, beauty, sensitivity, compassion, devotion, and the like—Léonce suffers from excessive concern with appearances, honor, family tradition, and loyalty to his superior social class. He is executed in September 1792, having joined, characteristically for him, the French royalist emigrants in their war against the revolutionaries. The tragedy of the novel, as of French history for Staël, lies in his reluctance to form a rational compromise with the revolutionary forces, emblematized by Delphine. It is that failed compromise that their unhappy romance represents.

Although internal defects in both protagonists play a role, the immediate blame in the plot for their failure to unite is laid at the feet of mothers, who act maliciously to undermine or destroy Delphine's reputation. Léonce's ultraconservative concern with appearances and honor, which leads him in the political realm to defend the royalist emigrants, causes him in the personal realm to believe those malicious mothers and lose faith in Delphine as a respectable aristocratic woman worthy of his love and esteem. In the first half of the novel, two mothers are chiefly responsible. One is Mme de Vernon, the mother of Delphine's cousin Matilde. During the courting stage of Léonce's relationship with Delphine, when he is betrothed against his will to Matilde,

Mme de Vernon betrays Delphine, her dear friend and confidant, by failing to
dispel Léonce's suspicions that Delphine was involved with another man,
M de Serbellane, the lover of her friend Thérèse d'Ervins. The other responsible person is Mme de Mondoville, Léonce's mother, who categorically rejects
Delphine's free manners and revolutionary political views and exerts strong
influence on Léonce to prevent his marriage to her. The second half of the
novel repeats with variations the first half. Mme de Vernon's role is played by
the equally deceptive Mme de Ternan, Léonce's aunt. Not only is she the
biological mother of two grown children. She serves as the mother superior of
the convent in which Delphine seeks refuge and thus she acts as Delphine's
substitute mother. But like Mme de Vernon, she is a bad mother to Delphine,
forcing her to profess vows by threatening to reveal her involvement with
M de Valorbe, who is wrongly assumed to be Delphine's lover. Mme de
Mondoville reappears in the second half of the novel, where she again actively
combats the union between Delphine and her son because of Delphine's nonaristocratic ways.

Despite what is unquestionably a consistently negative depiction of mothers' actions, however, *Delphine* does not represent women as the profound or
only cause of the failure of the union of the lovers and, symbolically, of the
aristocracy and revolution. Instead, aristocratic women are presented as victims of the regressive social forces that bring down progressive efforts such as
revolution. *Delphine* thus sets an example early in the century for the politicizing strategy that, as noted earlier in this book, Shelley adopted in her treatment of the queen several decades later in *The Last Man*. Staël develops this
strategy extensively, presenting in *Delphine* a detailed study of the effect of
patriarchal tyranny on women's lives. Some women fail to free themselves of
this tyranny, whereas others achieve some form of domestic freedom. Liberation of women within the family parallels for Staël that which occurs within
society; and the various ways in which women throw off husbands as tyrants
duplicate the ways in which the revolutionaries threw off despotic rule during
the revolution.

An illustrative case in point opens the novel. Delphine's friend Thérèse was
handed over as a young girl of fourteen to M d'Ervins, a man twenty-five years
her elder, with whom she bears a daughter, Isore. Within the family, both
mother and daughter have been subjected to despotic rule, which Ervins has
similarly exercised over the peasants who work on his land. At the time of the
revolution, however, liberation becomes possible in both the personal and
public arenas, as it does in society through revolution. The peasants rise up
against Ervins, and they are only appeased through the mediation of Serbel-

lane, an enlightened Italian who has come to France, significantly, because of his admiration for the revolution (I, 52). Serbellane becomes involved in the domestic arena as well, attempting to help Ervin's victimized wife, with whom he falls in love. Although the story ends badly—Serbellane kills Ervins in a duel; Thérèse retreats to a convent, Isore is handed over to Delphine to raise—it dramatizes the key issues of the death of tyranny, whether domestic or political, and freedom from oppression. Although violence, death, and loss of liberty by retreat into a convent result, the example of Thérèse's liberation has a positive legacy, as the revolution did according to Staël. As one character comments later in the novel, "This revolution . . . will be judged by posterity according to the liberty that it will insure in France"; "happiness, glory, virtue, everything noble in the human species is so intimately linked to liberty that history has always excused the event that brought it about" (II, 338).

Maternity plays a crucial role in the representation of the acquisition of revolutionary freedom in *Delphine*. Elise de Lebensei, an enlightened mother and the wife of an enlightened revolutionary, has a son, who survives. Thérèse, who frees herself from tyranny, has a daughter, who also survives, but who cannot remain with her mother, too weakened by tyranny to withstand the pressures of society. Later in the novel Henriette de Cerlebe, daughter of an enlightened father, presents another model of maternity, which she and other female characters in the novel actively promote as women's salvation. As Louise d'Albémar, Delphine's beloved sister-in-law, declares, "It is so difficult to have as a husband the man of your choice, the odds against happiness are so great, that Providence perhaps wanted the happiness of women to consist only in the pleasures of motherhood; that is their reward for the sacrifices that destiny imposes on them" (II, 35). This statement is not merely an encomium for women's domestic role, however. As the examples of Thérèse, Elise, and Henriette demonstrate, successful motherhood in *Delphine*—having offspring who survive and thrive—is reserved for women who achieve freedom from patriarchal tyranny within society, as within the family.

If one set of mothers embodies the liberation from patriarchal control as the positive revolutionary legacy, another group illustrates the ills to which the revolution almost immediately fell victim: dissimulation, fanaticism, selfishness, duplicity. Those bad mothers—Mme de Vernon, Mme de Mondoville, and Mme de Ternan—together conspire to thwart the union between Delphine and Léonce. The most decisive step in blocking Léonce's and Delphine's marriage consists of pushing Léonce to marry Matilde; that marriage occurs, significantly, on July 13, 1790, the eve of the first anniversary of the revolution. As this date clearly indicates, what has occurred is more than a purely private matter. By preventing the ideal union of the revolution and the aristocracy, which Delphine and Léonce represent, bad mothers undermine the initial positive phase of the symbolic union between the revolution and the aristocracy, just as the initial phase of the real revolution was similarly undermined, even before the end of its first year. Not surprisingly, we learn later that their progeny, unlike the children of good mothers, either die or turn against them. Successful maternity, as noted, is among other things for Staël a marker of successful politics. An allegiance to freedom in the public sphere is an indication of an allegiance to it within the family.

Looking closely at Staël's bad mothers can serve to bring out the reasons for the failures that she presents as occurring in the political sphere. The flaws of bad mothers in *Delphine*, in other words, can be read as those of the misguided aristocracy, who, according to Staël, were responsible for the destruction of the revolution. Women's use of language in this novel is especially revealing, as it has similarly been in other novels discussed in this book. Sophie de Vernon, whose first name echoes the false or sophistic use of language that characterizes her, hides or manipulates the truth from the start. She demands that silence surround Delphine's generous offer to provide Matilde's dowry (I, 25), and silence, as Matilde points out later in another context, is in itself a form of deception (II, 109). Sophie reveals to Delphine that she does not like to write (I, 34) or to read (I, 213). She often refuses to speak or hear the truth (I, 122, 169) and often manipulates it to suit her own selfish purposes. It is not surprising to discover that, besides her deathbed confession, her writing comprises only four letters, three of which are sent to men and all four of which are very short. Delphine, in contrast, along with such other women who are presented positively in the novel as Louise, Elise, and Henriette are expansive in their use of language, most often to convey their thoughts and feelings to other women.

Sophie de Vernon's deceptive use of spoken language brings to mind the artificial language and political rhetoric that, Staël suggests, often took the place of sincere political principles during the revolutionary period. It is that language—irresistibly appealing but without substance, like the sophistic Sophie herself—that political leaders often substituted for the true principles of the Enlightenment. *Talk* of freedom and virtue replaced the *truth* of freedom and virtue. Such an interpretation explains the extreme attraction that Sophie exercises over Delphine, even though the latter is repeatedly forewarned and alerted to Sophie's duplicity. Delphine is profoundly drawn to freedom, and she is unable to distinguish her own sincere commitment to it from the shallow trappings that others display.

In the second part of the novel, Delphine is similarly drawn to and deceived by the mother superior of her convent, Mme de Ternan, a bad mother who also uses language deceptively. Mme de Ternan succeeds in deceiving Delphine because she and her sister, Mme de Mondoville, take advantage of the uncanny resemblance of her voice to Léonce's to thwart once again the possibility of the two lovers' being united. And it is also worth noting in passing the onomastic element of the similarity of her name, Léontine, to Léonce's as well. Knowing that Delphine cannot resist the voice and name that remind her of her lost lover, Mme de Ternan exercises a linguistic power that she knows to be contrary to Delphine's wishes and happiness. Thus Delphine succumbs to the forced profession of religious vows: "Since heaven uses this voice to command me to die, it is useless to resist" (II, 288). Like Corday and many other feminine figures discussed in this book, aristocratic women are consistently depicted as using language to deceive.

Along with their deceptive use of language, bad mothers also submit to patriarchal control. The life of Mme de Ternan before she became a mother superior provides an example. True, she is a victim of patriarchy, as are the good mothers in the novel. Her husband and children fail to provide even minimal affection or support; and as she and other women in the novel bitterly complain, once they are past the age of thirty, society relegates them to a position of inactivity and unimportance. However, by using her position of authority in the church to subject Delphine and others to injustice, Mme de Ternan reinforces rather than rejects patriarchal authority, and thus she symbolically destroys revolutionary principles rather than upholding them. The same is true for the other members of her family, Mme de Mondoville and Matilde. Both are victims of excessively conformist, prejudiced, traditional upbringings, in which religious ignorance and superstition play major roles, but to the extent that they also perpetuate those false and regressive values, they are the objects of Staël's censure of mothers. Both also fall into the trap of excessive motherhood, of which Mme de Mondoville presents an extreme example. Vowing to prevent Léonce's marriage to Delphine at all costs, she declares, "I would gladly give my life for my son's happiness; but I cannot abide the thought that his happiness might lie in the hands of any other woman but me, and I feel hatred for any person whom he loves more than me" (II, 280.)

Sophie de Vernon's case is more nuanced than that of these other women, but she ultimately remains in the category of a bad mother and enemy of freedom. Orphaned at age three, handed over to a tutor, who forced her to marry a man she profoundly disliked, she developed her deceptive conduct in response to her enslaved condition: "I was confirmed in the idea I had held since I was a child, that my sex and the paltry resources I possessed made me an unhappy slave, who could resort to any form of deception against her tyrant. I did not reflect about morality at all, I considered that it did not affect oppressed peoples" (I, 331). Her deception is thus a response to patriarchal injustice, but at the same time it turns out to be a way of perpetuating it, as she does by actively deceiving Delphine and destroying her union with Léonce.

Sophie's ambivalent but ultimately regressive relation to patriarchal authority, which she passes on to her daughter Matilde, can be measured by contrasting their attitudes toward priests with Delphine's. She tells Delphine that after the death of her husband, M de Vernon, who in his lifetime had exercised complete control over their child Matilde's education, she chose to hand over the responsibility for raising Matilde to the Church (I, 41). Delphine's response—"But couldn't you guide your daughter yourself?" (I, 41)—reveals the high value that she places on the feminine exercise of authority and her concomitant reluctance to relinquish control over the education of daughters. Not surprisingly, Matilde goes on to perpetuate the example set by her mother. Her own son dies because she chooses, despite her weakened health, to nurse him, a decision that is supported by the priests to whom she turns for advice (II, 305). Delphine's decision to eschew the involvement of traditional figures of authority and to educate Isore herself represents a countervailing position. Even at the end, when Delphine's suicide leaves Isore motherless once again, Delphine is careful to stipulate that she be raised by Louise, another enlightened woman. Significantly, with respect to the notion of a feminine legacy, the novel opens and closes with Delphine's passing on parts of her fortune to younger women: at the beginning, to Matilde; at the end, to Isore. The financial legacy reinforces the intellectual one that, for Staël, women must pass on to each other, rather than yielding to patriarchy.

Delphine actually replaces the priest, for both Sophie and Léonce, as Corinne replaced the father for herself and Oswald. For both, her feminine voice is genuine and empowering, enabling her friends to face death with courage and strength. Sophie, regretting at the end of her life her earlier submission to patriarchy, rejects the intervention of established religion and cries out, "Above all I have an overwhelming aversion to opening up my soul to a priest, perhaps even to any person except you. . . . I do not want to interrupt the pleasure, alas too new, that sincerity allows me to experience" (I, 344–345). And near the moment of Léonce's death, Delphine tells him: "I replaced for you a man of the Church, who would have been truly worthy of speaking to you in the name of heaven; but a voice that is dear to you could penetrate your soul more profoundly" (II, 428). Complete sincerity is what Delphine, unlike priests, has to offer. With both Sophie and Léonce, however, she can only play that role at the moment of their deaths, even though both die protesting that they would have chosen her libertarian way over the patriarchal patterns of authority—tradition, opinion, rank, property—that marked their lives and separated them tragically from Delphine. But in the final analysis, it is less for them that Delphine's empowering voice is important than for the daughters and sons of believers in freedom, who will live on to receive the fruits of the liberty acquired in the family and society by their parents' generation.

It is interesting to reflect in closing this discussion of *Delphine* on the epistolary form that Staël adopted in this novel. Critics agree that this form, popular in the eighteenth century, was outdated in Staël's time; Gutwirth observes, moreover, that as a form that casts the heroine as a participating member of the polite society whose rules she rejects, that form ultimately clashes with the novel's unquestionably revolutionary and libertarian content. [11] There is another, more empowering side to Staël's use of the epistolary form, however. That women are empowered when their control of writing is highlighted has been seen on numerous occasions, and *Delphine* is very much a novel of feminine letters, unlike most other epistolary novels. *Delphine* indeed foregrounds the woman as both narrative sender and receiver, with approximately three-quarters of the novel's 220 letters written by and sent to women. Balayé points out that in addition to Delphine's, at least fifteen other women's destinies are explored, and she also notes that in Staël's complex treatment of the epistolary mode, women write their lives, recite them, send copies to other women, to mention just a few of the permutations that this unusual feminine epistolary novel develops. [12] It is indeed the fact of giving women, and especially mothers, a voice, albeit in a narrative form inherited from the previous century, that separates *Delphine* so strikingly from other nineteenth-century novels censuring mothers, of which Balzac's *La Rabouilleuse* provides a highly developed but not uncharacteristic example.

Although Balzac's negative attitude toward women in general and his own mother in particular is well known, there is a need to look closely at the ways

in which Balzac casts mothers in a negative light, notably through the distribution of vastly different narrative roles to men and women. Men in *La
Rabouilleuse* play active roles: not only as initiators of significant courses of
action, as one might expect, but also as viewers and describers of people and
scenes. Meanwhile, women—real and substitute mothers—play passive roles:
as symbols of revolutionary political forces and as the embodiment of confined,
constricting space. As a result of this distribution of roles, men assume the
power of judging and casting mothers in a culpable light.

That Balzac's consistent castigation of mothers in *La Rabouilleuse* has significant ties with the story of the French Revolution will be clear from a summary
of its intricate plot. The first sentence of the novel reads, "In the year 1792
the townsfolk [*la bourgeoisie*] of Issoudun were fortunate enough to have a
doctor of the name of Rouget who had the reputation of being an extremely
wily man [*un homme profondément malicieux*]" (23). Both the date and the
character of the doctor announce the dark side of the revolution, which the
novel will explore. Also, the doctor's name, Rouget, functions onomastically
to evoke both the revolutionary color of red (*rouge*) and, in the first syllable of
the name *Rouget*, the name of *Rousseau*, an association made still clearer by the
name of Rouget's son, Jean-Jacques. The doctor's name thus evokes what
Balzac saw as the negative legacy of both the Enlightenment and the revolution, which grew out of it. The novel also highlights revolutionary violence
by mentioning the execution of Rouget's brother-in-law, Descoings, who is
denounced by a *tricoteuse* of the Jacobin Club, arrested, and, despite all efforts
to obtain justice from Robespierre, executed in the spring of 1793. This
"incident in the reign of Terror" (*Episode sous la Terreur*), to cite the title of
another work by Balzac, prefigures the disorderly events that are dwelled on
later.

The first part of the novel, in which this incident occurs, casts the story of
the decline of the empire in terms of the decline of a family. Agathe has been
banished from Issoudun by her father, Dr. Rouget, who wrongly assumes that
she is illegitimate. She marries a devoted officer under Napoleon, Bridau, who
dies young, and although, after his death, she struggles to raise her two sons
in Paris, aided by her maternal aunt Mme Descoings, misfortunes befall her
at every turn. One of her sons, Joseph, who is undervalued by his mother, is a
genius—and, as the text points out, "a great artist is a king" (50)—but is
useless for helping to make ends meet; the other son, Philippe, who is adored
by his mother, becomes a distinguished soldier for a short time but, at the
end of Napoleon's reign, turns into a shiftless demobilized soldier (*un demi-
solde*). Between Mme Descoings's obsessive gambling and Agathe's obsessive

love for Philippe, which drives her to impoverish the family to grant all of his indulgent wishes, the substitute and the real mothers jeopardize the financial and moral stability of the family. So too, for Balzac, did substitutes for legitimate monarchy fail to uphold the integrity of French society.

The second part of the novel and the chief symbolic reenactment of the revolutionary events occur in Issoudun. Dr. Rouget has died and left his entire fortune to his simpleminded son Jean-Jacques, cheating Agathe and her sons of their inheritance, which two unscrupulous individuals in Jean-Jacques's entourage are trying to ensnare. One is Flore Brazier (*la rabouilleuse* [trapper of crayfish]), who can be read as a figure of the people and revolution; the other is her lover Maxence Gilet (Max), who can be read as emblematizing revolutionary violence and the Terror. In order to regain control over their grandfather's inheritance, first Joseph and then Philippe return to Issoudun. After Max incites a mob and comes close to bringing about Joseph's assassination, Joseph abandons all attempts to regain the fortune. Philippe, in turn, is successful; he kills Max and forces Flore to submit to his imperious control. At the close, Philippe loses everything and dies, whereas Joseph marries and flourishes, deservedly rich, titled, and renowned.

It is necessary to look now at various ways in which the censure of mothers plays a part in the symbolic story of the revolution, which is inscribed as a palimpsest beneath this complex plot about a lost inheritance and the rise and fall of a family. The first way consists of attributing to femininity generally and the matrilineal line specifically all that is socially and politically defective. Thus one observes that, although the characters who initiate significant courses of action are presented as highly masculine, they are also tainted by a moral defectiveness that is associated with maternal weakness and feminine traits. Whereas they appear as positive and masculine in their ability to act, they appear as negative and feminine in their moral defects.

The pattern begins with what for Joseph and Philippe is the defective maternal Rouget line, which lives on in Philippe. The fact that this line begins with a doctor emphasizes, as Jameson observes, "the close relationship, in the original seventeenth century concept of *libertinage*, between scientific knowledge (materialism, atheism, etc.) and unbridled licence: the primacy of the body as the ultimate limit of scientific inquiry or as the horizon of the quest for *bonheur*."[13] Masculine and patriarchal in his acquisition of wealth and establishment of a family, Rouget embodies the negative maternal line in his propensity toward the unbridled licence that will be unleashed during the revolution. In contrast, the paternal line of Bridau—suggesting *brider* (to bridle or restrain)—introduces the patriarchal control that is so lacking in the

revolutionary doctor. Rouget's defects are the ones that are passed on, matri-
lineally, to Philippe, who is characterized, significantly, as resembling his
mother physically (44) and his maternal grandfather morally: "The young
man, subtle in his selfishness, as his behavior later in the story will reveal, was
much more like his grandfather Rouget than his virtuous father" (82). Like
the doctor, he is masculine in his resolute, ambitious, vigorous nature, but at
the same time he is flawed by the doctor's bent toward violence and moral
licence. Like Napoleon and the empire, to which he clings tenaciously, even
after the Restoration, his strength and power are not of the legitimate, royalist
sort, which Joseph will symbolically represent.

The other active male character, Max, is also tainted by feminine, maternal
weakness. The illegitimate son of a peasant woman and a noble father, he has
grave moral flaws, which can be traced to his mother's side, that are hidden
from view to most of the inhabitants of Issoudun, whereas "his true father's
noble blood was dazzlingly evident" (156). It is undoubtedly to emphasize
Max's tainted moral character that Balzac depicts him, like de Marsay in *La
Fille aux yeux d'or*, as a hybrid, whose masculine beauty has a strongly feminine
quality. Thus along with his "martial countenance," his "fiery eyes," his
"shoulders that would have borne the destiny of a Marshal of France and a
chest broad enough to wear all the decorations in Europe," he displays the face
of a virgin, "a set of thirty-two teeth fit to adorn the mouth of any society
belle," and "white and fairly beautiful hands" (155–156).

Politically Max conforms closely to the negative maternal pattern observed
also in Rouget and Philippe, and thus he serves for Balzac as a fitting representative of revolutionary violence and excess. Not surprisingly, we learn that he
was born, with the revolution, in 1789 (140). Leader of the criminal band of
the Knights of Idleness (Chevaliers de la Désoeuvrance), who "spread a kind
of terror throughout Issoudun" (139), Max functions as a provincial Robespierre, whose first name, Maximilien, is echoed in his, Maxence. The connection is to be expected since, in Balzac's symbolic system, Max's maternal and
lower-class origins predispose him to violence. And indeed, the masses are
Max's great supporters: "If Max was underestimated by people of the middle
class, this unfavourable opinion was counterbalanced by the working class's
admiration for his character. His fine presence, courage and resoluteness were
bound to appeal to the masses, to whom in any case his depravity was un-
known—for not even the middle classes suspected its full extent" (145). In
addition to Max's maternal and lower-class origins, there are suggestions of
symbolic incest: there are false rumors that Max is Dr. Rouget's illegitimate
son, rumors that the doctor encourages by paying for Max's education. Since

Max becomes the lover of Flore, mistress to both the doctor and Jean-Jacques, the specter of symbolically incestuous relations of all sorts and thus of further impurity arises.

Turning now to a more positive masculine character, the good son Joseph, we find women and mothers again cast in a negative light. To understand how this occurs, it is necessary first to spell out this character's privileged narrative and descriptive role. Seemingly omniscient, *La Rabouilleuse* in fact bears telling signs of focalization centered on Joseph, especially in the series of descriptions it contains: five developed portraits, one extended landscape, and such brief descriptive sketches as the following: "Madame Bridau's windows looked down on to the cells, which (with iron bars across their windows) were an exceedingly dismal sight" (38). It is the young Joseph's eye as a painter that one can most easily imagine capturing this and other similar scenes. Elsewhere, it is with the painter's eye for artistic quality that his father's portrait is described: "Above the sofa, Bridau's portrait—a pastel drawn by a friend [*une main amie*]—at once commanded attention." Throughout this portrait, evaluative comments recur: "Although perhaps the picture lacked artistic finish," "The serene expression of his eyes . . . was well delineated," "The shrewdness, clearly evidenced by his prudent lips, and the frank memory and facial expression . . . had been conveyed faithfully, if not brilliantly" (39). There are even indications that many years after the story is over, Joseph possesses the portraits of its participants and, by implication, is in a position to recall or recount the events of their lives. Thus one reads that Agathe's portrait "still exists in Bridau's studio" and that "numerous artists ask our great painter today: 'Is that a copy of a Raphael head?'" (30). As Mozet observes, "Joseph, who is a painter . . . has at his disposal the resources to look and to represent. He can be his own historian." [14]

Because of Joseph's dominant narrative position as viewer and describer, he is in a unique position to make implicit judgments about himself and other characters, not the least among them his mother. Overall, these judgments might seem to be benign; thus Jameson, for example, speaks of Agathe's behavior as "witnessed indulgently by a *perceptive* son who is in fact its victim." [15] On close consideration, however, it becomes clear that Joseph's attitude toward his mother is often bitter and critical. For example, he praises Mme Descoings, "who loved him with a motherly, tender, confident, credulous and enthusiastic love so lacking in his own mother" (91), and even states outright at one point, "Oh! Mother, you are a mother in the way Raphael was a painter! And you'll always be a foolish mother! [*une imbécile de mère*]" (125). Comments such as these make it possible to view Joseph as a link in a chain of narrative participants whose role is to judge Agathe as a mother. That chain includes the authorial voice in the novel's dedication and the priest's judgment at the end, which were quoted earlier. It also includes Joseph's extension, the narrative presence that hovers over the text—call him the narrator-painter—who judges Flore in the following passage:

Perhaps my readers will accuse me of painting too crude a picture; perhaps they will say that Flore's outbursts are so close to the truth of human nature that the painter should leave them in the shadow? Well, this scene, which has been rehearsed a hundred times with the most terrifying variations, is typical—in its crude form and horrible truthfulness—of the scenes played by all women, at whatever point in the social scale they happen to be, when some self-interest or other has turned them away from the path of obedience and they have seized power into their own hands. (198)

It is also worth noting the religious and regal overtones that crop up at times in Joseph's presentations. He describes his mother, for example, as having "one of those faces . . . like the Virgin Mary's countenance" (30), and elsewhere we read about him, "He had his cross to bear, this poor artist!" (248). Not only do these remarks self-servingly cast Joseph in the martyred, victimized role of a Christ figure; they also establish Joseph's superiority over his mother. For as Susan Suleiman observes, summarizing Julia Kristeva's analysis in "Héréthique de l'amour," the myth of the Virgin Mother in a Christian discourse created by the fathers of the church presupposes "that the ultimate supremacy and divinity of the male be maintained in the person of the Son, before whom the Mother kneels and to whom she is subservient," and Suleiman adds that in Christian as well as in psychoanalytic discourse, "the mother is elevated precisely to the extent that she prostrates herself before her son; for Freud, the mother's greatest satisfaction is to see her favorite son attain glory." [16] It is in terms of precisely such subservience that allusions to Christ and Mary function in *La Rabouilleuse*.

Along with the religious overtones in Joseph's presentation there are regal ones. They too promote Joseph to the dominant position that enables him implicitly to control and judge his mother. Trying to convince Agathe to appreciate Joseph's vocation as a painter, the art professor Chaudet tells her, as noted earlier, that "a great artist is a king," and he goes on to add that in fact an artist is "even greater than a king: to begin with, he is happier, he is independent, he lives as he feels inclined; better still, he reigns over the world of imagination" (50). Mozet points out perceptively that, as I noted earlier,

Joseph is cast in the role of king when he is beset by a revolutionary mob in Issoudun and almost executed.[17] Joseph is also the recipient of a collection of priceless paintings from convents, a collection made possible, according to the narrator, by "the liberality of our kings and faithful worshippers" (164). That those paintings, the last remnants of nobility in Issoudun, ultimately remain in Joseph's possession reinforces his association with the aristocracy and kings.

Joseph's symbolic association with nobility is a predictable component of Balzac's politicizing of gender in *La Rabouilleuse* since he is the one who bears the mark of paternal rather than maternal lineage—"Joseph . . . took after his father, but only in the less favourable aspects of his father's nature [*mais en mal*]" (44)—and he, not Philippe, is in a position to carry on the family line at the end of the novel. Issoudun, we are told, is unique in France because it has no nobility, and it is not surprising that this is the city where terror arises and where a mob almost executes Joseph, the symbolic king. Not surprisingly, for Balzac, he is the son who survives, whereas Philippe meets his death—significantly, through decapitation. Joseph's prosperity reflects Balzac's sense that the Restoration was a restoring of power and land to those, like Joseph, who deserved to possess it and whose right to do so derived, as it must for Balzac, patrilineally. As Jameson observes, "Joseph—the image of the great artist—thus does double-duty for that other potential resolution to the narrative search for a social order which is the nostalgia for the old landed aristocracy."[18]

To turn now to the feminine characters in *La Rabouilleuse* is immediately to observe that the role assigned to Flore, who will serve as a substitute mother to Jean-Jacques Rouget, is that of a symbol of revolutionary disorder and licence. Consider the following description:"Born in 1787, she was brought up amidst the saturnalian revels of 1793–1798, whose repercussions extended as far as these country districts, in which there were no priests, no religion, no altars and no religious ceremonies, where marriage was legalized mating and where Revolutionary maxims made a profound impact, above all at Issoudun, with its rebellious tradition" (169). From the start, she is presented in close association with the revolution. When Dr. Rouget first discovers her, she is fishing for crayfish, in a special manner that consists of stirring up the waters, a clear analogy with revolution. Indeed, one apt if admittedly loose translation of the odd title of the novel, which literally designates a trapper of crayfish, might be "the revolutionary woman." When, in order to intimidate the girl and her uncle, the doctor points out that they have no right to fish on public property, the uncle declares, "Aren't we living under the united and

indivisible Republic?" (162), thereby declaring openly his and Flore's continued revolutionary allegiance a decade after the revolution. And in a similar
vein, when they arrive at the doctor's house, the cook announces them as
revolutionary subjects, "Citizen and Citizeness Brazier" (163).

Flore's political significance also arises from her close association with a
wide range of revolutionary symbols. She often appears as a feminine symbol
of the republic, an avatar of Marianne. Moreover, in describing her, Balzac
seems eager to stress such other well-known symbols of revolution as ragged
clothes, tricolor images, hats and cockades, trees and poles, and the woman's
uncovered breast. Consider Flore's appearance, which is presented as perceived
by Dr. Rouget and later reconstructed as a portrait by the painter's expert eye.

> Like some water-nymph, the little girl suddenly revealed one of the most
> beautiful, virginal faces ever imagined by a painter. . . . The girl was
> almost naked. She wore a shoddy short skirt full of holes and all torn, made
> out of a poor-quality woolen material with brown and white stripes. A leaf
> of coarse paper, kept in place by a willow twig, was all she had in the way
> of a head-covering. . . . Her pretty sunburnt chest showed patches of white
> beneath the sunburn, as did her neck which was covered by a tattered scarf
> that had once been a Madras handkerchief. Her skirt was fastened between
> her legs, and clipped up and attached to her waistline by a large pin; it
> reminded you of a swimming-costume. (161–162).

Elsewhere in this portrait of Flore, her blue eyes and the "reddish tone" of her
body combine with her white skin and striped clothing to evoke a tricolor
image. Also, her characteristic pose holding her *rabouilloir*—"a stout branch
whose twigs were splayed out in the shape of a racket" (162)—reinforces the
association with the staff Marianne typically holds and with liberty trees. In
terms of her beauty, too, Flore fits the description historians provide of the
typical feminine revolutionary symbol, who although she "was to look like an
ordinary woman, not like a superstitious icon" was almost always chosen
"much like a Carnival queen—the most beautiful woman of the village or the
neighborhood." [19] A similar figure, to be studied in the next chapter, is Sand's
Nanon.

Not only does Flore's close association with revolution cast her in a negative
light and render her guilty of collective sins, along with any personal ones she
may have committed. There is the further fact that her role as substitute
mother for Jean-Jacques—"Flore treated him as a mother treats her son"
(181)—implicates mothers generally in what is identified here as her un-

bridled, revolutionary desire for power. It also implicates her in symbolic mother and son incest. Not surprisingly, attempts are made throughout *La Rabouilleuse* to possess, control, and ultimately eliminate her and the revolutionary legacy she represents. With the exception of Joseph, whose royalist filiation clearly puts him above all compromise with revolution, as did Léonce's in *Delphine*, all of the other major male characters—Dr. Rouget, Jean-Jacques, Max, and Philippe—possess her physically and, with the exception of the less than normal Jean-Jacques, all of the others disown and attempt to destroy her.

Just as Flore, Jean-Jacques's substitute mother, is rendered implicitly guilty of the excesses of the revolution, Agathe, Joseph's and Philippe's real mother, is rendered implicitly guilty of the worst defects of the bourgeoisie, defects that are held up as inherently feminine and maternal in nature. Even as a child, we learn, "Agathe embodied the ideal of the housewife brought up in the provinces without ever leaving her mother's side" (30). The close association thus established among provincial life, maternal influence, and enclosed space is further reinforced by Agathe's mother's name, Descoings, connoting the constricting space of corners (*coins*). Significantly, when Agathe goes to Paris, she seems to take the provinces with her by moving into one of the most confining sections of the city. And to make matters worse, she not only rejects all suitors and thus all possibility for a renewed patriarchal support; she also throws in her lot with her maternal aunt and her children's substitute mother, Mme Descoings, whose defective financial conduct as a gambler was noted earlier. Not surprisingly, the word *coin* figures prominently in the description of the maternal residence of these two women:

> One of the most horrible corners of Paris [*coins de Paris*] is certainly that portion of the Rue Mazarine which runs from the Rue Guénégaud to the point at which it joins the Rue de Seine, behind the Palais de l'Institut. The tall grey walls . . . cast icy shadows across this part of the street [*ce coin de la rue*]. . . . The poor ruined widow took up residence on the third floor of one of the houses in this damp, dark, cold corner [*ce coin humide, noir et froid*].
> (38)

Overvaluation of maternity is one of Agathe's great sins, which she shares with Mme de Mondoville in *Delphine*. And we find that she "took after Dr. Rouget's mother" as well as "the Virgin Mary" (*Marie, mère de Notre Seigneur*) (30).

The negative features that mark Agathe's presentation in the novel— femininity, excessive maternity, bourgeoisie, provinces, confined space—also mark her native city of Issoudun. Its name is said to derive from Isis (129) and thus to reveal its inherently feminine nature. In mythology, Isis also connotes the faithful wife and devoted mother, the same qualities attributed by Balzac to the bourgeoisie. The city's insular spirit and unwillingness to change and expand also stem from what Balzac designates as a feminine kind of overvaluation of the confined world of the individual and the family. Issoudun thus ends in a state of economic decay that parallels Agathe's. Indeed, more generally, all of its defects can be viewed as embodied allegorically in her character. Not surprisingly, then, the same didactic tone adopted elsewhere to condemn her as a woman and mother is also directed at Issoudun.

> The event of this story will, moreover, depict the consequences of this state of affairs—a state of affairs which is by no means as unusual as you might think. Many French towns especially in the south are like Issoudun. The situation into which the triumph of the middle class has thrown this sub-prefecture is the same as awaits the whole of France and even Paris itself, if the middle class continues to direct the external and internal politics of our country. (135)

It is clear that Balzac's real target was less bad mothers as such than what he had identified as bad societal patterns, notably the replacement of the nobility by the bourgeoisie; as Mozet aptly observes, "For this concept of society to function it must be doubly polarized—sexualized, as it were." [20] But the fact remains that, unlike *Delphine* and other treatments of mothers and women generally in the nineteenth century, a work such as *La Rabouilleuse* contains distinctly misogynous elements. Consider the following remark that Philippe makes to Jean-Jacques: "Women are like naughty children [*des enfants méchants*]. They are inferior animals to men, and you must make them afraid of you, for the worst plight that can befall us is to be governed by the brutes" (281). [21] The vulgar, almost brutal tone of this statement is characteristic of Philippe and is not endorsed as such by the novel as a whole. But the concept that the worst condition for men is to be governed by women is familiar from the novel's dedication, where that concept is identified openly as the author's message. Thus although Balzac has the merit of having empowered women by dramatizing the key role of mothers in revolutionary and postrevolutionary society, he must also be held responsible for having not only reflected but actively contributed to promoting a negative empowerment of women, through such politicized feminine portrayals as those found in *La Rabouilleuse*.

6

Politicizing Marriage in *Shirley* and *Nanon*

THE EVENTS LEADING UP TO and surrounding marriage in nineteenth-century novels have been undervalued by many twentieth-century critics, who sharply divide the personal and domestic realm from the political and economic. In the past decade, however, critics have challenged traditional opinions about the significance of marriage in literature. As Armstrong and Miller were quoted earlier as reminding us, domestic issues do not stand outside politics; nor do they stand in opposition to the collective, public sphere. Marriage is a locus in the nineteenth-century novel for relationships of power, class, freedom, and equality, to mention the key issues highlighted in Brontë's *Shirley* and Sand's *Nanon*, two paradigms of the political ramifications of marriage. (A pictorial example, David's *Les Sabines*, will be looked at briefly in closing.) Whether representations of marriage function, as they typically did early in the century, to assert nonaristocratic values or, later, when Brontë and Sand wrote, to accommodate working-class culture, they clearly transcend merely sentimental, romantic matters.

An illustrative example of undervaluing domestic issues is provided in Simone de Beauvoir's *Le Deuxième Sexe*, a path-breaking work that nonetheless shows certain biases of gender and culture typical of the World War II era in which it was written. Beauvoir dismisses Sand quite summarily, claiming that she placed personal issues over such public causes as endorsing feminist groups: "George Sand calls for the right to free love but she refuses to collaborate on *The Voice of Women*; her claims are above all sentimental." [1] She similarly dismisses the Brontë sisters, along with Jane Austen and George Eliot, all of whom she admires, but not as much as such writers as Stendhal, Tolstoy, and Dostoyevski. What separates nineteenth-century female writers from male writers of that century for Beauvoir is precisely the women's focus on domestic matters. These women lack men's richness of experience, she claims, and as a result, "They do not contest the human condition, because they have barely begun to be able to make it integrally their own. This explains why their works generally lack metaphysical resonance." [2] Beauvoir thus privileges metaphysical concerns, placing domestic fiction and women writers' interest in marriage and family life in an inferior position, beneath or outside vital philosophical, political, and economic issues. Today, four decades after Beauvoir's assessment of Brontë and Sand, we need to learn to avoid readings of nineteenth-century fiction that, like hers, fail to acknowledge that women writers' representations of marriage do indeed address vital collective as well as personal issues. *Shirley* and *Nanon* constitute remarkable examples of the seriousness with which women writers treat marriage, both politically and economically, as can be discovered in the complex ties established in these works between marriage and the story of the French Revolution. Those ties are indirect in *Shirley*. Set in the years 1811–1812—near the end of the Napoleonic reign, at the time of the Luddite workers' revolts in England—*Shirley* is a palimpsest, in which the French Revolution is inscribed symbolically beneath a series of later workers' revolutionary uprisings. In contrast, the ties with the revolution are direct in *Nanon*, a work that spans the years from 1788 to 1795 and foregrounds a series of historical moments, from the fall of the Bastille to the end of the Terror. But it too is a palimpsest, although in reverse; written in 1872, it buries the later revolutionary events in France from 1848 and 1871 beneath the surface story of the earlier ones.

Indirect or direct, the story of the revolution is equally central, however, to the marriages that constitute the culminating events in the two novels. Both works contain couples who break down social barriers during the course of the novel in order to marry at the end, thereby forging syntheses of divergent class interests: those of the industrial bourgeoisie and the landowning gentry in *Shirley*, those of peasants and aristocrats in *Nanon*. Those bourgeois syntheses of upper- and lower-class values enable them to combine the conservative principles of order, stability, and protection of property with such ideals of the French Revolution as progress, freedom, and equality. Although both works dwell on how those ideals are tarnished during or after the revolution through violence by and against the people, the two novels also claim to show how those ideals are ultimately preserved when what the novels promote as "masculine courage" and "feminine compassion for the people" unite. The centrality of Brontë's and Sand's focus on the people is especially important, qualifying the two novels in an important sense as works both about and for the revolution.

In addition to the political focus in *Shirley* and *Nanon*, which would alone dispel any lingering suspicions that novels about marriage treat only personal and romantic matters, these two works are characterized by a similarly strong economic focus. Brontë's and Sand's common assertion that both women and workers have been denied certain basic needs—most notably, work, food, and education—explains their commitment to revolution, which both writers acknowledge as legitimate on economic grounds. It also explains the revolutionary thrust of their writing, which has not gone unnoticed. Moers points out that Marx ends *The Poverty of Philosophy* with a quote from Sand and that he singles out Brontë (along with Gaskell, Dickens, and Thackeray) as expressing important political and social truths.[3] Sand, as is well known, was also world renowned as a feminist, as well as a socialist and self-styled communist.

The parallel oppression of women and workers provides a key to understanding the political and economic nature of marriage in *Shirley* and *Nanon* and the feminist notion of the empowerment of women in marriage that these novels develop. Both authors conceive the general revolutionary goals of liberation, equality, and justice as corresponding and complementary processes within the family and society, and both symbolically represent marriage as an ideal means for reaching such specific goals that the revolution attempted or should have attempted to achieve as education, fair distribution of economic resources, and work. The ways in which these goals are met by the two members of the marriage serve as models of how they can be met in society. Developing strategies, albeit only literary ones, for meeting these goals is a crucial reason for these writers' choice to go back to the revolution and attempt to rectify its mistakes in the personal domain of the family. In the fictional home, Brontë and Sand fashion empowering roles for women—landowner, worker, educator, mother, writer, observer—that provide idealized literary representations of how oppressed people, women and workers, could acquire the power and knowledge needed to function in the modern, postrevolutionary world. Crucial to fashioning those empowering roles for women are a number of the key semiotic elements familiar from previous chapters of this book— hybrids, allegories of women, names, women's writing—that must be deployed anew in this chapter to show how the political and economic achieve representation in the current works.

To present the oppression of two groups, women and workers, as parallel, as the authors of *Shirley* and *Nanon* both do, is inevitably to invite charges, which recur in critical assessments of both Brontë and Sand, of shortchanging one or the other group and thus of deviating either from feminist or from liberal political views. But such charges often have the unfortunate result of detracting from the larger social significance of these women writers' works. One example is Terry Eagleton's otherwise incisive analysis of Brontë's writing. By focusing only on the admittedly real limitations to Brontë's socialism in *Shirley*, while leaving to the side her very significant feminism, he makes that work out to seem far more conservative than it is, concluding, for example, that Brontë "blends revolt and reverence in a way which tips the balance decisively on the side of the status quo."[4] He thus misses much of the politically and economically radical thrust of *Shirley*.

A similarly negative case has been made against Sand, but in reverse, for having prioritized the cause of the people, putting the cause of women in second place. But as Dennis O'Brien convincingly demonstrates, it is misleading to focus too narrowly on Sand's limitations as a feminist. O'Brien acknowledges that there are numerous, seemingly nonfeminist statements from her correspondence in which she expresses, for example, her approval of women's domestic role and obedience to husbands, her preference for men's company over women's, and her disapproval of women's active role in politics. But he also notes that there is a strongly feminist thrust to Sand's writing, for example, in her assertion of women's equality to men and her commitment to legal equality between partners in marriage.[5] And he points out that although Beauvoir justifiably highlighted Sand's refusal to participate in feminist movements of her time, the two women writers ironically had much in common: "Sand anticipated Simone de Beauvoir's belief that woman's inferior status is a function of bourgeois, capitalist society. Accordingly, Sand worked for the transformation of French society into a socialistic, or as she put it, 'communistic,' society. Likewise Sand used her literature as an instrument for advancing the cause of women."[6] Endorsing feminist positions is one way to empower women politically. But as both *Shirley* and *Nanon* show, providing new representations of marriage is another way, which although not more important for women in the large picture of history was perhaps a more immediately practical goal that women writers could achieve. As Georges Lubin explains of Sand,

> She was not opposed to women's entry into political life, indeed she predicted it, but in the future and conditional upon the abolition of women's dependency and upon the acquisition of equal rights for both sexes and

equal division of parental authority. Less inclined to improbable dreams than the authors of *The Voice of Women*, she thought that women should vigorously fight to acquire civil rights before asking for civic rights.[7]

It is important to focus, then, on the rights that women acquire through and within marriage in *Shirley* and *Nanon*. The eponymous heroines of these two novels not only themselves possess the wealth that before the revolution was controlled by the male aristocracy; they and the other women protagonists in these two novels, who share control of that wealth in marriage, provide examples of what Brontë and Sand as progressive women writers saw as the most valuable contribution that revolution did or could make for women and society generally: the establishment of egalitarian social relations between different classes and genders.

Beneath the surface of the multifarious events and characters in *Shirley* lies a now familiar story of revolution, which in the novel, as in history, passes through a series of phases. Those phases, which can be identified in the novel as patriarchal, revolutionary, and utopian, all function similarly to inextricably link personal and political issues. And thus it is not surprising that the two marriages that occur at the end of the novel are represented by Brontë as idealized syntheses of opposing genders, nationalities, and classes, and as symbolic resolutions to the demands of the people during the French Revolution. Those marriages serve to resolve the various conflicts and problems posed during the course of the novel's three phases. The first marriage unites the French-speaking manufacturer Robert Gérard Moore and Caroline Helstone, the niece of the clergyman Mr. Helstone; the second unites Robert's similarly French-speaking brother, the tutor Louis Gérard Moore, and Shirley Keeldar, a wealthy heiress and landowner. In addition to the semiotic element of French language, which in itself suggests a tie with French politics, *Shirley* brings to mind the revolution because it dwells on events culminating in a workers' revolt. Robert's textile mill is on the verge of bankruptcy because of the Orders of Council, trade restrictions that England imposed during the war against Napoleon and that severely curtailed English commerce abroad. Robert is thus forced to turn a deaf ear to his starving workers, who in one of the crucial scenes in the novel rise up in violent revolution against him. That revolution, which in the palimpsest of *Shirley* overlays the French Revolution, raises issues of power, justice, and equality, which must be resolved before the marriages of the four protagonists can take place at the end of the novel.

The first phase of the interrelated story of revolution and marriage in *Shirley* is an attack on patriarchy, which Brontë embodies largely in the clergy, as Sand will similarly do in *Nanon*. The attack is directed not at religion per se but at a certain irresponsible patriarchy, whose indifference or cruelty to the oppressed—workers and women—provokes the people to rise up and commit violence. It is as an alternative to that oppressive patriarchy that the ideal marriages at the end of *Shirley* need to be understood. A paradigmatic example of irresponsible patriarchy opens the novel, with the presentation of three shallow and selfish curates: Malone, Donne, and Sweeting. These unworthy clergymen, would-be suitors of Caroline and Shirley, revel in gluttony, at a time when the masses are starving, and they treat their landladies as they do their poor parishioners, with contempt. We read, for example, that Malone's way of looking at Mrs. Gale, who is serving the table, is "better suited to the owner of an estate of slaves, than to the landlord of a free peasantry."[8] By providing a caricatural version of the abuses of the ancien régime, the three curates at dinner illustrate symbolically the cause of revolution. The violence that results from their abuses is also illustrated in the first chapter through a premonition that a local madman, acknowledged in the novel as a Jacobin, is said to have had:

> All amongst the trees he saw moving objects, red, like poppies, or white, like May-blossom. . . . They were soldiers—thousands and tens of thousands. . . . A man in scarlet stood in the centre and directed them. . . . A column of smoke, such as might be vomited by a park of artillery, spread noiseless over the fields, the road, the common, and rolled, he said, blue and dim to his very feet. (49–50)

Sketched significantly in red, white, and blue—colors associated with the French revolutionary tricolor as well as the English flag—this picture prefigures the uprising of the people that will take place later in the novel and links that uprising to its historical antecedents in France.

Several other chapters near the beginning of *Shirley* serve to develop further the attack against patriarchy initiated in the opening presentation of the three curates and to develop firmly the link between patriarchal abuse in society and the family. The chief object of the attack against patriarchy is the well-intentioned but ultraconservative clergyman Mr. Helstone, Caroline's uncle, who scorns women and disapproves of the French Revolution. Helstone's patriarchal attitude is developed largely through contrast with the opposing attitudes of other masculine characters. One is the republican Mr. Yorke, who is kind to his wife and daughters and who defends the revolution: "To judge by his threats, he would have employed arbitrary, even cruel, means to advance the cause of freedom and equality. . . . Revolt was in his blood" (77). We learn that Helstone and Yorke were rivals when young for the same woman, Mary Cave, who chose Helstone over Yorke as her husband and died of neglect and sorrow because of Helstone's coldness and indifference toward her. Entrusted as a small child to Helstone's care, Caroline similarly feels like a "young captive," to cite the telling title of the French poem "La Jeune Captive," by the French revolutionary poet Chénier, which Caroline chooses to memorize (96). Only with the appearance of Caroline's long-lost mother Mrs. Pryor, the widow of Helstone's abusive, aristocratic-looking brother, does Caroline's loneliness come to an end. As the stories of Mary Cave, Mrs. Pryor, and Caroline illustrate, political affiliations have everything to do with marriage and family in *Shirley*. Unfeeling patriarchs in the family are likely to be upholders of the status quo and injustice in the public arena. Indifference to the fate of women is an indicator of a similar indifference to the plight of workers.

Helstone's patriarchal views on marriage and politics are contrasted not only with Yorke's but also with those of Robert Moore, Caroline's future husband. Contrasting Helstone and Moore is essential for indicating what the masculine partner in an ideal marriage can and cannot be. The contrast also helps to make the point that Robert is not by nature a representative of patriarchy, the negative perception of him by the workers and even at times by Caroline notwithstanding, and thus that he is not himself the cause of the revolutionary disorder that he cannot help but provoke. (A similar contrast established later in the novel serves to show that his brother Louis is profoundly different with respect to patriarchy from Shirley's despotic and conservative uncle Mr. Sympson.) Indeed, Robert is linked to both femininity and the revolution in a number of ways. He learned his native language, French, from his mother,[9] whose family business had "in the shock of the French Revolution . . . rushed down a total ruin" (60); their ruin then precipitated the bankruptcy of the Gérards' English partners, the Moores. Robert is also identified as a hybrid, as characters symbolically associated with revolution are for Balzac: "A hybrid in nature, it is probable he had a hybrid's feeling on many points—patriotism for one" (60). We learn also that at heart Robert is really for the freedom-loving French republicans and against patriarchal imperial figures like Napoleon. Thus he comments near the beginning of the novel,

> It puzzles me to this day how the conqueror of Lodi should have condescended to become an emperor, a vulgar, stupid humbug; and still more how a people, who had once called themselves republicans, should have sunk again to the grade of mere slaves. I despise France! If England had gone as far on the march of civilisation as France did, she would hardly have retreated so shamelessly. (70)

Only when Robert is restored at the end of the novel to the republican sentiments with which he has a natural affinity, only when he overcomes his apparent indifference toward the people, can he marry Caroline; for Brontë suggests that kindness toward the people and kindness toward women go hand in hand.

A semiotic element that serves to measure the gap between indifferent patriarchs and those, like Yorke and Moore, who care about women and the workers is the French language. Moore is a native speaker, and Yorke, the model of republican politics and happy marriage, is presented as a "French-speaking Yorkshire gentleman" (75). In contrast, the ultra-conservative, patriarchal Helstone, who is scornful of women, is suspicious of the idea of his niece's learning French, as he is similarly wary of the idea of incorporating French revolutionary elements into English society. At one point Helstone accuses Robert of Jacobin tendencies and forbids Caroline to study French with Robert's sister, Hortense: "She must give up French lessons. The language, he observed, was a bad and frivolous one at the best, and most of the works it boasted were bad and frivolous, highly injurious in their tendency to weak female minds" (185). In a similar vein, Shirley's conservative uncle Mr. Sympson accuses her later in the novel of excessively liberal ways: "You read French. Your mind is poisoned with French novels. You have imbibed French principles" (513). The patriarchs would quash all uprisings, leaving no place for the legitimate aspirations of the people for change.

Following the first phase in which patriarchy is attacked, the second phase in *Shirley* represents the rising up of women and the people in revolt. This phase contains, at the exact midpoint of the novel, Brontë's representation of a scene in which workers strike out in violence against economic injustice, a scene that Eagleton has examined in detail.[10] Instead of that scene, what I want to look at in the second phase are the indirect but symbolically revolutionary ways in which Caroline and Shirley parallel the workers' revolt by protesting against the social injustice inflicted on them as women. The injustice toward them will be seen to center on the issue of not marrying for Caroline and the issue of marrying for Shirley. The fact that symbolism that has been seen earlier to be linked to the French Revolution enters into the presentation of these issues—Medusan and revolutionary images of women, bad air, hybrids—brings home the point that women's domestic lives and men's public activities are inextricably linked. Brontë suggests in *Shirley* that similar upheavals arise in the private and public arenas and thus that similar solutions to social problems can be worked out within society and the family.

Social injustice in Caroline's life concerns the absence of work for bourgeois women, who are made virtual prisoners within the home. Their collective fate is that of the "jeune captive," Chénier's poem mentioned previously, which dates from the French Revolution and which Brontë treats as emblematic of woman's condition. Caroline's repeated attempts to find suitable outlets for her time and energies are thwarted, as are her hopes for marriage to Robert during the time of his financial crisis. Accordingly, she experiences a sense of oppression and injustice that parallels that of the starving workers. Brontë shows that being unmarried for Caroline's social class is tantamount to exclusion from society. In order for a bourgeois woman "to install herself as a full subject within a male-dominated culture," [11] she must have a family. Marriage is not only a romantic dream: it is a social and economic necessity.

That celibate women, designated in the novel as "old maids," are a symbolically incendiary force, like the workers, is hinted at through the symbolism of the Medusa, whose association with violent women during the Terror was noted earlier in Balzac's *La Fille aux yeux d'or*. The semiotic elements associated with the Medusa that Brontë makes use of in *Shirley* are the Medusa's role as chief of the Gorgons, her celebrated hair, and her icy gaze, which turned those who looked at it to stone. Significantly, the older, unmarried women in the novel are consistently associated with this mythological figure. Miss Mann, a compassionate and generous woman, is identified as a Medusa with a "Gorgon gaze" (194); Hortense is characterized by her strange habit of wearing her hair wrapped in curl papers (91–92); Mrs. Pryor is known for "her chill, repellent outside" (361). Unlike Balzac, however, Brontë valorizes these women, even as she associates them symbolically with revolution. Auerbach notes that for Brontë and some other writers of the Victorian period, the unmarried woman becomes "an authentic female hero," "an awesome paragon of courage, intellect, and love, whose heroic stature is inseparable from her spinsterhood." [12] Brontë suggests that single women, like workers, have been wronged, and if accordingly they have turned physically ugly or threatening, the reasons are neglect and abuse. Morally they are cast in a distinctly positive light.

In addition to befriending the Medusan feminine figures in the novel, the normally withdrawn and reserved Caroline gives verbal expression to feelings of rebellion, thereby affirming her ability to defend her own rights in marriage and society. On one occasion, she speaks out forcefully for women's right to work, making a Biblical reference to Solomon's "virtuous woman" and contrasting her with English women in the nineteenth century: "*She* had something more to do than spin and give out portions: she was a manufacturer—she made fine linen and sold it: she was an agriculturist—she bought estates and planted vineyards. *That* woman was a manager" (378). (Brontë's vision of Solomon's virtuous woman prefigures Sand's Nanon, who will be discussed shortly). And on another occasion, Caroline lashes out against an opponent, "It is my right to speak as I think proper" (390).

The most striking symbolic expression in Caroline's private life of what revolution represents in the public domain is illness: a violent upheaval of the biological organism that mirrors the upheaval of the social organism through revolution. Illness serves in *Shirley*, as in other novels discussed in earlier chapters, as a semiotic marker of a character's participation in or sympathetic response to revolution. It also serves as a sign of degeneration, a notion that, as noted earlier, linked social, political, physical, and moral phenomena in nineteenth-century thought and even, as Robert A. Nye observes, in the field of medicine: "Degeneration was the perfect expression of a hygienic medicine whose primary concern was the health and moral well-being of a whole population." [13]

In *Shirley*, Caroline falls ill in an atmosphere fraught with personal and political crises, struck by what readers of this book will easily identify as the same "bad air" that brought low the characters in *The Last Man*. Echoes of Shelley's novel indeed resound strongly in the description of the onset of Caroline's illness: "The future sometimes seems to sob a low warning of the events it is bringing us, like some gathering though yet remote storm, which in tones of the wind . . . announces a blast strong to strew the sea with wrecks; or commissioned to bring in fog the yellow taint of pestilence, covering white Western isles with the poisoned exhalations of the East" (399). It is significant that Caroline is infected the very night when her French-speaking future brother-in-law arrives from abroad, thereby symbolically importing the germ of revolution, which Brontë, like many other English writers of her time, both feared and admired. Each of the three other protagonists—Louis, Shirley, and Robert—will similarly undergo personal illnesses, which enable them to interiorize the people's suffering and the revolutionary legacy. Their survival and successful marriages at the end of the novel depend on the fact that they, like Lionel in *The Last Man*, were able both to contract and to resist the infection. Rather than fearing revolution as a fatal malady, as so many of their English compatriots did, Brontë and Shelley both suggest that it is a malady that can be endured and used to strengthen the English social organism.

The parallelism of upheavals in the private and public arenas is even more pronounced with Shirley than with Caroline. Only introduced into the novel during the second phase, she immediately constitutes a revolutionary presence, who calls into question the very basis of women's subordination to men in marriage. Her empowerment is stressed repeatedly. Mockingly she refers to herself, or conjures up images of herself, as esquire, captain, churchwarden, magistrate, colonel, and justice of the peace (213). And as Caroline observes to her, "My uncle, who is not given to speak well of women, says there are not ten thousand men in England as genuinely fearless as you" (267). Although Helstone is profoundly misogynistic and does not normally favor strong women, he does not hesitate to arm Shirley during the workers' revolt. And the text suggests that she, too, like Robert, is a hybrid, a semiotic marker of revolution for Brontë, as for the other writers considered in this book. Although she is feminine in her sexual and social identity, she is masculine in her economic power and her first name (*Shirley* has masculine connotations in England); as she observes, "They gave me a man's name; I hold a man's position: it is enough to inspire me with a touch of manhood" (213).

Shirley's full revolutionary potential as a woman manifests itself in a highly significant scene near the midpoint of the novel, a scene that reveals the terms on which Shirley's marriage later in the novel will be negotiated. In this scene, where Shirley and Caroline are seated outside the church and talking to two working-class men during a church service, the intermingled factors of language, gender, and revolution are to the forefront. Not only is this scene revolutionary by virtue of the women's rejection of patriarchal values: their refusal to hear the sermon and their transgression of class boundaries. Revolutionary violence, which will erupt in the next chapter, colors the landscape ("rosy reflections on hill-side," "red hills" [314]), as it will in a similar scene in *Nanon* to be discussed later. And revolutionary feminist arguments are advanced directly. Thus Shirley counters one of the workers' regressive views on women's domestic role by emphasizing that her command of language and knowledge of politics are in no way inferior to a man's and thus that she will not accept a submissive role as a wife: "Politics are our habitual study, Joe. Do you know I see a newspaper every day, and two of a Sunday? . . . I read the leading articles, Joe, and the foreign intelligence, and I look over the market prices: in short, I read just what gentlemen read" (321).

This scene is also one of several in which Shirley develops the kind of epic, heroic images of women mentioned in earlier chapters—Staël's Corinne, Shelley's Evadne, Sand's Lélia—who sharply contrast with traditional nineteenth-century wives. Rejecting Milton's patriarchal version of creation—and this at the very moment when Helstone is delivering his sermon inside the church—Shirley states: "Milton tried to see the first woman; but, Cary, he saw her not. . . . I would beg to remind him that the first men of the earth were Titans, and that Eve was their mother. . . . The first woman's breast that heaved with life in this world yielded the daring which could contend with Omnipotence. . . . The first woman was heaven-born" (315). What Shirley does with Milton she then goes on to do with Saint Paul, whose words Joe cites as an authority for women's bowing to men's opinions in marriage.[14] Even Saint Paul's words could, she maintains, be rewritten from a woman's viewpoint: "It would be possible, I doubt not, with a little ingenuity, to give the passage quite a contrary turn; to make it say, 'Let the woman speak out whenever she sees fit to make an objection'" (323).

Elsewhere in the novel Shirley similarly articulates images of women that are heroic and revolutionary, and thus she sets the foundation for the notion of independent women in marriage and society. At one point she conjures up an epic image of revolutionary violence as a cross between a feminine sea monster and a mermaid: "Anger crosses her front; she cannot charm, but she will appal us: she rises high, and glides all revealed, on the dark waveridge. Temptress terror! monstrous likeness of ourselves!" (249). When Caroline responds, "But, Shirley, she is not like us: we are neither temptresses, nor terrors, nor monsters," Shirley answers, "Some of our kind, it is said, are all three. There are men who ascribe to 'woman,' in general, such attributes" (250). This description of feminine heroism is not unusual in Victorian literature, according to Auerbach, who observes that commonly in that literature, "Mermaids . . . submerge themselves not to negate their power, but to conceal it," and concludes that they are "an amalgam of imprisonment and power."[15]

On another occasion, a different heroic image of women is evoked. We learn that as a student, Shirley wrote an epic story entitled "La Première Femme Savante," a feminist rewriting of the Bible. Like Shelley's last man, Shirley's first woman, Eva, is evoked "utterly alone—for she had lost all trace of her tribe"; like him, "she asked, was she thus to burn out and perish, her living light doing no good, never seen, never needed,—a star in an else starless firmament,—which nor shepherd, nor wanderer, nor sage, nor priest, tracked as a guide, or read as a prophecy?" (457). The story goes on to tell how Eva acquires knowledge and marries Genius. Brontë suggests that knowledge and learning are the salvation of women, an insight that Sand extends in *Nanon* to the people. It is not surprising then that Shirley and Nanon both marry their teachers. Far from constituting a passive submission to authority, these marriages represent an active acquisition of strength, knowledge, or power.

A number of symbolic scenes involving animals provide further instances of the revolutionary symbolism attached to Shirley.[16] On one occasion, she demonstrates her fearlessness by engaging symbolically in a battle involving a bull, stating afterward, "I was not startled from self-possession when Mr Wynne's great red bull rose with a bellow before my face, as I was crossing the cowslip lea alone, stooped his begrimed, sullen head, and made a run at me" (267). This depiction of Shirley, near the time of the battle against the workers, confronting the "great red bull," with his "begrimed, sullen head," suggests that animals serve in Brontë's novel as analogues for the people. On another occasion, a dog receives similar symbolic treatment. Mr. Donne and Mr. Malone, attracted by Shirley's fortune, come to court her. But their efforts are rendered ridiculous from the start when they ignobly hide, terrified, from Shirley's dog Tartar, thereby supporting her intuition that you can judge men by the way they act toward animals (224). More is at issue, however, than a dog. In the following description typical of many in the novel, the description of animals is evocative of the oppressed workers:

> She was caressing the said Tartar: he lay crouched at her feet, his fore-paws stretched out, his tail still in threatening agitation, his nostrils snorting, his bulldog eyes conscious of a dull fire. He was an honest, phlegmatic, stupid, but stubborn canine character . . . quiet enough he was, unless struck or threatened with a stick, and that put a demon into him at once. (276–277)

It is easy to read the dog as an analogue of the people, whom Brontë depicts in *Shirley* as violent only when mistreated. Donne and Malone fail completely to understand either people or dogs, and thus they are depicted as subject to extreme and irrational feelings of fear. Shortly after Donne calls Tartar a brute, whom he wants hung (279), he refers to the people as brutes (285). He thereby provokes Shirley's rage and causes her to lose control of herself and, although he is a respected member of her society, to banish him from her home. Although on the surface level of the plot, her action seems insignificant, it serves symbolically as a strong assertion of her politically revolutionary concern for the people.

In contrast, we learn later that Louis not only loves and is beloved by dogs (430) but he even looks like one! Describing Louis's face, Shirley states: "It looks like Tartar: you are my mastiff's cousin: I think you as much like him as a man can be like a dog" (575). And Louis loves the people so much that his life is endangered by the "bad air" he is exposed to in their midst: "Louis Moore had perhaps caught the fever . . . in one of the poor cottages of the district, which he, his lame pupil, and Mr Hall, were in the habit of visiting together" (450); Shirley warns him: "I hear you often visit the sick in Briarfield, and Nunnely too, with Mr Hall: you should be on your guard: temerity is not wise" (451). In contrast with Louis are those who do not love the people, the ultimate sin in *Shirley*, as it will similarly be in *Nanon*. Both novels take the position that the people, like dogs, are essentially good if only they are not mistreated. As Shirley states, "It is only against the weak affectation and futile pomposity of a would-be aristocrat they turn mutinous" (345).

Having looked at the phases in which patriarchy is attacked and in which women and the people revolt, it is time now to consider the third and last phase in the novel, in which a series of compromises aimed at preserving the revolutionary legacy are developed. It is in this final phase that the two couples marry, an ending that for many critics belies the strong feminist thrust found elsewhere in the novel. Leslie Rabine calls the ending a "utopian account of patriarchal marriage and paternalistic capitalism" and concludes,

> It is as if Brontë, faced with the larger power system into which an author sends her finished work, had to hide the feminist conclusion behind the patriarchal discourse and ideology of the overt conclusion. Yet if we consider some of the qualities of the fragmentary and silent feminine discourse she produced in the body of the text, we can remember that it gives a lesser importance to the linear plot, and we might conclude that the last word does not come at the end.[17]

Carol Ohmann calls the ending the "bourgeois, liberal dream" of a paternally ruled family, and she concludes that in *Shirley*, "the Industrial Revolution accelerates without disturbing either the peace or the usual relationships of classes."[18] And Susan Gubar considers that Brontë exaggerates the happy ending to alert us to her skepticism about marriage as a solution.[19]

If marriage is seen in relation to the story of revolution in *Shirley*, however, its meaning is far different. One critic who has the merit of situating the ending of *Shirley* in relation to the larger political meaning of the novel is Enid Duthie, who emphasizes Brontë's sympathy for revolution: "Though she distrusted theorising, and the use of violent action to remedy social evils, Charlotte Brontë could not be indifferent to aspirations for freedom or hatred of tyranny"; she highlights the importance of statements by Brontë such as "Every struggle any nation makes in the cause of Freedom and Truth has something noble in it." It is in relation to such political views that Duthie also grasps the symbolic nature of marriage as a mediating structure in *Shirley*. She notes that the fable of the first woman represents "the ideal relationship of the sexes," and she observes the close relationship of the concepts of marriage in the works of Brontë and Sand, both of whom depict the breaking down of class barriers through marriages between heiresses and their lovers.[20] Therein lies to a significant extent the feminist thrust of their novels, in contrast, for example, with Staël's *Corinne*, which, as Moers observes, "does not argue for an adjustment of marriage to female requirements" and thus, with respect to marriage at least, "is not, in any polemical sense, a feminist work."[21]

I would like to look closely at two ways in which equality is established symbolically through marriage at the close of *Shirley* in order to make the point that the ending of Brontë's novel rejects patriarchy in society and the family and also develops positive models for preserving the egalitarian legacy of the French Revolution. The first way consists of "unmanning" the strong, to use the term that Brontë applies to Robert during his illness (542). As noted earlier, Robert, a hybrid, is not himself a patriarchal force or the cause of revolution. But he is presented as unduly masculine in his commitment to power, money, and family pride. Only when a series of events succeeds in "unmanning" him—his illness, Shirley's rejection of his marriage proposal, his travels among the poor while in Birmingham—does he learn that he must go beyond his own narrow self-interest to concern himself with others. Only then is his masculine pride sufficiently mitigated for him to marry Caroline. Only then, too, can he accept that even if the mill were to fail, he could accept the life of a worker: "I can work, as Joe Scott does, for an honourable living: in such doom, I yet see some hardship, but no degradation" (554).

Unmanning the strong is equally important with respect to Shirley, also a hybrid, who has all the courage, power, and strength normally granted to men. Unmanning Shirley is not tantamount, however, to disempowering her. Rather Brontë suggests that regardless of the gender of the dominant partner, equality is essential in marriage. As an aristocrat, Shirley has too much au-

thority and control, and thus like Robert she is brought down to size. As
Rabine observes, Brontë made an interesting choice by not simply reversing
the standard plot and placing Shirley in the traditional position of a man;
rather, she chose to challenge the underlying values and assumptions of that
standard plot.[22] To do so requires subjecting Shirley to the same kind of
diminution that other excessively masculine figures must undergo.

Shirley's unmanning occurs symbolically through the curious episode of a
dog bite, which terrifies the otherwise unflappable heroine to an extent that is
only truly comprehensible in light of the political symbolism of animals
developed elsewhere in the novel. Thus an apparently insignificant event
becomes comparable to an attack by the violent mob during the Terror: "On
account of that little mark, I am obliged to look forward to a possibility that
has its terrors" (476). It is significant that the dog in question has been
mistreated, as have the workers, and that it is female, as are such other
feminized representations of revolutionary violence as Balzac's marquise. It is
also significant that its name, Phoebe, signifies the moon in classical mythology. Phoebe's bite brings to mind Barthes's analysis of Girodet's *Endymion*,
in which the male—in Brontë's novel, the formerly masculinized Shirley—is
penetrated and feminized by the moon, thereby producing a gender reversal.
And indeed it is only after the dog bite that Shirley relinquishes her masculine
attitude of superiority toward Louis. She now needs him to protect her symbolically against outside terrors. Only he can reassure her: "I doubt whether
the smallest particle of virus mingled with your blood" (479). It is precisely
at the moment of Shirley's change with respect to gender that Brontë evokes
Endymion. Shirley's feminization is expressed metaphorically as the feminization of the moon: "The Moon reigns glorious, glad of the gale; as glad as if
she gave herself to his fierce caress with love. No Endymion will watch for his
goddess to-night" (485).

The second way in which equality is established symbolically at the close of
Shirley, the opposite of unmanning the strong, is empowering the weak, again
of both genders. Regarding Louis, one might think at first glance that because
he is a man, his economic empowerment at the end of the novel constitutes
an affirmation of patriarchal values. Thus, for example, Gubar concludes,
wrongly to my mind, that Shirley sells out by handing over the control of her
land to her husband: "By the end of the novel, Shirley is a bondswoman in the
hands of the hero of a patriarch."[23] I would see the ending, rather, as a
symbolic affirmation of the need to divide resources equitably between the
rich and the poor. The ending affirms, as Duthie observes,

the liberal belief in the equality of both sex and class, which was part of the republican ethos, and in which the half-Belgian Louis Moore believes as wholeheartedly as the wealthy Victorian Sympson rejects it. The pride of the heiress in her love for the tutor . . . is something more truly revolutionary in the Victorian novel than Jane Eyre's confession of her love for the patrician Rochester.[24]

Shirley's love is doubly revolutionary in duplicating a plot element—the male teacher's seduction of his aristocratic female pupil—penned by an author whom many associated with the principles of the French Revolution, Rousseau, celebrated for the shocking inclusion of a love affair between Saint-Preux and Julie in *La Nouvelle Héloïse*. Moers provides a list of numerous poor, socially inferior but intellectually superior "teacher-lovers" in nineteenth-century novels, whom she describes as "the feminist's fantasy of perfect love—foolish perhaps, but the result of pride rather than humility." Only because these men were poor, Moers observes, "was it possible for the heroine of a novel to give herself voluntarily to the lover of her choice."[25] Far from representing patriarchal rule, then, Louis as a teacher embodies the revolutionary aspirations to freedom of the poor. Thus Shirley and Louis succeed in promoting within their marriage the goals of the revolution, freedom and equality. When they decide to marry, he states, "I have such a thirst for freedom—such a deep passion to know her and call her mine," and he evokes the woman he desires as Liberty: "I am certain Liberty will await me" (571). And she asks him, "Are we equal then, sir? Are we equal at last?" (578).

Empowering the weak also occurs with Caroline, although in a subtle way that critics have not fully acknowledged. That way consists of her control over language. From the start, Caroline evinces a special ability to read, for example, in an emblematic episode near the beginning of the novel in which she corrects Robert's reading of Shakespeare's *Coriolanus* in order to warn him against "the proud patrician who does not sympathize with his famished fellow-men" (116). That rereading is even the occasion for her to express republican sentiments: "I cannot help thinking it unjust to include all poor working people under the general and insulting name of 'the mob'" (118). As in this episode, so in the novel as a whole, Caroline functions as a narrator and fictional author of sorts, a role she can be imagined to assume at the end, when she has the peace of mind and leisure time to undertake a retrospective look at the events recounted in the novel. And indeed there is evidence that she, like Jane Eyre, indirectly plays a privileged narratological role.[26] She is the one who can show others how to bridge the gap with the people through compassion, who has the special link with the region that is attributed to the narrator, who speaks French and is sensitive to nature as the narrator is. The frequent uses of an authorial *I*—"I did not find it easy to sketch Mr Yorke's person" (76)—fit with Caroline's experience. And on other occasions, Caroline's close identification with the narrator is even acknowledged: for example, "What I have just said are Caroline's ideas of the pair: she felt what has just been described" (254). In short, as Eagleton observes, "*Shirley*, a third-person novel, secretes a tacitly first-person narration—that of Caroline Helstone— within it"; another critical assessment of the novel mentions "Bronte speaking in her own thinly disguised voice, often through Caroline." [27]

Emphasizing Caroline's special relation to language and narration is important for grasping the nature of her marriage to Robert. Like Louis, who toward the end of the novel also at times assumes a privileged narratological role, Caroline is the weaker member of the couple, and language, Brontë suggests, is one way in which women or oppressed people acquire the strength that allows for equality in marriage. Caroline's privileged link with language is something she shares, significantly, with her mother, whose "voice, even in speaking, was sweet and silver-clear; in song, it was almost divine" (407). Brontë thus valorizes two key elements of what Cixous was quoted earlier as designating as feminine writing: the mother and the woman's voice. [28] The emphasis on Caroline's privileged link with language is also something she shares with the women whom Staël and Sand sought to empower symbolically as speakers, poets, and writers. The fact that Brontë did not openly acknowledge Caroline's role should not lead us to overlook its importance; and thus I disagree with such assessments as the following:

> Throughout Brontë's work the basic need of women is to make a love-match. By excluding the importance of the self-expression of which her novels are themselves the practice, Brontë also excludes her own solution, that of being a professional woman writer. Only Barrett Browning is able to inscribe this radical alternative within the text itself, and to centre it in the structure of her narrative. [29]

Not only do I disagree because Staël in fact prefigured Barrett Browning's achievement. More importantly, I disagree that women's self-expression is excluded from *Shirley* and that the need for marriage is primordial for Brontë. Both language and marriage are part of a larger story in *Shirley*, the story of the revolution, in which both women and the people achieve freedom, justice, and equality in diverse and often symbolic ways.

In *Nanon*, Sand singles out the Jacobins' failure to provide the people with basic rights to education, property, and work as the shoal on which the revolution foundered in 1793. Her utopian model for how to achieve those rights is provided in the idealized, egalitarian marriage between Nanette Surgeon (Nanon), a poor orphaned peasant, and Emilien de Franqueville, scion of a venerable aristocratic family. Not only does their marriage at the end of the novel, in 1795, bring together and symbolically blend opposing classes and genders. It culminates a series of personal phases in the evolution of the couple, personal phases that mirror the political phases in the development of the revolution. The idealized way in which the couple passes successfully through those phases in order to form the perfect marriage, marked by complete equality, justice, prosperity, and peace, constitutes Sand's utopian vision of what revolution should be. Moreover, Nanon's passage through those phases provides a symbolic representation of Sand's utopian vision of the empowerment of women in the postrevolutionary era.

The first phase, chapters 1 through 9, dwells on two conditions necessary for the ideal evolution of the couple and the revolution during the early phase from 1788 to 1792: liberation from the feudal control exercised by the clergy and education of the people. The novel begins in 1788 with the episode of Nanon's acquisition of a sheep, the result of years of saving by her impoverished but generous uncle. Through her hard work and intelligence, she raises her sheep and prospers, unlike the lazy, wasteful monks, whose fortunes decline. The text notes, significantly, that Nanon was "a *good shepherdess* in every sense of the word."[30] For it is Nanon who will gradually replace the clergy and perform the functions that the monks were supposed to perform: leading the pastoral flock, teaching the peasants, protecting and helping them, and the like. One recalls Delphine's similar replacement of priests in Staël's novel, considered in chapter 5. But Nanon's success is not hers alone. She meets Emilien when, as a newly arrived young monk, he allows her to graze her sheep on the church property during a drought, a privilege that the monks normally denied to the peasants. This small but significant detail whereby Nanon and Emilien find a way to make use of the land prefigures many episodes in the novel where the two young people similarly devise new ways, acting together as a couple, to accomplish the goals set by the revolution.

The outbreak of the revolution during the first phase provides further ways for the couple and society to replace the feudal control of the clergy. Nanon as a peasant and Emilien as a monk, a condition forced on him by his unfeeling aristocratic parents, are liberated by the revolution from their formerly enslaved conditions. With the decline of patriarchal authority, Nanon and Emilien, like Chateaubriand's couples discussed in chapter 4, form a sibling-like relationship ("We loved each other as if the same mother had brought us into the world" [94]), in which fraternity and equality replace the authority of the church. Nanon and Emilien also form a symbolic compromise with the vestiges of the patriarchal order they replace. Together they liberate the enlightened prior Fructueux, imprisoned by his fanatical religious brothers for his liberal position on the issue of the sale of church property. The name *Fructueux*, which echoes the fruitfulness that the revolution strove to bring to the people, points to the prior's acceptance of the new goals. By saving him, the couple salvages the best in the clergy, which they choose to help rather than to oppose. They also save Emilien's haughty and capricious sister Louise, whose name, the feminized version of the royal name *Louis*, designates her aristocratic commitment to the monarchical values of the past. With Louise, a vestige of the aristocracy, and the prior, a vestige of the clergy, Nanon and Emilien form a free society that inhabits the old monastery, the former bastion of feudalism, now owned by the bourgeois patriot M Costejoux.

Another condition for the formation of the couple and the realization of revolutionary goals during the first phase in *Nanon* is education. That Emilien is the one who most directly performs the role of educating both the people and his future wife Nanon is appropriate in light of his first name, which recalls the ideal student Emile created by Rousseau, a writer hailed by Sand and others on the Left, as noted earlier, as a forerunner of the revolution. As with Nanon's acquisition of pastoral responsibilities, so too with Emilien's role as educater, both partners in the couple are involved. Barely literate when he arrives at the monastery, Emilien is put to shame by Nanon for his ignorance and his inability to teach her and others like her. Emilien thus acquires the ability to read and write in order to be able to pass on knowledge to Nanon and her compatriots, as he does, for example, in informing the town of their newly acquired rights under the revolution:

My friends, you are free men! It has been decided at last to publish and put in force the decree of last year abolishing compulsory labor throughout France. After this, you will be paid for your labor and make your own terms. There are no more tithes, no more compulsory service. The monastery is no longer lord of the manor or creditor, and soon it will cease to own the land even. (48)

Emilien, an aristocrat by birth, thus leads the way in educating the people, as the aristocracy led the way in bringing about the revolution during its initial phase. It is indeed as an education that the people's experience of the revolution is presented in *Nanon*: "Being compelled to leave their homes, to concert measures with one another, to go in search of news and to hear what was said outside of the ravine and even in the large towns, they began to understand what the Bastille was, and war and famine and the king and the National Assembly" (43).

Emilien's education of Nanon provides an especially striking example of how the development of the couple mirrors the progress of the revolution. It is at the very moment of the great fright (*la grande peur*), when the terrified people from the town go off to do battle against supposed "brigands" spreading through the countryside, that Emilien teaches Nanon to read, thereby laying the groundwork for her upward mobility, which will culminate eventually in their marriage. Her education, the basis for her empowerment as a woman, parallels that which Sand identifies as one of the positive results of the revolution for the people. It is significant that learning to read is represented symbolically in the novel as the semiotic process of learning to read the meaning of the revolution. After having learned the alphabet, she begins to read and interpret landscape, which formerly she was unable to do: "It was the first time I had ever noticed such things." Now she can observe that the region is marked with the revolutionary color red ("The sun was setting to our right; the chestnut trees and beeches seemed to be on fire. The fields were aflame" (*les prés en étaient rouges*); she can interpret red as a sign of war and can see "red and blue letters in the sun's beams" (46). What is accomplished in this scene is the conjunction of a cluster of forces: woman, language, revolution, and class. Revolution and education enable a peasant woman to pass through the first phase of her social and personal evolution. At the end of this phase, as she observes, "Beginning with 1792, I ceased to be a peasant, except in costume and in constant work" (105).

Another scene in the first phase, which dwells on education of the people, marks a key point in the parallel evolution of the couple and the society. On the first anniversary of the revolution, the festival of Federation occurs. Again it is Emilien, the aristocrat, who leads the people: he is the one who arranges the special altar made for the occasion of fruits, vegetables, plants, animals, and flowers. But in order to grasp the meaning of the altar—to understand its symbolic significance as a representation of the peasants' newly acquired access to the fruits of the land that they work—it is necessary to read its inscription, which Nanon alone among the peasants is able to do. Having read the inscription ("This is the altar of the grateful poor whose toil, being blessed in heaven, will be rewarded on earth" [56]), Nanon is placed on "the altar of their fatherland" to play the role of "an angel figure praying for the poor" (57). Like Corinne's similar role as an allegory of freedom and a positive, feminine representation of revolution, Nanon's role depends on her privileged access to language. Corinne, a member of the elite, brings poetry to the people; Nanon, a peasant, brings reading and thus knowledge to them. As Emilien says when addressing the people during the festival, "What she knows she does not keep for herself, but she is in haste to teach it to others" (58). The people will thereby be able to understand their newly acquired rights to purchase national property.

The second phase in *Nanon*, chapters 10 to 20, dwells on the period of the Terror, and it posits further leveling of class and gender differences, beyond those developed in the first phase, as the condition for the development of both the ideal marriage and the ideal revolution. With respect to class, the utopian solution that Sand develops in the second phase is a sharing of control over the direction of the revolution between the people and the bourgeoisie. The two classes cooperate in obtaining the release of Emilien, who has been imprisoned as an aristocrat, despite his exemplary commitment to revolutionary and patriotic principles. Nanon and Emilien's trusted former servant Dumont, both peasants, contribute much hard work and careful planning to obtaining his release. But they also receive invaluable assistance from the well-intentioned bourgeois lawyer and landowner Costejoux, who for idealistic reasons has shifted politically from the moderate Girondins to the radical Jacobins. *Nanon* suggests that it is only through such cooperation among classes that the ideal revolution could occur. As the enlightened prior observes at the beginning of the second phase, on hearing of the king's flight to Varennes, "Louis XVI was afraid of his people . . . that is to be regretted [*c'est mal*], for the people are not ill-meaning" (106). Loving the people, as Emilien loves Nanon, is a prerequisite for the success of the revolution.

A telling episode involving the key semiotic element of women's writing illustrates symbolically how competing class interests are synthesized in

Nanon. Learning that both she and Emilien will need certificates of citizenship to travel after his release from prison, Nanon takes it on herself to forge them. She makes her own by "imitating Monsieur Costejoux's handwriting" (163). The revolutionary authority vested in the bourgeois man during the Terror is thus written over—that is, usurped and given new and greater legitimacy— by the peasant woman, who chooses to free the aristocracy symbolized by Emilien rather than violently suppressing it. In a similar spirit, Nanon then forges the name of the fanatical former monk and evil Jacobin Pamphile in order to produce Emilien's certificate. She thus writes over both the former power of the clergy and the present authority of the Jacobins.

The leveling of gender differences is also necessary for Emilien's liberation, as it is for an ideal marriage and society in Sand's novel. Nanon's first efforts to reach Emilien require, significantly, that she walk "as far as an ordinary man would walk in a day" (133). Later Emilien compliments her for her "manly courage" (*un courage d'homme*) (170). In order to accomplish their plan, she and Dumont decide to disguise her as a boy, his nephew Lucas, and thus she is initially dressed in masculine attire during this phase of the revolution. And she observes, while performing manual tasks, "Since I had been a boy I had become adroit and strong with my hands in boy's work" (185).

Sand's conception in *Nanon* of what gender should and should not be with respect to the revolution is illustrated in the second phase by a number of representations of women who play a real or symbolic public role. One negative representation, which Nanon glimpses during a republican festival at the height of the Terror, is the Jacobin goddess of liberty. Nanon decries that festival as "purely fanciful" and a "senseless performance" (167). The goddess, "a very handsome, tall woman in antique costume" (166), is referred to, significantly, by the ostensibly aristocratic name "La Grand' Marquise." (In fact, her name derives from the fact that "she was the daughter of a cobbler whose name was Marquis" (166). The name of Sand's goddess of liberty recalls Balzac's marquise in *La Fille aux yeux d'or*, also a symbolic representation of feminine excess in association with the Terror. Unlike Nanon's own modest and respectful role in the earlier festival of Federation, the marquise's role is depicted as wanton and arrogant. One distasteful element of the marquise's representation of the republic from Nanon's point of view is "a half-naked child representing the *child of love*" (166) at the foot of the altar. Another element is the marquise's way of stepping down, by ordering a bourgeois suspected of royalism to serve as her stepping stool.

Another negative feminine representation in the public sphere, the queen, is discussed by Emilien, who is severe in his antiroyalist views. Paralleling the opposition between David and Staël in judging the queen noted in the last chapter, Emilien is far more severe in his judgment than Nanon. For her, she observes, the "death of the queen made more impression on me than anything else in the Revolution"; like Staël, Nanon attempts to defend her: " 'Why put a woman to death?' I said; 'what harm can she have done? Wasn't it her duty to obey her husband and think as he did?'" (196). Emilien counters that women have a moralizing function to play in the family and society, and "in many cases the husband obeys the wife" (196). His assessment of the queen is thus harsh: "It has always been said that the queen wanted to bring the enemy into France, or to take the king away. So she did him a great injury, and it may be that she is the prime cause of the frenzy into which the Revolution has plunged" (197). One is reminded of the myriad other negative representations of aristocratic women observed in the other chapters of this book. Despite the harshness of Emilien's judgment of the queen, I might add, some compassion does show through, which is consonant, I believe, with representations of the queen by women writers. Whereas David, a masculine artist, denies her all dignity, Emilien, the creation of a feminine novelist, at least counterbalances his condemnation of her with an acknowledgment of her courage: "It has always been said that she was proud and brave; she must have died bravely, saying to herself that it is the fate of the heads of a nation to stake their lives against those of their people, and that she has lost the game" (197). Emilien even grants her the power of speech at the moment of her death that David has been seen to deny her.

During the second phase, Nanon, in contrast with the marquise and the queen, plays the positive public role of a maternal embodiment of the republic. That role also contrasts with the negative role that Balzac was seen in the last chapter to assign to mothers in *La Rabouilleuse*. Having served as Emilien's sister in the first phase, Nanon becomes his symbolic mother in the second phase when she, Emilien, and Dumont are in hiding, after Emilien's liberation. Together, they form a new revolutionary family, with Dumont's playing the role of the substitute, peasant father and Nanon's playing the role, as the following remark by Emilien reveals, of the substitute, peasant mother: "Be my mother, I am willing; for I imagine that, if I had had a real mother, I should have loved nobody else in the world" (188). That role of the mother has significant ties with the republic is evident at the end of the second phase, when Costejoux tries to excuse the violence that has occurred during the Terror on the grounds that the beleaguered republic has had no other way to defend itself: "Robespierre and Saint-Just have only a few more obstacles to overcome to make the Republic, freed from all its foes, what it should be—a loving mother who gathers all her children into her arms and provides them all with happiness and security" (218).

The third and last phase in the development of the couple and the revolution, chapters 21 to 28, covers the period after the ninth of Thermidor and the end of the Terror, from 1794 to 1795. There are several final goals for Nanon and Emilien, and for French society generally, that are achieved during this phase: equitable distribution of property; faith in the people, despite the violence of the unruly urban mob; and again, as in the other phases, equality of gender and class. Marriage in the final chapters of *Nanon* depends on the ways in which these goals are achieved by the various characters in the novel.

Achieving an equitable distribution of property at the end of *Nanon* involves diverse classes of society. The bourgeoisie in this case takes the lead, as the aristocracy did in the first phase. Costejoux generously proposes advantageous terms that enable Nanon to purchase the monastery, which she has carefully restored and maintained. She thereby again replaces the clergy, as she did earlier in filling its pastoral function. Through this purchase, she also achieves a sense of self-worth, having completed through the acquisition of land the upward mobility that began with her education. In this phase, Nanon emerges as a true capitalist, who carefully calculates the means to acquire her independent fortune: "I began to reckon, and I discovered that at the price at which land was held at that moment, one might in a few years make it yield a revenue that would triple the value of the land itself" (240). Similar comments abound as Nanon completes her social ascension to the landowning class. There is even a question very briefly of Costejoux's proposing marriage to her, a proposal that he prefaces by saying, "I am no more aristocratic than you by birth; what property I have I owe to my father's labor and my own" (256). Even without this marriage, however, Nanon has achieved an empowerment through control of the land. Most significantly from an economic standpoint, Fructueux dies and leaves a sizable fortune to the couple, thus giving Nanon access to the riches of the clergy, along with its land, which she had already acquired.

If economic matters are resolved successfully for all narrative participants through the utopian ending of *Nanon*, social and political matters are only resolved successfully by Nanon and Emilien, in sharp contrast with Costejoux and Louise, whose unhappy marriage unites two classes that have lost all faith in the future and the people. Louise, ever the aristocrat, like Léonce in *Delphine*, never ceases to uphold the values of the past and to the end remains incapable of integrating herself into modern, nonaristocratic society. Her fate, an early death, bespeaks that of her social class. As she states near the close of the novel, "My race is accursed and blotted out" (283). Costejoux, the bour-

geois Jacobin, completely reverses his political position; having gone to all
lengths in the name of the people, he now has only hatred for them: "I am
disgusted with them, with the people of the cities, with everything" (256).
Only through Nanon's intervention is Costejoux prevented from a suicide
prompted by profound political disappointment: "The Republic is expiring
all about me and within me. Yes, I can feel it dying here in my cold bosom;
my faith is leaving me!" (316). Even his own marriage to Louise is for him a
sign of the corruption of his revolutionary ideals: "The third estate is sleeping,
satisfied with the increased importance it has acquired. It is already corrupted;
it forgives, it holds out its hand to the clergy, it mimics the nobility and
consorts with them, and the women of the nobility are trampling us under
foot again, beginning with myself, who am in love with a Franqueville whose
father I detested and despised" (317). Blaming "the women of the nobility"
for the corruption of the republic is, of course, a familiar politicizing strategy
that has been observed in many other nineteenth-century novels examined in
this book.

The marriage between Nanon and Emilien, in contrast, is based on love for
the people and optimism for the future. Emilien, having chosen to defend the
revolutionary government as a soldier and having lost an arm in battle, can
declare at the end, "I have atoned for my noble birth" (303). He lost his arm,
he says, not only for the sake of his country but "also for the cause of liberty
throughout the world" (303). And although, like Costejoux, he knows that
difficult times lie ahead for republican government, he declares: "Whatever
happens I shall retain my political creed, but I shall not hate my fellow-
countrymen, whatever they may do" (302). Nanon has similarly retained her
faith in the revolution and the people, as she is called on to explain to
Costejoux:

> It was left to me, a poor ignorant girl, to prove to him that all the mighty
> efforts of his party were not wasted, and that some day—soon per-
> haps—enlightened public opinion would apportion blame and gratitude.
> In order to explain my meaning as clearly as possible, I said a great deal of
> the indubitable progress of the common people and of the great privations
> from which the Revolution had delivered them. (318)

In the light of Nanon's great faith in the people and the revolution, it is not
surprising to learn that as an elderly woman she eventually dies from what in
these pages stands out as the revolutionary illness par excellence: helping the
sick during an epidemic!

Nanon's and Emilien's marriage is also based on equality of gender and class.

It is true that Nanon tells Louise, "Emilien, if he is my husband, will be my master, and I shall be content to obey him" (291). But it is also true that he says to her near the end, "I shall always consider that what you desire is what I should desire. Take me for your steward; command, and it will be my delight to obey" (301). She brings the peasant's hard work and energy to the marriage. For his part, he brings the aristocrat's courage and honor, which are represented symbolically through the restoration of his title, marquis de Franqueville, after the deaths of his father and older brother. Although at the end of the novel, Sand's peasant heroine is referred to as the marquise de Franqueville, it is important to remember that she has acquired her wealth and land herself: her husband gives her only his noble social status, which as Mozet observes is like his sleeve, an empty sign.[31] Thus the marquise de Franqueville can stand apart from such other negative "marquises" as the Goddess of Liberty, presented earlier in *Nanon*, or Balzac's marquise de San Réal in *La Fille aux yeux d'or*. Significantly, until the end of their lives, Nanon and Emilien follow the odd linguistic practice, adopted in their youth, of his addressing her with the familiar form *tu* while she uses the respectful, formal form of *vous* for him. Although at first glance this practice might seem to be sexist or indicative of class prejudice, I believe that it serves instead as a sign of Nanon's humility and enduring ties with her peasant roots: precisely what separates her from the negative "marquises."

Further indication of the class and gender equality that prevails in Nanon's and Emilien's marriage is provided through the presentation of the two partners as hybrids: not in the negative sense that Balzac's use of that semiotic element assumes but in the same positive sense that Brontë has been seen to develop in *Shirley*. The names of the two characters are revealing. *Emilien de Franqueville* combines the aristocratic *de* with the bourgeois connotation of *ville franche*, in which freedom from taxes favored commerce. His last name thus evokes a character who synthesizes class differences by retaining the social advantages of the aristocracy while acquiring the economic, physical, and moral strengths of the nonaristocratic classes. Regarding Sand's heroine, it is significant that her real name *Nanette* was changed at the beginning of the novel by Emilien to the less distinctly feminine *Nanon*. This change suggests her hybrid role, often acting as both a man and a woman. As Costejoux says to her, "You are an exception. You are neither woman nor man; you are both together, with the best qualities of both sexes" (248). *Nanon*, significantly, is the name that she, as the marquise de Franqueville, retains to the end of her life. She thereby preserves in her first name the distinctly lower-class connotation that women's names ending in *on* typically assume in French, a connotation echoed in her maiden name *Surgeon* as well. Significantly, Sir Walter Scott noticed that connotation, which as a conservative he was quick to associate negatively with women in the revolution. Thus he refers to "Citoyenne Roland, who piques herself on the plebeian sound of her name, Manon Philipon."[32] In contrast with Scott, Sand views connotations of lower class and revolution positively.

The equality that Nanon and Emilien achieve as hybrids is passed on, significantly, to the next generation, notably through those among their five children who receive special mention in the novel. Their son, Pierre de Franqueville, marries one of the two daughters of Costejoux, whose bourgeois line of the family thus unites with Nanon's peasant and Emilien's aristocratic lines. More importantly, Nanon's matrilineal legacy is emphasized in the marriage of one of her daughters to the son of her peasant cousin Pierre: "One of his sons, remaining a peasant, although he was well educated, married one of the Demoiselles de Franqueville" (322). In this marriage, the bourgeoisie is excluded, as in Nanon's and Emilien's utopian union. But as with the parents, so too with the children, education will enable this "well educated peasant" to achieve all the wealth, power, and knowledge that the bourgeoisie possesses.

It is time now to look at the larger picture of Sand's ideal marriage in *Nanon* and the utopian social vision that it represents. Admittedly, there are limitations to Sand's social vision, as there similarly were to Brontë's. Sand wrote *Nanon* at the time of the Commune, when her faith in the revolution was dealt a heavy blow, as it had been earlier at the time of the revolution of 1848. Her faith was shaken to the point that she had difficulty in endorsing either the people's participation in the Commune or the newly declared Third Republic. And there is little doubt that one of her chief goals in *Nanon* was to pit the peasants against the proletariat: to promote the image of peace-loving peasants, whose example she naively admonishes the urban masses to follow. As Mozet observes, "George Sand openly expresses her suspicions about the workers and chooses the side of the French countryside. . . . There is reason to believe that she made the wrong choice. . . . Her socialism is completely based on the need for agrarian (not collectivist) reform and on the importance of small peasant property."[33] Sand, like Brontë, was not consistently able to face squarely the radical consequences of promoting the people's cause in an industrial age.

Like her English counterpart, and perhaps to an even greater extent, however, Sand held firm in her commitment to the people and revolution. As Yves Chastagnaret insightfully explains, Sand profoundly understood and valued the legacy of the revolution, her reservations about the problems that had arisen in its implementation notwithstanding:

> The author of *Nanon* understood that the French Revolution could not be summed up in several magical dates. Her merit is to have contributed—in her own way, and well before Jean Jaurès—to anchoring socialism in the Republic. . . . Too much has been said about the "value" of the French Revolution and not enough about what that value represents in economic and social terms. George Sand's claim boils down to one sentence: while doing away with one evil—absolutist privileges—1789 created another—inequality—which is more surreptitious and thus harder to erase.[34]

Like Brontë, she never failed to propose narrative solutions for erasing that inequality. Despite the pessimism that marked her outlook in the 1870s, during the writing of *Nanon* and the few short years she had to live after completing it, she continued to hold the belief that with the proper education and economic integration into French society, the people could achieve the goals of the revolution. That belief was shared by many others on the Left in the 1870s, when education was widely viewed as a way to win the people over to the republic and eliminate class struggle.[35]

In *Nanon*, Sand's vision of equality for the people coincides with her vision of equality for women, as does Brontë's in *Shirley*. Nanon provides a truly liberated and empowering image of both femininity and the people: she works, frees prisoners, acquires and controls property, educates others. And most importantly perhaps, she controls the narration, imposing the vision specific to her gender and class on the revolutionary events. As she observes near the beginning of her first-person narration, "I can say how the peasant looks at things, as I was born in that class" (36). For both women novelists, representing women in marriage was a convenient vehicle for conveying that vision in novelistic form.

The striking way in which David's *Les Sabines* politicizes marriage can serve to encapsulate this chapter's claim that the personal and political are profoundly linked in the nineteenth century as well as to point in the direction of the next

9   Jacques-Louis David, *Les Sabines*, 1799. Courtesy of the Musée du Louvre, Paris.

chapter's focus on the centrality of women of action in narratives of the revolution. Unlike Brutus's passive, grief-stricken wife and daughters, David's Sabine women play active roles as wives and mothers, the kind of roles that Brontë and Sand have been seen to assign to women in *Shirley* and *Nanon*. The painting depicts a moment, some years after the celebrated episode of the rape, when the Sabine leader Tatius and his soldiers have come to avenge the earlier crime. His daughter Hersilia, along with other women who have married the Romans and borne their children, intervene and succeed in separating the two warring factions.[36] As Roberts points out, "Women are seen pushing through the space occupied by the men. In pictorial terms it is the women who are dominant."[37] A similarly dominant role will be attributed to women in Dickens's *A Tale of Two Cities*. Indeed, *Les Sabines* contains one feminine figure who bears a striking resemblance to Dickens's *tricoteuses*. Bryson observes that the hostile arm gestures and reddish dress of the woman behind the central, conciliatory figure of Hersilia suggest "the previous era of bloody conflict" during the Terror: the same violent era evoked through other revolutionary images such as the Phrygian caps of the Romans on the left side of the painting and the wolf, a reference to the founding of the Roman republic and to David's earlier valorization of republican virtue in *Brutus*.[38] Hersilia's role in the painting is to put an end to this violent era and promote peace and reconciliation. The fact that *Les Sabines*, with its acknowledgment of the active, public role of wives, dates from 1799—ten years after *Brutus*—supports my claim in this book that, although women's legal and political role was not improved and was even worsened in many cases, their cultural role was enhanced in the years following the French Revolution.[39]

David's representation of wives and women of action differs in a number of significant ways, however, from that developed by Brontë and Sand, women writers who, as I have also claimed in this book, tend to be more progressive in their politicizing of gender than their male counterparts. One difference can be observed in the fact that, unlike Brontë and Sand, David emphasizes women's physical nature. David uses women's thin or ripped clothing and fully or partially exposed breasts to accentuate their sensuality, as Girodet did in *Atala au tombeau*. Paradoxically, his men, who are represented nude, are not sensuous objects but instead appear as sublime, idealized Greek heroes. Another difference can be seen in the representation of the trio of children at the center of the painting. (This trio—along with such other features as the nurturing, bare-breasted mother in the foreground, the tower in the background, the division of the characters into two factions on the left and the right—bear striking resemblance to Victor Hugo's representation of the revolution in *Quatrevingt-Treize*.) Roberts observes perceptively that the child to the right of the trio is visibly male and that the two children to the left seem to be boys because they are fighting, imitating the actions of their adult models. Roberts notes that the function of the woman in front, who is turned toward Tatius, is "pointing out to him that the boys, like the men, are fighting" and implicitly asking him, "Is it not time for such behavior to end?"[40] David thus symbolically suggests that the fate of the nation lies in the male line. In a related vein, the written words that appear in the painting—*Roma* on a shield on the Roman side, *David* on a stone block on the Sabine side—are tributes to a masculine control of war and art, not to the kind of feminine control of language and human values celebrated in Brontë's and Sand's far different politicizing of marriage in *Shirley* and *Nanon*.

7

Epilogue:
A Tale of Two Cities

As the preceding chapters have shown and as an analysis in this closing chapter of Dickens's *A Tale of Two Cities*, with its unforgettably lurid descriptions of Mme Defarge and other feminized forces of revolutionary violence, will confirm, politicizing gender is fundamental to nineteenth-century representations of the French Revolution. By showing that a semiotic method can shed light even on Dickens's celebrated novel, which has been subjected to exhaustive critical scrutiny, I wish to support the claim that the method used in this book for studying the politicizing of gender has an illuminating relevance for all nineteenth-century works of art and literature that tell the revolutionary story. The productive application of my method to the much studied *A Tale of Two Cities* is intended to stand for its application to the many other revolutionary works in the nineteenth century that time does not permit me to consider. Focusing in this Epilogue on the recurrent narrative strategies and semiotic elements observed in the earlier chapters will also serve to provide a summary and synthetic overview of them, with *A Tale of Two Cities*'s serving as a paradigmatic example that combines them all.

My analysis of *A Tale of Two Cities* in this closing chapter is also intended to illustrate the fact that, although all nineteenth-century works about revolution use women in similar ways, these works display varying degrees of political and feminist progressiveness, and that the cultural patterns examined in this book can help to assess the degree of that progressiveness, with *A Tale of Two Cities* as a test case. Although I have found that politicizing gender occurs to an equal extent and in similar ways in all works about revolution—whether the writers or artists in question are women or men, French or English, pro- or antirevolution—I have also found that significant variations exist in the choice of semiotic elements and that those choices reflect the degree of progressiveness: for example, in more conservative versions of the revolutionary story, revolution and femininity are linked through women engaged in acts of violence (as with Balzac, a male writer on the Right), whereas in more liberal versions, revolution and femininity are linked through acts of language (as with Staël and Sand, female writers on the Left). Evaluating *A Tale of Two Cities*, which has recourse to characteristically conservative as well as liberal cultural practices, in terms of its political and feminist progressiveness is especially enlightening. Dickens's ideologically mixed utilization of a wide range of semiotic elements supports my earlier contention that there is no strict dichotomy according to gender lines in representations of the French Revolution, that is, that there is not here a neat division into the two opposing camps of men and women or of those who empower women and those who do not. Whereas *A Tale of Two Cities* is far more regressive overall from the standpoint of feminism than the novels written by women studied in this book, it also has a progressive side, which merits the attention of feminist and other literary scholars alike. As noted earlier with regard to Balzac, even at their most regressive, male writers often empower women by the very fact of casting them in symbolically public, political roles. Whether very regressive, very progressive, or somewhere in between, as with Dickens and many of the other writers discussed in this book, feminized representations of revolution merit critical attention because they all belong to the culture of the nineteenth century and shed light on its workings. It will prove especially enlightening in this closing chapter to dwell on comparisons and contrasts between Dickens and the other novelists and artists who treated the French Revolution. These comparisons and contrasts make it possible to obtain the kind of broad cultural perspective that is normally missing from studies of individual authors.

The analysis here of *A Tale of Two Cities* follows the multiphase pattern, frequently encountered in the preceding chapters, consisting of a patriarchal phase, followed by a feminized and revolutionary phase, ending in a compromise or utopian phase that attempts to articulate the revolutionary legacy. For Dickens's novel, I have chosen to identify the major characters in connection with the phase in which they play the most important role. Thus the patriarchal phase highlights Jarvis Lorry, Dr. Manette, and the marquis d'Evrémonde; the revolutionary phase, Jerry Cruncher, Miss Pross, and Mme Defarge; and the compromise phase, Charles Darnay, Lucie Darnay, and

Sidney Carton. Admittedly, this multiphase pattern imposes a stricter sequentiality on the presentation of events and characters than the novel itself displays. A similar caveat obtains to the application of this pattern in other chapters of this book. It can be useful, however, as long as it has been "deconstructed," that is, as long as it has been identified as an interpretive device—itself a cultural practice—necessary for the coherence of a critical argument, rather than being passed off as a natural outgrowth of the works analyzed.

Deconstruction of critical or narrative categories is especially appropriate for Dickens, who himself consistently calls categories and oppositions into question, even ones that his representation of the revolution requires him to adopt. Indeed, much of the complexity and interest of *A Tale of Two Cities* lie in what I would call its deconstructive side, its tendency to expose to view, through a variety of narrative strategies to be examined shortly, the questionable validity of such absolute oppositions as revolution versus order, freedom versus imprisonment, victims versus oppressors. The novel itself even deconstructs the opposition that the title foregrounds and the story develops between "two cities": London at peace and Paris in turmoil. Dickens makes readers aware that the opposition between two cities corresponds more closely to the structure of the novel than to that of history. Perhaps the best lesson to be learned from representations of the French Revolution, whether they are forged by authors like Dickens or critics like me, is that ideology and culture function both to limit the categories through which we can understand the past and to give us an awareness of the limitations of our tools. Deconstruction gives us the ability, if not to correct as much as possible, at least to be aware of the cultural and ideological distortions that are inherent in our concepts for treating the past.

It may seem surprising to group together and label as patriarchal such diverse figures as Jarvis Lorry, a kindly English banker at Tellson's Bank; Dr. Manette, a former Bastille prisoner and victim of aristocratic despotism; and the marquis d'Evrémonde, the symbol of the abuses of the ancien régime. But there is an important sense in which all three characters share certain fundamental social and political affiliations that link them to patriarchal social institutions. The key to discovering their common ground is Tellson's Bank, a bastion of ancien régime conservatism and the economic anchor and meeting place in London for French émigré aristocrats. As Lorry states, "Yes. We are quite a French House, as well as an English one." [1] Lorry's and Manette's innocent and pure motives notwithstanding, they are as profoundly linked to Tellson's as Evrémonde is linked to the old order in France. Nicholas Rance observes perceptively that although the doctor "has been victimised by the old regime in France, the Manettes' safety is linked with that of the money in Tellson's vaults." [2] Ironically, Tellson's, which assists Manette to escape from the Bastille, is itself a prison of sorts, complete with iron bars on the windows. Outside the bank, we learn, you could see "the heads exposed on Temple Bar with an insensate brutality and ferocity worthy of Abyssinia or Ashantee," and the narrator adds:

> But indeed at that time, putting to death was a recipe much in vogue with all trades and professions, and not least of all with Tellson's. . . . Tellson's, in its day, like greater places of business, its contemporaries, had taken so many lives, that, if the heads laid low before it had been ranged on Temple Bar instead of being privately disposed of, they would probably have excluded what little light the ground floor had, in a rather significant manner. (84)

As James M. Brown observes of Tellson's, the "suggestion that the material wealth of the prosperous classes is based on unsavoury and insecure foundations is directly relevant to the scenes in revolutionary Paris"; so too, according to Brown, is Dickens's presentation of Lorry as a prisoner of sorts at Tellson's, who no less than Manette was "buried alive." [3]

Placing the three figures together and linking them through their association with patriarchal social institutions make it possible to see in them as a group a broad range of the semiotic elements that have characterized the representations of real and substitute fathers considered in this book. It also makes it possible to see the blend of conservative and liberal cultural practices that characterizes *A Tale of Two Cities*, a blend that makes it an ideologically mixed work with respect to both political and feminist issues. All three figures linked with patriarchy belong to what *René* depicts as a depleted, nonregenerative system. At the end of Dickens's novel, no one lives on to bear the name Lorry, Manette, or Evrémonde. Lorry is elderly. Evrémonde meets the same fate as other public and domestic despots such as Ervins in *Delphine*: the uprising or liberation of oppressed people spells his doom. Manette has been rendered physically and mentally weak through long imprisonment. Weakness, one will recall, is the condition that was repeatedly associated with the deposed monarch Louis XVI, for example, in Shelley's symbolic representation of the end of monarchy in *The Last Man* and in Gillray's satiric drawing of the royal family. Manette also brings to mind Louis XVI inasmuch as both men sought respite from their troubles through manual labor.[4] Such diminished or dissolute patriarchal figures discussed in this book as Balzac's Goriot and Lord Dudley also come to mind in connection with Manette because of the suggestions of incest that surround him, which several critics have noticed.[5]

Placing the three figures of Lorry, Manette, and Evrémonde together also makes it possible to see certain progressive features of Dickens's representation of revolution in *A Tale of Two Cities*. Dickens does not adhere to the English stereotype whereby patriarchy is embodied in the oppressive, corrupt French monarchy as opposed to the enlightened, peaceful English system. Although Lorry is well intentioned and forward thinking, much like Sand's Fructueux—both men leave their fortunes, significantly, to the nonpatriarchal figures in the novel, who can carry on the legacy of the revolution—Lorry is part of the patriarchal system embodied in Tellson's. Dickens's political progressiveness consists of his willingness to criticize the English system along with the French. He thereby shares certain liberal tendencies with writers such as Staël and Brontë and stands apart from the conservative attitudes of Burke and his many followers in the nineteenth century.

Another progressive element in Dickens's treatment of patriarchy lies in the fact that Dickens attributes to male aristocrats certain negative characteristics that are attributed stereotypically in nineteenth-century literature to their female counterparts. Secrecy and deception, notably, surround Lorry and Manette, not Lucie or other female characters. The action of the novel begins with Lorry and other travelers on the mail coach, shrouded in layers of fog and clothing: "There was a steaming mist in all the hollows, and it had roamed in its forlornness up the hill, like an evil spirit"; "Each was hidden under almost as many wrappers from the eyes of the mind, as from the eyes of the body, of his two companions" (38). The emphasis in this passage on an ancien régime mode of covering up is reinforced by the secrecy surrounding Lorry's mission: "I carry about me, not a scrap of writing openly referring to it" (58). Lorry stands as a polar opposite of Marat, whose open disclosure of his republican body and writing is celebrated in David's painting. The same covering up holds for Evrémonde and his twin brother, who are described as young men, hidden from view by clothing: "I observed that they were both wrapped in cloaks, and appeared to conceal themselves" (349). Manette, too, carries with him the secrecy of the ancien régime, notwithstanding his fate as a victim of its most egregious form, the lettre de cachet. When his beloved son-in-law Charles is brought to trial near the end of the novel and condemned on the basis of Manette's prison diaries, it becomes apparent that Manette is the one who not only has insisted that Charles's identity be kept a secret from Lucie but opposes the revelation of truths about the former abuses of the ancien régime.

The Evrémonde family represents a particularly interesting case of a reversal of the stereotype of the negative aristocratic woman. We are told that Charles's mother—the young wife of the marquis's twin brother—sought actively and openly to right the wrongs that her husband and his tyrannical brother inflicted on their feudal subjects. She openly revealed to Manette and later to her son the hideous acts of the Evrémondes. Not surprisingly, Charles adopts her name, "slightly changed" (166), rather than Evrémonde: "D'Aulnais is the name of his mother's family" (214). Charles's uncle the marquis, in contrast, is guilty of all of the aristocratic sins attributed in other nineteenth-century works to aristocratic women such as David's Corday or Shelley's queen. Whereas Balzac shunts much of de Marsay's moral decadence onto his feminine look-alike, Margarita, Dickens confines it to men—Charles's father and his twin brother, the marquis.

The patriarchal phase in *A Tale of Two Cities* is followed by the revolutionary phase, in which revolution and femininity are inextricably linked for Dickens, as they are for all the writers and artists considered in this book. Once again, Dickens has recourse to conservative as well as liberal practices, with the result that his presentation of the various characters associated with this phase—Jerry Cruncher, Miss Pross, Mme Defarge, female and male revolutionaries—is two-sided, displaying both a progressive and a regressive side.

The progressive side is apparent in Dickens's refusal to attribute the revolutionary evil to France alone, as his treatment of Jerry Cruncher and Miss Pross reveals. Although both characters are English and although neither displays the overtly frenzied behavior of the French insurrectionists, both are marked from the start of the novel with seemingly insignificant but in fact telling revolutionary semiotic signs. With Jerry, one sign is his Medusan hair: "He had stiff, black hair, standing jaggedly all over . . . more like the top of a strongly spiked wall than a head of hair" (45). Not only does an Englishman thus display wild, snakelike hair, a trait that has been seen repeatedly in this book to mark characters associated with revolutionary disorder—Margarita,

Amélie, Brontë's "old maids"; he displays a trait that has most often been attached to women. Another telling detail is Jerry's occupation as grave robber, which, although it does not consist of killing people, does entail defiling human bodies, as the revolutionaries do, and does result in his hands' turning red from rust, as theirs are turned red metaphorically by blood.

Miss Pross is marked by equally telling signs associated with revolution. These signs, apparent only here and there in the novel, are all the more remarkable inasmuch as they run counter to the overall impression of this character as a prim and conservative English lady. They contribute, then, to Dickens's efforts to represent revolutionary violence as not confined merely to the French. At the same time, however, they are part of the general association of revolutionary violence with women that marks the novel as a whole. Consider the emphasis in the initial description of Pross on wildness and the color red, both of which are semiotic elements signifying revolution: "A wild-looking woman, whom even in his agitation, Mr Lorry observed to be all of a red colour, and to have red hair" (58). In a similar vein, this description highlights Pross's mixed gender, another telling marker of revolution. Thus Lorry observes in seeing her for the first time, "I really think this must be a man!" (58). And indeed, despite the cool, prim English manner that characterizes Pross most of the time, she is referred to on several other occasions in the same revolutionary terms: "the wild red woman" (125); "wild, and red" (129). Moreover, there are a number of episodes in the novel in which she is presented as a true wild woman and perpetrator of violence. In one episode, she and Lorry decide to destroy the shoemaker's bench that Manette used during his imprisonment in the Bastille and that they fear continues to remind him of his unhappy past. During that act of destruction, we read, Pross "held the candle as if she were assisting at a murder—for which, indeed, in her grimness, she was no unsuitable figure" (235). As John Kucich observes, this act is "oddly congruent with the revolutionary destruction of the French mob."[6] It also prefigures Pross's active role in combating and ultimately killing Mme Defarge. Although the victory over Mme Defarge may seem at first glance to be wholly out of step with Pross's normal behavior, the description of her after she performs that act supports the novel's earlier intimations that wildness was inherent in her nature. That description is indeed not without analogy to the lurid description of Balzac's Margarita, dripping with blood after killing Paquita: "The marks of gripping fingers were deep in her face, and her hair was torn, and her dress (hastily composed with unsteady hands) was clutched and dragged a hundred ways" (398).

Dickens's representation of the revolutionary woman—Pross and, as will be seen shortly, Mme Defarge as well—differs substantially from Balzac's, however. Although Pross is associated on at least one occasion with the telling sign of mixed gender, she is never stigmatized as are such other bearers of that marker of revolution as Corday or Balzac's characters in *La Fille aux yeux d'or*: Lord Dudley, de Marsay, and Margarita. True, Pross is a hybrid, not only through her sexuality but even, as Dickens somewhat humorously emphasizes, through her cuisine, "half English and half French" (129). But she is also a heroine, who displays a truly inspiring and empowering moral and physical strength, as her look at the moment of taking on Defarge reveals: "Miss Pross had nothing beautiful about her; years had not tamed the wildness, or softened the grimness, of her appearance; but, she too was a determined woman in her different way, and she measured Madame Defarge with her eyes, every inch" (395). She thus joins the small but select camp of such women of action alluded to in earlier chapters as Corday and Evadne.

Far more prominent, of course, than Jerry or Pross in the second, revolutionary phase of *A Tale of Two Cities* are the feminine revolutionaries, depicted as wild, bloodthirsty *tricoteuses*: "The fingers of the knitting women were vicious, with the experience that they could tear" (250–251). From knitting, these women pass in a flash to the most violent crimes. Mme Defarge is presented, "not knitting to-day. Madame's resolute right hand was occupied with an axe, in place of the usual softer implements, and in her girdle were a pistol and a cruel knife" (244). Elsewhere in the novel, passages such as the following describing her and her sidekick The Vengeance abound:

> The drum was beating in the streets, as if it and a drummer had flown together by magic; and The Vengeance, uttering terrific shrieks, and flinging her arms about her head like all the forty Furies at once, was tearing from house to house, rousing the women. The men were terrible, in the bloody-minded anger with which they looked from windows, caught up what arms they had, and came pouring down into the streets; but, the women were a sight to chill the boldest. From such household occupations as their bare poverty yielded . . . they ran out with streaming hair, urging one another, and themselves, to madness with the wildest cries and actions. . . . (252)

> She put her foot upon his neck, and with her cruel knife—long ready— hewed off his head. . . . The blood of tyranny and domination by the iron hand was down—down on the steps of the Hôtel de Ville where the gover-

nor's body lay—down on the sole of the shoe of Madame Defarge where she had trodden on the body to steady it for mutilation. (249)

Dickens's hyperbolic evocation of a savage femininity that far outstrips masculine violence is unparalleled. His women utter "terrific shrieks" and perform "the wildest cries and actions." They are "a sight to chill the boldest." They are treacherous, with their hidden "cruel knife." Their actions are mutilating and symbolically castrating—"She put her foot upon his neck, and . . . hewed off his head"—and they are performed with wild enthusiasm, abandon, and hatred.

The very fact of thus highlighting violence has political implications. In his representation of revolutionary women, Dickens parts company with writers and artists who stand on the political Left—Staël, David, Sand—who refrain from emphasizing the violence of the Terror. With David, only Marat's stab wounds attest to Corday's violent acts. With Staël, who ends *Delphine* with an allusion to the September Massacres of 1792, no acts of violence are actually described. With Sand, who directly recounts the Terror in *Nanon*, violence is similarly elided. Dickens, in contrast, makes use of narrative strategies typical of the political Right. In Balzac's palimpsests of the revolution in *La Fille aux yeux d'or* and *La Rabouilleuse*, notably, images of violence, the Terror, and revolutionary women are prominent. Margarita, dripping with blood and panting with the desire for revenge, forms a close analogy to Mme Defarge, even more than she does to Pross. Through his emphasis on violence and through his attribution of that violence especially to women, which makes it seem more horrible, Dickens reveals a distinctly nonliberal side, which counterbalances certain of his progressive tendencies.

Women are further stigmatized through other associations with revolution. When the revolutionaries dance the Carmagnole, feminine elements are highlighted in the most negative and deprecating way: "Such grace as was visible in it, made it the uglier, showing how warped and perverted all things good by nature were become. The maidenly bosom bared to this, the pretty almost-child's head thus distracted, the delicate foot mincing in this slough of blood and dirt, were types of the disjointed times" (307–308). Inevitably the bare breast of the republic makes its predictable appearance. But here, in conjunction with the "slough of blood and dirt," the bare breast of freedom has unambiguously negative connotations.

A further stigmatization of women applies to the guillotine, which, like the plague in Shelley's *The Last Man*, is gendered as feminine. Not only is *la guillotine* grammatically feminine, but Dickens identifies it as a woman as well, as did other authors in the nineteenth century such as Hugo, who variously refers to it as a widow, a virgin, and a daughter.[7] Dickens's description of the guillotine is especially negative: "Above all, one hideous figure grew as familiar as if it had been before the general gaze from the foundations of the world—the figure of the sharp female called La Guillotine. . . . It superseded the Cross. Models of it were worn on breasts from which the Cross was discarded, and it was bowed down to and believed in where the Cross was denied" (302). Although the feminized guillotine replaces Christ, as have other feminized figures—Marat, Amélie, Atala—the replacement here is negative, involving none of the redeeming social values developed by David, Chateaubriand, or Girodet.

A similar negativity marks Dickens's feminization of revolutionary men, in contrast with the ambivalent and at times even positive feminization observed in earlier chapters with such figures as Marat and Chactas. Like Chactas, Dickens's revolutionaries are savage, with "shaggy black hair" (259), "their matted locks now flung forward over their eyes, now flung backward over their necks" (291). And like both Chactas and Marat, Dickens's male figures consistently display such features as the color of blood, nakedness, and feminized dress: "Shouldering one another to get next at the sharpening-stone, were men stripped to the waist, with the stain all over their limbs and bodies; men in all sorts of rags, with the stain upon those rags; men devilishly set off with spoils of women's lace and silk and ribbon, with the stain dyeing those trifles through and through" (291).

There is another side, however, to Dickens's representation of revolutionary femininity, as there is with other writers, even Balzac. To emphasize feminine violence is also to emphasize women's strength and role in the public sphere, as Balzac has been seen to do in his characterizations of both Margarita and Flore. Consider the following description of Mme Defarge:

> Of a strong and fearless character, of shrewd sense and readiness, of great determination, of that kind of beauty which not only seems to impart to its possessor firmness and animosity, but to strike into others an instinctive recognition of those qualities. . . . Such a heart Madame Defarge carried under her rough robe. Carelessly worn, it was a becoming robe enough, in a certain weird way, and her dark hair looked rich under her coarse red cap. Lying hidden in her bosom, was a loaded pistol. Lying hidden at her waist, was a sharpened dagger. Thus accoutred, and walking with the confident tread of such a character, and with the supple freedom of a woman who had

habitually walked in her girlhood, bare-foot and bare-legged, on the brown sea-sand, Madame Defarge took her way along the streets. (390–391)

Balzac's Flore especially is evoked by Mme Defarge's "confident tread," attributed to "the supple freedom of a woman who had habitually walked in her girlhood, bare-foot and bare-legged, on the brown sea-sand." Elsewhere, too, the text posits a positive viewpoint on Mme Defarge: "Her husband smoked at his door, looking after her with admiration. 'A great woman,' said he, 'a strong woman, a grand woman, a frightfully grand woman!'" (216). Defarge draws on his wife's energy and authority, just as de Marsay was seen to draw on the wealth and passion of his sister.

It is also important to note the ways in which Mme Defarge is *not* described, in contrast with other revolutionary women considered in these pages. Although, like Flore, she is of the people, she is not selfish or motivated by greed. On the contrary, her motives are pure and political, although undoubtedly in the eyes of Dickens and most readers they are misguided to a significant extent. Unlike Balzac's Agathe and many of Staël's characters, she is not a mother and thus suffers neither from excessive maternity nor from the other flaws of bad mothers. Most importantly perhaps, she is not represented as tainted by sexuality, homosexual or heterosexual, as are such proletarian characters as Balzac's Paquita and Flore. Nor like those characters is she or her social group—women or the working class—obliterated at the end of the novel. Unlike that of Balzac, Dickens's attitude toward participants in the Terror was ambivalent, as Sterrenburg explains:

> On the one side, he does indeed call for a completion of the Revolution and a reimmersion into primitive or cannibal states of being. . . . Yet on the other side, he also retains an aversion toward the primitive and the cannibalistic. This side of him hopes that the Terrors will not have to be reenacted, but rather that some currently moribund aristocratic force will revive itself and impose a communal model from the top. Either way, he remains opposed to the current bourgeois social order, and to its comfortable belief that the world has been reformed and radical changes are therefore no longer necessary.[8]

The need to bring about those radical changes is dramatized through Mme Defarge and the other women participants in the Terror.

A further word must be said about the privileged relationship that Mme Defarge, like such other feminine figures examined in this book as Corday and

Nanon, holds with language, defined broadly here to include various ways of conveying meaning, not only through written or spoken words. Mme Defarge is the one who controls the semiotic system of the revolution, a system that differs from the ancien régime's by its openness. Admittedly, the revolutionary code must be learned. Unlike Lorry, however, who never carries "a scrap of writing" openly referring to Tellson's political and economic affairs, Mme Defarge knits the record of the names and crimes of her victims in public: "Knitted, in her own stitches and her own symbols, it will always be as plain to her as the sun" (202). Equally public is her use of a rose in her headdress to indicate the presence of the enemy (209). At Charles's trial, she reverses the secrecy of the ancien régime by proclaiming orally the secrets hidden in Manette's written account, just as Nanon was seen earlier to rewrite and thus give new meaning to Jacobin authority during the Terror. On another occasion, Mme Defarge appears in the most public of settings, in the streets, as a conveyor of meaning to the crowd during public executions: "Madame Defarge's frequent expressions of impatience were taken up, with marvellous quickness, at a distance: the more readily, because certain men who had by some wonderful exercise of agility climbed up the external architecture to look in from the windows, knew Madame Defarge well, and acted as telegraph between her and the crowd outside the building" (253). That through the language of gestures a woman thus achieves the power and authority to determine the meaning of the revolution is an empowering practice that at least partially mitigates the denigration of Mme Defarge and other revolutionary women as forces of wildness and disorder.

In the third and final phase of the revolutionary drama discernible in Dickens's *A Tale of Two Cities*, a triad of characters—Lucie, Charles Darnay, Sidney Carton—serves to articulate symbolic solutions to the problems that the revolution posed for Dickens. Like many of the other writers discussed in this book, Dickens had ambivalent feelings toward the political issues surrounding the revolutionary events. John P. McWilliams sums up Dickens's political ambivalence when he speaks of his "attack upon the evils of both the old and new orders," his yearning for "a synthesis of aristocratic order and popular energy."[9] McWilliams further observes:

> It is not surprising that Dickens should declare himself a "Liberal" in a letter of 1842, a "Reformer" in 1855, a "Radical" in 1857, yet should also state that he "infinitely prefers a liberal Monarchy" to the American Republic, and should even contend . . . that he "believes in the virtues and uses

of both . . . Aristocracy and People . . . and would elevate or depress neither, at the cost of a single just right belonging to either." [10]

It is not surprising, then, that Dickens has recourse to the same kinds of mediating structures that served other writers discussed in this book to explore symbolic solutions to political conflicts: marriage and maternity; hybrids of class, gender, and nationality; and the like. Comparing Dickens to other writers, I find overall that, although *A Tale of Two Cities* is less progressive with respect to women, in ways that will be noted shortly, than the works of Staël or Sand, it is generally forward-thinking with respect to politics. Not surprisingly, as noted in the last chapter, Marx praised Dickens for expressing important social and political truths. In *A Tale of Two Cities*, Dickens's politically progressive side is especially visible in his acknowledgment of the positive legacy of the French Revolution.

Charles Darnay shares features with a considerable number of moderate, hybrid characters examined in these pages—Lionel in *The Last Man*, Louis and Robert in *Shirley*, Emilien in *Nanon*—who embody compromises of class, gender, or nationality and who thus differ profoundly from such uncompromising male aristocrats, incapable of adapting to the changes brought on by the revolution, as Oswald in *Corinne* or Léonce in *Delphine*. Indeed, Charles is presented in *A Tale of Two Cities* as a man ready and willing to accept and adapt to the future. Like Brontë's Louis, he is a teacher and thus a person who is committed to the future development of others in postrevolutionary society. Like Sand's Emilien, he renounces his class privileges, marrying a nonaristocratic woman and choosing a bourgeois existence far away from ancien régime France. As much as Charles differs from uncompromising aristocrats like Oswald and Léonce, he also differs from figures of upheaval such as Mme Defarge and other members of the proletariat. Eigner perceptively observes that as the name *Darnay* suggests, he is a mender, who prefers reform to violent change. [11] Enlightened and adaptable though he may be, he remains an aristocrat, whose commitment to order in society never wavers. And Sterrenburg also stresses Charles's role as a figure of moderation, noting that he participates in Dickens's dream of a politically viable, revitalized aristocracy:

For Carlyle, Dickens, and the Fraserians, the solution to ancien regime evils is the emergence of new, responsible aristocracy that will provide a social model, instead of simply preying upon and devouring its subjects. In their respective ways, these writers all distinguish between the aristocrats of the old regime (or the Regency), and a new breed of aristocrats, perhaps resembling Dickens's Charles Darnay, who will undergo a conversion, renounce their despotic past, and assume positions of responsibility in the post-Revolutionary age. [12]

An interesting comparison could be drawn between Charles's life after the revolution, which admittedly Dickens refrains from developing, and that of Emilien, the marquis de Franqueville, in *Nanon*. Presumably after the revolution, Charles would, like Emilien, be entitled to his aristocratic privileges once again. He and Lucy would, in principle, be the marquis and marquise d'Evrémonde, potential participants in Dickens's nostalgic dream of an idealized aristocracy, working in cooperation with other progressive forces in society.

Lucie plays an equally, if not more, symbolic role in *A Tale of Two Cities* than Charles. Like her husband, she is a positive hybrid. Daughter of an English mother and a French father, she has lived in England since the age of two but, curiously, has a "clear and pleasant young voice; a little foreign in its accent" (52). Although anomalous, her accent functions symbolically to emphasize her hybrid nature. Similarly the novel emphasizes her daughter's hybrid role by describing her as bilingual: "Little Lucie . . . chattered in the tongues of the Two Cities that were blended in her life" (240). It is as the promise of a political and cultural synthesis of those two cities that Lucie's female offspring should be viewed. Although Lucie lacks the intellectual and artistic development that the real or substitute mothers conceived by Staël pass on to their daughters, she does represent a highly positive maternal figure, who establishes a matrilineal pattern of descent: Lucie's and Charles's son, significantly, does not survive. Like Juliette in *Corinne*, Clara in *The Last Man*, and Isore in *Delphine*, Lucie's daughter is the hope of the future, a hope that is embodied, significantly, in feminine form and nurtured or taught by women. And if it is true that Lucie's lessons to her daughter are undoubtedly more conformist than Corinne's to Juliette, it is also true that even embodiments of moderate, English domestic values like Dickens's Lucie or Shelley's Idris assert values that are essentially republican and egalitarian in nature.

Several aspects of Lucie's presentation in *A Tale of Two Cities* that are especially reminiscent of other feminine figures considered in this book help to understand the mediating political role she plays in Dickens's novel. Her appearance near the beginning of the novel, at the time of her father's release from the Bastille, recalls such other feminine liberators and allegories of freedom described in this book as Corinne, Idris, Atala, Delphine, and Nanon. Admittedly, she does not herself perform the act of liberating her father. But the novel consistently attributes to her the role of symbolic liberator and symbol of liberty. Like Atala rescuing the imprisoned Chactas, Lucie appears as an apparition of freedom to her father: "She stood, like a spirit, beside him" (74). We also learn that she provided the means for his spiritual liberation during his imprisonment. Manette recounts pleading with his captors to be allowed to keep a memento of his daughter with him, saying of the few strands of her hair that he wished to keep: "They can never help me to escape in the body, though they may in the spirit" (75). And when father and daughter are reunited, we read, Manette's "cold white head mingled with her radiant hair, which warmed and lighted it as though it were the light of Freedom shining on him" (76). Her name, *Lucie*, signifies the light of freedom that she brings into the life of the former Bastille prisoner.

Another important aspect of Lucie's presentation, her role as a refuge from and alternative to revolutionary violence, also recalls other feminine figures considered in this book, notably Chateaubriand's Amélie and Balzac's Agathe. Lucie plays this role, significantly, at the very beginning of the novel, when she meets Lorry at an English inn before joining her father in France. Before their meeting, Lorry goes out and looks at the stormy sea, which is described in much the same way that the sea outside Amélie's convent is described in *René*. In both novels, it symbolizes the menace of revolution: "The sea did what it liked, and what it liked was destruction. It thundered at the town, and thundered at the cliffs, and brought the coast down, madly" (51). In sharp contrast, when Lorry visits Lucie's room in the inn, absolute silence and order reign. Later in the novel, Lorry will similarly escape from the disorder of public life to the quiet home that Lucie keeps for her husband and father. The political importance of that home cannot be overestimated. As Michael Tinko writes, "Dickens, as did so many of the writers of his age, linked the welfare of the nation with that of the state of the family in that nation . . . domestic tranquility meant, indeed, national peace and tranquility." [13] As Eigner observes, Dickens is careful to place Lucie's and Charles's marriage in the central chapter of *A Tale of Two Cities*, a highly significant position that points to "marriage as the novel's central meaning." [14] Lucie is as centrally placed in Dickens's novel as a figure of mediation as Atala is in Girodet's painting.

Drawing the comparison between Dickens's Lucie as a domestic refuge and Balzac's Agathe in *La Rabouilleuse* is instructive. Through a curious instance of intertextuality, Dickens chooses to dwell on the same signified—*coin* for Balzac, corner for Dickens—to emphasize the confined space of domesticity.

With Balzac, one will recall, the word *coin* was even echoed in Agathe's name, *Descoings*. In chapter 6 of the novel alone, which provides a description of the lodgings that Lucie shares with her father and later with Charles and her children, the word *corner* appears as many as ten times. Dickens presents the domestic corner as "a very harbour from the raging streets" (123). In sharp contrast to Balzac, however, Dickens does not condemn the wife and mother who provides the refuge for the masculine characters in the novel and society generally. Whereas Agathe's symbolically royalist son judges and implicitly condemns her for what Balzac stigmatizes as negative or overvalued maternity, Dickens pays tribute to women's domestic role in society, as did both Brontë and Sand. Not surprisingly, neither the Manette nor the Evrémonde maternal line is stigmatized, as the maternal line typically is with Balzac. Whereas Balzac identifies mothers as the modern nation's downfall, Dickens views them as its salvation. Although Dickens can be criticized by feminists for failing to envision the kind of symbolic solutions proposed by Staël and Sand, in which women replace patriarchy or share power with men, he also deserves some credit for having avoided Balzac's openly misogynistic attitudes.

Such mediating structures examined thus far as the hybrid, marriage, and maternity do not suffice, however, to bring about the symbolic solution to the political conflicts addressed by Dickens in *A Tale of Two Cities*. Not only is Sidney Carton fundamental, as critics and general readers would all agree, to the plot and to the larger philosophical meaning of the novel; he participates to a profound extent in its political meaning as well. To understand his role, it is crucial to take note of the revolutionary symbolism that marks his presentation throughout the novel. Like such Medusan figures as Jerry and French revolutionary men, Sidney is described early on with "his hair straggling over the table" (116), and his hair, as a signifier of wildness, is accentuated repeatedly, including at the moment of his execution. As he goes to his death, we read, "He shakes his hair a little more loosely about his face" (400). Other links between Sidney and revolution abound. Kucich observes that the scene of the bursting wine casket

> has the effect of linking the mob's exuberant expenditure of energy with Carton's drunkenness, as does the code name of the insurgents, the Jacques, link them with Carton and his sobriquet: the Jackal. . . . Like Carton's, too, the insurgents' drives for extremity have a metaphysical cast—though they do not consciously articulate it—in their collective willingness to risk life for something more valuable even than life: undefined, limitless freedom.[15]

Also noteworthy is Sidney's linguistic tie with France, a clear marker in other novels—most notably Brontë's—of political ties with France and French politics. It is not insignificant, then, that Sidney refers, speaking to his colleague Stryver, to the time when they were "fellow-students in the Student-Quarter of Paris, picking up French, and French law, and other French crumbs that we didn't get much good of" (120). Sidney mirrors not only Charles's physical appearance but his speech as well. Thus on his arrival in France, he is told, "You speak like a Frenchman . . . a perfect Frenchman!" (341).

It is also important to observe that Sidney's role as a sacrificial Christ figure at the end of *A Tale of Two Cities*, a role that is widely acknowledged by critics, is an integral part of the revolutionary symbolism that surrounds him. His Medusan hair and the castrating effect of the decapitation that awaits him at the end of the novel bespeak a feminization that, in addition to marking Dickens's representation of French revolutionary men, also marks David's Christ-like representation of Marat. A similar symbolism surrounds the character of Gauvain in Hugo's *Quatrevingt-Treize*, whose substitution for his uncle at the guillotine duplicates Sidney's substitution for Charles. In addition to his feminization, Sidney is like David's Christ-like revolutionary hero in sacrificing his life for others: for the people generally in Marat's case, for the Darnay family specifically in Sidney's. But it would be wrong to see the one death, Marat's, as a sacrifice for a public cause and the other, Sidney's, as a sacrifice for a merely private, domestic one; for, as noted repeatedly in this book, the domestic is inextricably linked with public and political issues in the nineteenth century.

Two women evoked in the closing pages of *A Tale of Two Cities* further accentuate the similarity between Dickens's novel and David's painting because they similarly make femininity a vital ingredient in the depiction of the revolutionary hero. One of those women is the poor seamstress, who goes to the guillotine with Sidney. She too is a Christ-like figure of sacrifice who, like Girodet's Atala, is sufficiently masculinized through virginity to bear analogy with Christ and who, like Chateaubriand's Amélie, gives her life affirming her belief in others. As she walks to her death, the seamstress expresses the hope that the republic will improve the lot of the people and thus that her death, like Christ's, will not be in vain. Speaking of another poor young girl, her beloved cousin, she states: "If the Republic really does good to the poor, and they come to be less hungry, and in all ways to suffer less, she may live a long time: she may even live to be old" (403). This simple expression of the meaning of the revolution helps to enhance the meaning of Sidney's sacrifice, just as the letters by Corday and to the widow helped to enhance the meaning of Marat's sacrifice. The seamstress is a humble heroine of the revolution, with whom Sidney joins in the same kind of symbolic union that Amélie and René form in Chateaubriand's novel. Thus the seamstress's last words, spoken to Sidney, are "Am I to kiss you now? Is the moment come?"; his last word to her is the positive, hope-affirming declaration "Yes." After that exchange of words, we read, "She kisses his lips; he kisses hers" (403). Their union also recalls Amélie's and René's inasmuch as they are described as "two children of the Universal Mother" (402), and he addresses her as "my gentle sister" (403). Theirs is a symbolically incestuous union of siblings that, like the similar unions evoked in Chateaubriand's novel and other nineteenth-century works, makes a place for republican values. As noted earlier, the proletariat is not eliminated at the end of Dickens's novel, as it is in Balzac's, but rather is subsumed and preserved as part of the revolutionary legacy.

The other woman, whose memory is evoked in the closing pages of *A Tale of Two Cities*, is the historical figure of Mme Roland, whom many of Dickens's readers would have recognized and knowledgeable readers would recognize still today from the following description: "One of the most remarkable sufferers by the same axe—a woman—had asked at the foot of the same scaffold, not long before, to be allowed to write down the thoughts that were inspiring her" (404). This description, which conjures up an image of Mme Roland writing at the moment of her death, enables the narrator to introduce the long monologue that is supposed to approximate Sidney's thoughts at the moment of his death. That monologue begins with the sentence "If he had given an utterance to his [thoughts], and they were prophetic, they would have been these" (404). Mme Roland thus constitutes, as does the seamstress, a vital ingredient in Sidney's depiction as a revolutionary hero. It is her account of her death that he "rewrites," as Nanon rewrote Costejoux's authority as a Jacobin leader, but in Nanon's case, a woman gives new legitimacy to a man's writing, whereas here a man draws on a woman's writing to bolster his own legitimacy.

Interpreting Sidney's monologue is the final step in interpreting both his role and Dickens's representation of women and revolution in *A Tale of Two Cities* generally. What is at issue is the significance of the masculine legacy that at the moment of his death Sidney imagines Lucie's bringing forth:

> I see Her with a child upon her bosom, who bears my name. . . . I see that I hold a sanctuary in their hearts, and in the hearts of their descendants, generations hence. . . . I see that child who lay upon her bosom and who

bore my name, a man winning his way up in that path of life which once was mine. . . . I see him, foremost of just judges and honoured men, bringing a boy of my name, with a forehead that I know and golden hair, to this place—then fair to look upon, with not a trace of this day's disfigurement—and I hear him tell the child my story, with a tender and faltering voice. (404)

Not surprisingly, several critics have attributed nonfeminist significance to Sidney's monologue. Chris R. Vanden Bossche states, "Carton interposes a male line (mentioning his father and imagining a yet unborn son and grandson) for a female line that goes from Darnay's mother to Lucie to her daughter"; Diane F. Sadoff says of Sidney, "As his death approaches, he discovers his sonly feelings for Jarvis Lorry, banker at 'Tellson's,' and becomes the figurative apotheosis of sonhood, Christ, the dying son who, choosing death, redeems the nearly dead to life in the name of the Father." [16]

Although the masculine element of Sidney's monologue is pronounced, that element needs to be understood in relation to the feminine elements—Medusan hair, castration through decapitation, union with the seamstress, assumption of Mme Roland's voice—that surround it. I would not want to argue that Dickens affirms a matrilineal heritage in the way that Staël, for example, does in *Corinne*. But I would want to acknowledge that with Dickens, as with David, the feminine is included as well as excluded from representation in an attempt to mediate the meaning of the revolution. Just as with social class, so too with gender, Dickens tries to incorporate and synthesize opposing forces: the aristocracy and the people, masculinity and femininity, London and Paris. As with David, the masculine has the last word but not the only word. The closing image of Sidney, a heroic English man meeting his death, coincides with the image of the seamstress, a heroic French woman meeting hers. Similarly, the "tale of two cities" ends with the evocation of Lucie and Charles—hybrids and émigrés—whose offspring, male and female, will carry on the revolutionary legacy.

Appendix
of Semiotic Elements

(Numbers in parentheses refer to chapters
containing analyses of the semiotic elements.)

1. **Allegories of liberty, revolution, or the republic:** Marianne (1), Corinne (2), the "tricoteuses" (2, 7), Corday (2), Rome (2), living allegories (2), the sibyl (2), Idris (2), Evadne (2), Marat (3), Amélie (4), Atala (4), Chactas (4), Delphine (5), Max (5), Flore (5), Shirley's sea monster (6), dogs (6), Nanon (6), the marquise (6), the Sabine women (6), Mme Defarge (7), the seamstress (7), Mme Roland (7), Lucie (7)

2. **Bad air and illness:** Corinne (2), Lionel and humankind generally (2), Amélie (4), Caroline (6), Shirley (6), Robert (6), Louis (6), Nanon (6)

3. **Bare breast:** Delacroix's *La Liberté guidant le peuple* (4), Atala (4), Flore (5), the Sabine women (6), the mother in Hugo's *Quatrevingt-Treize* (6), revolutionary women (7)

4. **Clothing:** Brutus's wife and daughter in softly draped clothing (2), Corinne "en gaule" (2), Evadne disguised as a soldier (2), revolutionaries clothed in feminized dress (2, 7), Marat draped in white fabric (3), Corday dressed in wet cloth (3) and in masculine attire (3), de Marsay dressed as a woman (3), Amélie clothed in thin muslin (4), Atala shrouded in white (4), Aubry fully dressed (4), Chactas scantily dressed (4), Marie Antoinette

stripped of royal dress (4, 5), Flore dressed in ragged clothing (5), Nanon disguised as a man (6), the Sabine women in thin or ripped clothing (6), Lorry and Evrémonde wrapped in cloaks (7)

5. **Feminized men:**   revolutionaries (2, 3, 7), Lionel (2), Adrian (2), Marat (3), Christ (3), de Marsay (3), René (4), romantic heroes (4), Chactas (4), Endymion (4), Max (5), Sidney (7)

6. **Foreign women:**   The last English queen—Austrian (2), Marie Antoinette—Austrian (2, 5), Evadne—Greek (2), Margarita—Spanish and English (3), Paquita—Asian, European, and tropical (3), Mme de Mondoville—Spanish (5), Hortense—Belgian (6)

7. **French language:**   Robert (6), Louis (6), Mr. Yorke (6), Shirley (6), Caroline (6), Charles (7), Lucie (7), Lucie's daughter (7), Sidney (7)

8. **Incest:**   Goriot and daughters (1), Marie Antoinette and son (1, 4), Lord Dudley and de Marsay (3), de Marsay and Margarita (3), René and Amélie (4), Atala and Chactas (4), Goethe's lilies (4), "marriages of the first-born of men" (4), Max and Flore (5), Jean-Jacques and Flore (5), Nanon and Emilien (6), Manette and Lucie (7), Sidney and the seamstress (7)

9. **Masculinized women:**   Corday (1, 3), Evadne (2), Medusa (3), Margarita (3), Lélia (4), Atala as a virgin (4), the moon (4, 6), Shirley (6), Nanon (6), Pross (7), the seamstress as a virgin (7)

10. **Matrilineal descent:**   women authors (1, 2), Corinne and Italy (2), Juliette (2), Clara (2), Lionel's reader (2), the Natchez (4), Isore (5), Nanon's daughter (6), little Lucie (7)

11. **Medusan hair or Gorgon eyes:**   revolutionary women according to Hugo and others (3), Margarita (3), Amélie (4), Chactas (4), Miss Mann (6), Hortense (6), Mrs. Pryor (6), Jerry (7), revolutionaries (7), Sidney (7)

12. **Names:**   Corinne (2), feminine classical names (2), Marat—Marsay—Margarita—marquise—Mariquita (3), Philip (4), Sophie (5), Léontine—Léonce (5), Rouget (5), Jean-Jacques (5), Descoings (5), Max (5), Bridau (5), Shirley (6), Fructueux (6), Louise (6), Emilien de Franqueville (6), Nanon (6), Lucie (7), Darnay (7), Jacques—the Jackal (7), Tellson's (7)

13. **"Others," hybrids, deviants:**   Vautrin (1), Corday (1, 3), Evadne (2), Marat (3), de Marsay (3), Margarita (3), Paquita (3), Paris (3), Mauriac's marquise (3), workers (3), Lord Dudley (3), Max (5), Roger (6), Shirley (6),

Nanon (6), Emilien (6), Charles (7), Lucie (7), Sidney (7), Pross (7), little Lucie (7)

14.   **Patriarchal substitutes:**   Mme Vauquer (1), Corinne (2), Marat (3), de Marsay (3), Margarita (3), the Thirteen (3), René (4), Amélie (4), Chactas (4), Delphine (5), Agathe (5), Flore (5), Issoudun (5), Shirley (6), Nanon (6)

15.   **Patrilineal descent:**   Brutus (2), Joseph (5), the Romans' male children (6), Sidney's vision of the future (7)

16.   **Pietà and Christ-like figures:**   Goriot (1), Marat (2, 3), Amélie (4), Atala (4), Joseph (5), *la guillotine* (7), Sidney (7), the seamstress (7)

17.   **Sexualized women:**   Marie Antoinette in Burke's account (2, 3), Evadne (2), prostitutes (2), Margarita (3), Paquita (3), Amélie (4), Atala and her mother (4), Flore (5), the Sabine women (6)

18.   **Stigmatized aristocratic women:**   Marie Antoinette (1, 2, 5, 6), the last English queen (2), Evadne (2), the plague (2), Corday (3), Margarita (3), Paris (3), Mme de Vernon (5), Mme de Mondoville (5), Mme de Ternan (5), Louise (6)

19.   **Teachers:**   Delphine (5), Louis (6), Saint-Preux (6), Emilien (6), Charles (7)

20.   **Threatening weather:**   Amélie—stormy seas (4), Atala—storm in the forest (4), Shirley and Caroline—reddish landscape (6), Nanon—reddish landscape (6), Lucie—stormy seas and raging streets (7)

21.   **Utopian unions:**   Idris and Lionel (2), Amélie and René (4), Atala and Chactas (4), Christian brotherhood (4), Endymion and the moon (4), Caroline and Robert (6), Shirley and Louis (6), Eva and Genius (6), Nanon and Emilien (6), Nanon's daughter and the son of her peasant cousin (6), Lucie and Charles (7), Sidney and the seamstress (7)

22.   **Women's language:**   Corinne's voice (2), the narration by the sibyl—author—Lionel (2), Evadne's letter (2), Corday's letter (3), Margarita's letter (3), Paquita's body (3), Amélie's letter (4), Atala's words inscribed in the grotto (4), Delphine's and other women's letters (5), Mme de Ternan's voice (5), Caroline's narration (6), Shirley's mythical stories (6), Mrs. Pryor's voice (6), Nanon's narration (6), Mme Defarge's signs (7), Mme Roland's reflections (7)

23.   **Women of action, militants, or assassins**: Wittig's "guérillères" (2), Evadne (2), Corday (3), Margarita (3), Atala (4), Shirley's "first woman" (6), Nanon (6), the Sabine women (6), Mme Defarge (7), La Vengeance and *les tricoteuses*, (7), *la guillotine* (7), Pross (7)

Notes

1. Introduction

1. Honoré de Balzac, *Le Père Goriot* (Paris: Garnier, 1963), 8. The omission occurs in *Père Goriot*, trans. Jane Minot Sedgwick (New York: Dodd, Mead and Co., 1954), 3; the mistranslation, in *Old Goriot*, trans. Ellen Marriage, ed. George Saintsbury (New York: Walter J. Black, 1946), 9.

2. Quoted by Michel Delon, "La Fiction immédiate," in *La Mort de Marat*, ed. Jean-Claude Bonnet (Paris: Flammarion, 1986), 264.

3. Regarding the undermining of patriarchal authority in *Le Père Goriot* and the issue of incest see Janet L. Beizer, *Family Plots: Balzac's Narrative Generations* (New Haven: Yale University Press, 1986), chap. 3; regarding the pension Vauquer in relation to the revolution and Madame Vauquer in relation to prostitution, see Pierre Barbéris, *Le Père Goriot de Balzac* (Paris: Larousse, 1972), 200–215.

4. Along these same lines, Mary Poovey observes, "The French Revolution, with its accompanying economic, political, and ideological ferment, posed a direct threat to the principle of subordination, of which feminine propriety was a part, and thus brought the issue of 'women's rights' to the attention of men and women alike." Mary Poovey, *The Proper Lady and the Woman Writer* (Chicago: University of Chicago Press, 1984), 30.

5. Mona Ozouf, *Festivals and the French Revolution*, trans. Alan Sheridan (Cambridge, Mass: Harvard University Press, 1988), 212.

6. Marina Warner, *Monuments and Maidens* (New York: Atheneum, 1985), 19, 27.

7. Lynn Hunt, *Politics, Culture, and Class in the French Revolution* (Berkeley: University of California Press, 1984), 13, 26.

8.   For the historical link, see Natalie Z. Davis, *Society and Culture in Early Modern France* (Stanford, Calif.: Stanford University Press, 1975), 147–50. The psychological interpretation is offered by Neil Hertz, "Medusa's Head: Male Hysteria under Political Pressure," *Representations* 4 (1983): 27–54.

9.   Joan B. Landes, *Women and the Public Sphere in the Age of the French Revolution* (Ithaca, N.Y.: Cornell University Press, 1988), 138.

10.   Nancy Armstrong, *Desire and Domestic Fiction* (New York: Oxford University Press, 1987), 5, 10.

11.   Nancy K. Miller, *Subject to Change* (New York: Columbia University Press, 1988), 170.

12.   Germaine de Staël, *Oeuvres complètes*, vol. 1 (Geneva: Slatkine Reprints, 1967), 245.

13.   University of Essex English Studies Group, "Strategies for Representing Revolution," in *1789: Reading Writing Revolution*, ed. Francis Barker et al. (Essex: University of Essex, 1982), 84.

14.   Fredric Jameson, *The Political Unconscious* (Ithaca, N.Y.: Cornell University Press, 1981), 188.

15.   See François Furet, *Marx et la Révolution française* (Paris: Flammarion, 1986).

16.   Jonathan Culler, *The Pursuit of Signs* (Ithaca, N.Y.: Cornell University Press, 1981), 48, 62.

17.   Clifford Geertz, *The Interpretation of Cultures* (New York: Basic Books, 1973), 89.

18.   Patricia O'Brien, "Michel Foucault's History of Culture," in *The New Cultural History*, ed. Lynn Hunt (Berkeley: University of California Press, 1989), 36.

19.   Geertz, *Interpretation of Cultures*, 6.

20.   Ibid., 20.

21.   Naomi Schor, *Reading in Detail* (London: Methuen, 1987), 4.

22.   Roger Chartier, *Cultural History: Between Practices and Representations*, trans. Lydia G. Cochrane (Ithaca, N.Y.: Cornell University Press, 1988), 13–14.

23.   Nina Auerbach, *The Woman and the Demon* (Cambridge, Mass.: Harvard University Press, 1982), 188.

24.   Landes, *Women and the Public Sphere*, 13. In a similar vein, Poovey observes, "To say that women were legally or economically marginal or even that they were characteristically relegated to the object term of cultural grammar is not to say that they were denied all forms of power": *Proper Lady*, xi.

25.   Charlotte Smith, *Desmond*, vol. 3 (London: Robinson, 1792), 131.

26.   Naomi Schor, *Breaking the Chain* (New York: Columbia University Press, 1985), 145.

27.   Naomi Schor, "The Portrait of a Gentleman: Representing Men in (French) Women's Writing," *Representations* 20 (1987): 114.

28.   Hélène Cixous, "The Laugh of the Medusa," trans. Keith Cohen and Paula Cohen, *Signs* 1, no. 4 (1976): 875–93.

2. Allegorizing Women
Corinne and *The Last Man*

1.   George Sand, *Lelia*, trans. Maria Espinosa (Bloomington: Indiana University Press, 1978), 30.

2.   Ellen Moers, *Literary Women: The Great Writers* (Garden City, N.Y.: Doubleday, 1976), 174.

3.   Another striking example of Staël's female lineage is the daughter of the French writer Sophie Gay, Delphine Gay de Girardin, who inherited the first name of Staël's other well-known heroine Delphine and who, like Corinne, was crowned with laurels and famous for her poetry.

4.   Mary Shelley, *Lives of the Most Eminent French Writers* (Philadelphia: Lea & Blanchard, 1840), 342.

5.   For more on Staël and neoclassicism, see Madelyn Gutwirth, *Madame de Staël, Novelist* (Urbana: University of Illinois Press, 1978), 175–181. See also Gutwirth's "Corinne et l'esthétique du camée," in *Le Préromantisme: Hypothèque ou Hypothèse*, ed. Paul Viallaneix (Paris: Klincksieck, 1975), 153–168.

6.   Norman Bryson, "Centres and Margins in David," *Word and Image* 4, no. 1 (1988): 46.

7.   Bryson, "Centres and Margins," 46.

8.   For more details on the involvement of the family of Brutus's wife in the monarchist conspiracy, see Anita Brookner, *Jacques-Louis David* (London: Chatto & Windus, 1980), 90.

9.   Bryson, "Centres and Margins," 47.

10.   Simone Balayé, "'Corinne' et la presse parisienne de 1807," in *Approches des lumières, mélanges offerts à Jean Fabre* (Paris: Klincksieck, 1974), 11–12.

11.   Henri Coulet, "Révolution et roman selon Mme de Staël," *Revue d'histoire littéraire de la France* 87, no. 4 (1987): 638–60.

12.   Carla L. Peterson, *The Determined Reader* (New Brunswick, N.J.: Rutgers University Press, 1987), 57–58.

13. Charlotte Hogsett, *The Literary Existence of Germaine de Staël* (Carbondale: Southern Illinois University Press, 1987), 66.

14. Gutwirth, *Madame de Staël, Novelist*, 175.

15. Germaine de Staël, *Corinne, or Italy*, trans. Avriel H. Goldberger (New Brunswick, N. J.: Rutgers University Press, 1987), 21.

16. Marina Warner, *Monuments and Maidens* (New York: Atheneum, 1985), 288–289.

17. Brookner, *David*, 12.

18. Gutwirth, "Corinne et l'esthétique du camée," 242–243.

19. See also Gérard Gengembre's and Jean Goldzink's discussion of Italy versus England in "L'Opinion dans *Corinne*," *Europe* 64 (1987): 48–57.

20. Marie-Claire Vallois, "Les Voi(es) de la Sibylle: Aphasie et discours féminin chez Madame de Staël," *Stanford French Review* 6, no. 1 (1982): 38–52.

21. Vallois, "Voi(es) de la Sibylle," 45.

22. Peterson, *The Determined Reader*, 48, 61.

23. Julia Kristeva, *Powers of Horror*, trans. Leon S. Roudiez (New York: Columbia University Press, 1982), 152–153.

24. Regarding the notion of degeneration, see Sander L. Gilman, "Sexology, Psychoanalysis, and Degeneration: From a Theory of Race to a Race to Theory," in *Degeneration: The Dark Side of Progress*, ed. J. Edward Chamberlin and Sander L. Gilman (New York: Columbia University Press, 1985), 72–96; Robert A. Nye, *Crime, Madness, and Politics in Modern France* (Princeton, N.J.: Princeton University Press, 1984), 42–45; and Nancy Stepan, "Biological Degeneration: Races and Proper Places," in *Degeneration: The Dark Side of Progress*, ed. J. Edward Chamberlin and Sander L. Gilman (New York: Columbia University Press, 1985), 97–120.

25. Monique Wittig, *Les Guérillères* (Paris: Minuit, 1969).

26. Maija Lehtonen, "Le Fleuve du temps et le fleuve de l'enfer: Thèmes et images dans *Corinne* de Madame de Staël," *Neuphilologische Mitteilungen* 69 (1969): 106–107.

27. Mary Shelley, *Last Man* (Lincoln: University of Nebraska Press, 1965), 4.

28. Lee Sterrenburg, "*The Last Man*: Anatomy of Failed Revolutions," *Nineteenth Century Fiction* 33, no. 3 (1978): 327.

29. Sterrenburg, "Anatomy of Failed Revolutions," 341.

30. Joan B. Landes, *Women and the Public Sphere in the Age of the French Revolution* (Ithaca, N.Y.: Cornell University Press, 1988), chap. 1.

31. Warner, *Monuments and Maidens*, 289.

32.   W.J.T. Mitchell, *Iconology: Image, Text, Ideology* (Chicago: University of Chicago Press, 1986), 143–144.

33.   Nancy Armstrong, *Desire and Domestic Fiction* (New York: Oxford University Press, 1987), 178.

34.   Doris Y. Kadish, *The Literature of Images* (New Brunswick, N.J.: Rutgers University Press, 1987), 98–99.

35.   Sterrenburg, "Anatomy of Failed Revolutions," 337–338.

36.   Ibid., 332, 343.

37.   Mary Poovey, *Proper Lady and the Woman Writer* (Chicago: University of Chicago Press, 1984), xv.

3. Mixing Genders in *Marat assassiné* and *La Fille aux yeux d'or*

1.   Marie-Hélène Huet, *Rehearsing the Revolution* (Berkeley: University of California Press, 1982), 64.

2.   It is significant, too, that the main events of the story take place in April 1815, during the Hundred Days, when according to Balzac and other monarchists Louis XVIII and his followers allowed Napoleon to take control of the country through substitution.

3.   Martine Saint-Pierre, "Le Bruit des noms," *Etudes françaises* 23, no. 3 (1988): 109.

4.   Dorothy Kelly, *Fictional Genders* (Lincoln: University of Nebraska Press, 1989), 2.

5.   Ibid., 42.

6.   Ronald Paulson, *Representations of Revolution (1789–1820)* (New Haven: Yale University Press, 1983), 31, 34.

7.   David Lloyd Dowd, *Pageant-Master of the Republic: Jacques-Louis David and the French Revolution* (Lincoln: University of Nebraska Press, 1948), 80–99.

8.   The painting analyzed in this book is found in the Musées Royaux in Brussels. Two other versions, which do not bear David's signature but were presumably made under his supervision, are attributed to the painters Gérard and Sérangeli: see Jean-Rémy Mantion, "Enveloppes A Marat David," in *La Mort de Marat*, ed. Jean-Claude Bonnet (Paris: Flammarion, 1986), 229–230.

9.   For Corday's exclusion from the painting, see Gilbert Lascault, *Figurées, Défigurées* (Paris: Union Générale d'Editions, 1977), 32–37, and Erica Rand, "Depoliticizing Women: Female Agency, the French Revolution, and the Art

of Boucher and David," *Genders* 7 (1990): 47–68. For women's exclusion from politics, see Jane Abray, "Feminism in the French Revolution," *American Historical Review* 80, no. 1 (1975): 43–62; and Claire Goldberg Moses, *French Feminism in the Nineteenth Century* (Albany: State University of New York Press, 1984), chap. 1.

10.   Neil Hertz, "Medusa's Head: Male Hysteria under Political Pressure," *Representations* 4 (1983): 30.

11.   Rand argues that ironically Hertz himself performs a similar exclusion by treating women revolutionaries only as symbolizations of male castration anxiety ("Depoliticizing Women," 64).

12.   See Chantal Thomas, "Portraits de Charlotte Corday," in *La Mort de Marat*, ed. Jean-Claude Bonnet (Paris: Flammarion, 1986), 271–286, especially the section "Le féminisme de Marat." See also Léopold Lacour, "Marat féministe," *La Grande Revue* (1902): 575–602.

13.   Warren Roberts, *Jacques-Louis David, Revolutionary Artist* (Chapel Hill: University of North Carolina Press, 1989), 41–43.

14.   Ibid., 25–41, 85–89.

15.   I have used the translations of the two letters provided by Luc de Nanteuil, *Jacques-Louis David* (New York: Abrams, 1985), 112.

16.   Huet, *Rehearsing the Revolution*, 49–50, 5, 7.

17.   Milton W. Brown, *The Painting of the French Revolution* (New York: Critics Group, 1938), 72.

18.   Daniel Wildenstein and Guy Wildenstein, *Louis David* (Paris: Fondation Wildenstein, 1973), no. 674.

19.   Michael Fried, *Absorption and Theatricality: Painting and Beholder in the Age of Diderot* (Berkeley: University of California Press, 1980); Anita Brookner, *Jacques-Louis David* (London: Chatto & Windus, 1980), 114.

20.   George De Batz, "History, Truth and Art," *Art Quarterly* 8 (1945): 257.

21.   Margaret Walters, *The Nude Male* (New York: Penguin Books, 1978), 213–214.

22.   Thomas, "Portraits de Charlotte Corday," 271.

23.   Jacques Guilhaumou, "La Mort de Marat à Paris," in *La Mort de Marat*, ed. Jean-Claude Bonnet (Paris: Flammarion, 1986), 71.

24.   Brookner, *David*, 113.

25.   Lynn Hunt, *Politics, Culture, and Class in the French Revolution* (Berkeley: University of California Press, 1984), 94.

26.   Norman Bryson, *Tradition and Desire: From David to Delacroix* (Cambridge, England: Cambridge University Press, 1984), 96. The details depicting Marat's

frugality are perhaps not clearly visible in the reproduction: the patch is found at the lower left side of the sheet; the stain, near the upper left edge of the box. As for the truth about the simplicity of the apartment, there are competing accounts. De Batz gives credence to historical records according to which Marat's apartment was large and "rather lavishly furnished": "History, Truth and Art," 249–250. This is the kind of elegant bourgeois setting found in *La Mort de Marat*. Lacour, in contrast, credits records that show it as the kind of poor household seen in *La Mort du patriote*, and he attributes the report of its lavish furnishings to Michelet, repeating a false report by Mme Roland: "Marat féministe," 601.

27.   Walters, *Nude Male*, 10.

28.   Frank Bowman, "Le 'Sacré-Coeur' de Marat (1793)," in *Colloque de Clermont-Ferrand (1974)*, ed. Jean Ehrard and Paul Viallaneix (Paris: Société des Etudes Robespierristes, 1977), 155–180.

29.   René Verbraeken, *Jacques-Louis David jugé par ses contemporains et par la postérité* (Paris: Léonce Laget, 1973), 123.

30.   Guilhamou, "Mort de Marat," 71.

31.   Michael Marrinan, "Images and Ideas of Charlotte Corday: Texts and Contexts of an Assassination," *Arts Magazine* 54, no. 8 (1980): 162.

32.   Nancy Stepan, "Biological Degeneration: Races and Proper Places," in *Degeneration: The Dark Side of Progress*, ed. J. Edward Chamberlin and Sander L. Gilman (New York: Columbia University Press, 1985), 114.

33.   Honoré de Balzac, *The Girl with the Golden Eyes* (La Fille aux yeux d'or), in *History of the Thirteen*, trans. Herbert J. Hunt (London: Penguin Books, 1974), 372.

34.   As I have attempted to demonstrate elsewhere, the structure of the hybrid also applies to each section of the novel, including its long and seemingly gratuitous prologue: Doris Y. Kadish, "Hybrids in Balzac's *La Fille aux yeux d'or*," *Nineteenth-Century French Studies* 16, nos. 3–4 (1988): 270–278.

35.   Roland Barthes, *S/Z*, trans. Richard Howard (New York: Hill and Wang, 1974), 40.

36.   Shoshana Felman, "Rereading Femininity," *Yale French Studies* 62 (1981): 30–31.

37.   As quoted in Mantion, "Enveloppes A Marat David," 222.

38.   Leyla Perrone-Moisés, "Le Récit euphémique," *Poétique* 17 (1974): 36.

39.   Nicole Mozet, "Les Prolétaires dans *La Fille aux yeux d'or*," *L'Année balzacienne* (1974): 109.

4. Sexualizing Family Relations
in *René*, *Atala*, and *Atala au tombeau*

1.   Pierre Barbéris, *René de Chateaubriand* (Paris: Larousse, 1974), 212, 43–44.

2.   Allegations of incest between Marie Antoinette and her brother-in-law the comte d'Artois, who later became Charles X, had also been made: Yvonne Korshak, "Paris and Helen by Jacques Louis David: Choice and Judgment on the Eve of the French Revolution," *Art Bulletin* 69, no. 1 (1987): 103–105.

3.   As reported in Meade Minnigerode, *The Son of Marie Antoinette* (New York: Farrar & Rinehart, 1934), 208–211. For David's report of his interrogation of Louis Charles, whose statements David described as "awful words" and "infamous turpitudes," see Daniel Wildenstein and Guy Wildenstein, *Louis David* (Paris: Fondation Wildenstein, 1973), no. 575.

4.   E. Daniel Wilson, "Science, Natural Law, and Unwitting Sibling Incest in Eighteenth-Century Literature," *Studies in Eighteenth Century Culture* 13 (1984), 249–270.

5.   Patricia Joan Siegel, "Chateaubriand, révolutionnaire politique," in *Chateaubriand and Today*, ed. Richard Switzer (Madison: University of Wisconsin Press, 1970), 181; François-René de Chateaubriand, *Mémoires d'Outre-Tombe*, vol. 1(Paris: Gallimard, 1966), 1129.

6.   Wilson, "Unwitting Sibling Incest," 260, 262.

7.   Margaret Waller, "*Cherchez la Femme*: Male Malady and Narrative Politics in the French Romantic Novel," *PMLA* 104, no. 2 (1989): 149.

8.   François-René de Chateaubriand, *Atala/René*, trans. Irving Putter (Berkeley: University of California Press, 1952), 85.

9.   René Galand, "Chateaubriand: Le Rocher de René," *Romanic Review* 77, no. 4 (1986), 331.

10.   Galand, "Rocher de René," 331.

11.   Barbéris, *René de Chateaubriand*, 104, 160.

12.   Michèle Respaut, "*René*: Confession, répétition, révélation," *French Review* 57, no. 1 (1983): 16.

13.   Chateaubriand, *Mémoires*, 1: 392.

14.   Jean-Pierre Richard, *Paysage de Chateaubriand* (Paris: Seuil, 1967), 11.

15.   Diana Knight, "The Readability of René's Secret," *French Studies* 37, no. 1 (1983): 43, 45.

16.   Respaut, "Confession, répétition, révélation," 16.

17.   Richard, *Paysage de Chateaubriand*, 141, 159.

18.   The notion of a novel of mothers and a novel of fathers in Staël's writing is developed by Madelyn Gutwirth, *Madame de Staël, Novelist* (Urbana: University of Illinois Press, 1978), 157.

19.   Naomi Schor, *Breaking the Chain* (New York: Columbia University Press, 1985), 145.

20.   Marina Warner, *Monuments and Maidens* (New York: Atheneum, 1985), 277.

21.   David Wakefield, "Chateaubriand's 'Atala' as a Source of Inspiration in Nineteenth-Century Art," *Burlington Magazine* 120 (1978): 20, 21.

22.   Ann Hollander, *Seeing Through Clothes* (New York: Viking Press, 1978), 85, 117–118, 211.

23.   Comparing Girodet's *Atala au tombeau* with Chateaubriand's *Atala*, George Levitine emphasizes the originality of Girodet's attribution of Christian symbolism to Atala, which he calls "surenchère visuelle" (visual one-upmanship): "Some Unexplored Aspects of the Illustrations of *Atala*," in *Chateaubriand and Today*, ed. Richard Switzer (Madison: University of Wisconsin Press, 1970), 145. But the case for Girodet's originality is less clear-cut when *Atala au tombeau* is considered in a broader context including other closely related works such as *René*.

24.   Hollander, *Seeing through Clothes*, 373.

25.   Warner, *Monuments and Maidens*, 64.

26.   Barthes, *S/Z*, 70.

5. Censuring Maternity
Delphine and *La Rabouilleuse*

1.   Honoré de Balzac, *The Black Sheep* (La Rabouilleuse), trans. D. Adamson (London: Penguin Books, 1970), 21.

2.   Fredric Jameson, "Imaginary and Symbolic in *La Rabouilleuse*," *Social Science Information* 16 (1977): 62.

3.   J. M. Thompson, *The French Revolution* (Oxford: Basil Blackwell, 1966), 436.

4.   Warren Roberts, *Jacques-Louis David, Revolutionary Artist* (Chapel Hill: University of North Carolina Press, 1989), 75.

5.   Germaine de Staël, *Oeuvres complètes*, vol. 1 (Geneva: Slatkine Reprints, 1967), 25.

6.   Germaine de Staël, *Correspondance générale*, vol. 4, ed. Beatrice W. Jasinski (Paris: Pauvert, 1972–1978), 326.

7.   Simone Balayé, "Destins de femmes dans *Delphine*," *Cahiers Staëliens* 35, no. 1 (1984): 58.

8. Madelyn Gutwirth, "La *Delphine* de Madame de Staël: Femme, révolution et mode épistolaire," *Cahiers Staëliens* 26–27 (1979): 161–162.

9. For a detailed examination of the novel's historical background and references to the revolution, see Laurence Viglieno, "*Delphine*, roman de la Révolution?" in *Hommage à Claude Digeon*, forward by Claude Faisant (Paris: Belles Lettres, 1987), 129–139.

10. Germaine de Staël, *Delphine*, 2 vols. (Paris: Editions des Femmes, 1982), 1:423; 2:12.

11. Gutwirth, "*Delphine* de Madame de Staël," 163–165.

12. Balayé, "Destins de femmes," 42.

13. Jameson, "Imaginary and Symbolic," 76.

14. Nicole Mozet, *La Ville de province dans l'oeuvre de Balzac* (Paris: Société d'édition d'enseignement supérieur, 1982), 243.

15. Jameson, "Imaginary and Symbolic," 66.

16. Susan Rubin Suleiman, "Writing and Motherhood," in *The (M)other Tongue*, ed. Shirley Nelson Garner, Claire Kahene, and Madelon Sprengwether (Ithaca, N.Y.: Cornell University Press, 1985), 368–369.

17. Mozet, *Ville de province*, 243.

18. Jameson, "Imaginary and Symbolic," 77.

19. Lynn Hunt, *Politics, Culture, and Class in the French Revolution* (Berkeley: University of California Press, 1984), 65.

20. Mozet, *Ville de province*, 240.

21. In a similar but far less virulent vein, Hugo's narrator in *Quatrevingt-Treize* observes, "What makes a mother sublime is that she is a sort of animal. The maternal instinct is divinely animal. The mother is no longer a woman, she is a female. Children are her young": Victor Hugo, *Quatrevingt-Treize* (Paris: Garnier, 1963), 280.

6. Politicizing Marriage
in *Shirley* and *Nanon*

1. Simone de Beauvoir, *Le Deuxième Sexe*, vol. 1 (Paris: Gallimard, 1949), 140. This passage is omitted from the English translation, *The Second Sex*, trans. H. M. Parshley (New York: Alfred A. Knopf, 1968).

2. Beauvoir, *Deuxième Sexe*, 2:555.

3. Ellen Moers, *Literary Women: The Great Writers* (Garden City, N.Y.: Doubleday, 1976), 31, 20.

4. Terry Eagleton, *Myths of Power: A Marxist Study of the Brontës* (London: Macmillan, 1975), 52. For a critique of Eagleton's assessment of *Shirley*, see the Marxist-Feminist Literature Collective, "Women's Writing: *Jane Eyre, Shirley, Villette, Aurora Leigh*," *Ideology and Consciousness* 1, no. 3 (1978): 27–48.

5. Dennis O'Brien, "George Sand and Feminism," in *George Sand Papers, Conference Proceedings, 1976*, ed. Natalie Datlof (New York: AMS, 1976), 76–91.

6. O'Brien, "George Sand and Feminism," 82.

7. Georges Lubin, "George Sand en 1848," in *George Sand Papers, Conference Proceedings, 1976*, ed. Natalie Datlof (New York: AMS, 1976), 28–41.

8. Charlotte Brontë, *Shirley* (New York: Penguin Books, 1974), 42.

9. Although the home of the Gérard family, the French-speaking city of Anvers, is situated in Belgium, historical records show that it was taken over by the French in 1792 during the revolution, occupied by the French at the time when the events recounted in *Shirley* occur and successfully defended against the Dutch in 1832 by a French military leader, whose name, significantly, was Gérard. Moreover, Moore is careful to specify that although his mother was from Anvers, she was of French lineage (87).

10. Eagleton, *Myths of Power*, 47–49.

11. Marxist-Feminist Literature Collective, "Women's Writing," 33.

12. Nina Auerbach, *The Woman and the Demon* (Cambridge, Mass.: Harvard University Press, 1982), 111.

13. Robert A. Nye, *Crime, Madness, and Politics in Modern France* (Princeton, N.J.: Princeton University Press, 1984), 45.

14. "Outside the church Shirley briefly rewrites the Bible and Milton too, making men and women equal at the time of their creation": Carol Ohmann, "Historical Reality and 'Divine Appointment' in Charlotte Brontë's Fiction," *Signs* 2, no. 4 (1977): 765.

15. Auerbach, *Woman and the Demon*, 7, 11.

16. For Brontë's similarly extensive symbolic use of bird imagery in *Jane Eyre*, see Doris Y. Kadish, *The Literature of Images* (New Brunswick, N.J.: Rutgers University Press, 1987), 178–181.

17. Leslie Rabine, *Reading the Romantic Heroine* (Ann Arbor: University of Michigan Press, 1985), 131, 132–133.

18. Ohmann, "Historical Reality and 'Divine Appointment,'" 766.

19. Susan Gubar, "The Genesis of Hunger, According to *Shirley*," *Feminist Studies* 3, nos. 3–4 (1976): 19.

20. Enid L. Duthie, *The Foreign Vision of Charlotte Brontë* (London: Macmillan, 1975), 110, 141, 196.

21. Moers, *Literary Women*, 207.

22. Rabine, *Reading the Romantic Heroine*, 107.

23. Gubar, "Genesis of Hunger," 18.

24. Duthie, *Foreign Vision*, 142.

25. Moers, *Literary Women*, 156–157.

26. For Jane Eyre's role as narrator and fictional author, see Kadish, *Literature of Images*, 160–168.

27. Eagleton, *Myths of Power*, 80; Marxist-Feminist Literature Collective, "Women's Writing," 38.

28. "In women's speech, as in their writing, that element which never stops resonating, which, once we've been permeated by it, profoundly and imperceptibly touched by it, retains the power of moving us—that element is the song: first music from the first voice of love which is alive in every woman": Hélène Cixous, "The Laugh of the Medusa," trans. Keith Cohen and Paula Cohen, *Signs* 1, no. 4 (1976): 881.

29. Marxist-Feminist Literature Collective, "Women's Writing," 46.

30. George Sand, *Nanon*, trans. G. Burnham Ives (Philadelphia: George Barrie & Son, 1901), 10.

31. Nicole Mozet, "Introduction," in *Nanon* (Paris: Editions de l'Aurore, 1987), 16.

32. Walter Scott, *The Life of Napoleon Buonaparte*, vol. 1 (Exeter, England: J. & B. Williams, 1828), 70.

33. Mozet, "Introduction," 6.

34. Yves Chastagnaret, "George Sand et la révolution française," *Dix-Huitième Siècle* 20 (1988): 445–446.

35. See Roger Magraw, *France 1815–1914: The Bourgeois Century* (Oxford: Oxford University Press, 1983), 194–195.

36. David provided the historical facts about the Sabine women in a booklet that was issued to accompany the public exposition of the painting in 1799. The booklet is reproduced in Daniel Wildenstein and Guy Wildenstein, *Louis David* (Paris: Fondation Wildenstein, 1973), no. 1326.

37. Warren Roberts, *Jacques-Louis David, Revolutionary Artist* (Chapel Hill: University of North Carolina Press, 1989), 116. The dominant role of women in *Les Sabines* finds further expression in the booklet that accompanied the painting, which includes an extended speech delivered by Hersilia.

38. Norman Bryson, "Centres and Margins in David," *Word and Image* 4, no. 1 (1988): 47–48.

39.   I disagree with Rand's contention that David uses a "maternal overlay" in *Les Sabines* to mitigate women as activists and thus that from *Les Horaces* to *Les Sabines*, there is little or no change in David's treatment of women. Erica Rand, "Depoliticizing Women: Female Agency, The French Revolution, and the Art of Boucher and David," *Genders* 7 (1990): 61.

40.   Roberts, *David*, 117.

7. Epilogue
A Tale of Two Cities

1.   Charles Dickens, *A Tale of Two Cities* (London: Penguin Books, 1970), 50.

2.   Nicholas Rance, *The Historical Novel and Popular Politics in Nineteenth-Century England* (New York: Barnes & Noble, 1975), 97.

3.   James M. Brown, *Dickens: Novelist in the Market-Place* (Totowa, N.J.: Barnes & Noble, 1982), 119, 121.

4.   This detail about Louis XVI was reported by Carlyle according to Earle Davis in *The Flint and the Flame* (Columbia: University of Missouri Press, 1963), 249.

5.   Edward M. Eigner observes, "There is frequently the suggestion . . . that the father's feeling for his daughter is not purely parental and that he views her favored lover, Charles Darnay in this novel, with more than a touch of sexual jealousy": "Charles Darnay and Revolutionary Identity," in *Charles Dickens's* A Tale of Two Cities, ed. Harold Bloom (New York: Chelsea House, 1987), 96. Lawrence Frank draws attention in a similar vein to "the ambiguity of Manette's love for his daughter, who has entered his life not as an asexual child, but as a young woman": "Dickens's *A Tale of Two Cities*: The Poetics of Impasse," *American Imago* 36, no. 3 (1979): 228.

6.   John Kucich, "The Purity of Violence: A Tale of Two Cities," in *Charles Dickens's* A Tale of Two Cities, ed. Harold Bloom (New York: Chelsea House, 1987), 62.

7.   Victor Hugo, *Quatrevingt-Treize* (Paris: Garnier, 1963), 163, 165, 449, 485.

8.   Lee Sterrenburg, "Psychoanalysis and the Iconography of Revolution," *Victorian Studies* 19, no. 2 (1975): 256.

9.   John P. McWilliams, "Progress without Politics: *A Tale of Two Cities*," *Clio* 7, no. 1 (1977), 20, 27.

10.   McWilliams, "Progress without Politics," 22.

11.   Eigner, "Charles Darnay and Revolutionary Identity," 104.

12.   Sterrenburg, "Psychoanalysis and the Iconography of Revolution," 249.

13.   Michael Tinko, "Splendid Impressions and Picturesque Means: Dickens, Carlyle, and the French Revolution," *Dickens Studies Annual* 12 (1983): 181–182.

14.   Eigner, "Charles Darnay and Revolutionary Identity," 105.

15.   Kucich, "Purity of Violence," 63.

16.   Chris R. Vanden Bossche, "Prophetic Closure and Disclosing Narrative: *The French Revolution* and *A Tale of Two Cities*," *Dickens Studies Annual* 12 (1983): 220; Diane F. Sadoff, *Monsters of Affection* (Baltimore: Johns Hopkins University Press, 1982), 32.

Bibliography

Abray, Jane. "Feminism in the French Revolution." *American Historical Review* 80, no. 1 (1975): 43–62.

Agulhon, Maurice. *Marianne into Battle.* Translated by Janet Lloyd. Cambridge, England: Cambridge University Press, 1981.

Armstrong, Nancy. *Desire and Domestic Fiction.* New York: Oxford University Press, 1987.

Auerbach, Nina. *The Woman and the Demon.* Cambridge, Mass.: Harvard University Press, 1982.

Balayé, Simone. "'Corinne' et la presse parisienne de 1807." In *Approches des lumières, mélanges offerts à Jean Fabre,* 1–16. Paris: Klincksieck, 1974.

———. "Destins de femmes dans *Delphine.*" *Cahiers Staëliens* 35, no. 1 (1984): 41–59.

Balzac, Honoré de. *The Black Sheep* (La Rabouilleuse). Translated by D. Adamson. London: Penguin Books, 1970.

———. *History of the Thirteen* (Histoire des Treize). Translated by Herbert J. Hunt. London: Penguin Books, 1974.

———. *Le Père Goriot.* Paris: Garnier, 1963.

Barbéris, Pierre. *Le Père Goriot de Balzac.* Paris: Larousse, 1972.

———. *René de Chateaubriand.* Paris: Larousse, 1974.

Barthes, Roland. *S/Z.* Translated by Richard Howard. New York: Hill and Wang, 1974.

Beauvoir, Simone de. *Le Deuxième Sexe.* 2 vols. Paris: Gallimard, 1949.

Beizer, Janet L. *Family Plots: Balzac's Narrative Generations.* New Haven: Yale University Press, 1986.

Bowman, Frank. "Le 'Sacré-Coeur' de Marat (1793)." In *Colloque de Clermont-Ferrand (1974),* edited by Jean Ehrard and Paul Viallaneix, 155–180. Paris: Société des Etudes Robespierristes, 1977.

Brontë, Charlotte. *Shirley*. New York: Penguin Books, 1974.

Brookner, Anita. *Jacques-Louis David*. London: Chatto & Windus, 1980.

Brown, James M. *Dickens: Novelist in the Market-Place*. Totowa, N.J.: Barnes & Noble, 1982.

Brown, Milton W. *The Painting of the French Revolution*. New York: Critics Group, 1938.

Bryson, Norman. "Centres and Margins in David." *Word and Image* 4, no. 1 (1988): 43–50.

———. *Tradition and Desire: From David to Delacroix*. Cambridge, England: Cambridge University Press, 1984.

Chartier, Roger. *Cultural History: Between Practices and Representations*. Translated by Lydia G. Cochrane. Ithaca, N.Y.: Cornell University Press, 1988.

Chastagnaret, Yves. "George Sand et la révolution française." *Dix-Huitième Siècle* 20 (1988): 431–448.

Chateaubriand, François-René de. *Atala/René*. Translated by Irving Putter. Berkeley: University of California Press, 1952.

———. *Mémoires d'Outre-Tombe*. Vol. I. Paris: Gallimard, 1966.

Cixous, Hélène. "The Laugh of the Medusa." Translated by Keith Cohen and Paula Cohen. *Signs* 1, no. 4 (1976): 875–893.

Coulet, Henri. "Révolution et roman selon Mme. de Staël." *Revue d'histoire littéraire de la France* 87, no. 4 (1987): 638–660.

Culler, Jonathan. *The Pursuit of Signs*. Ithaca, N.Y.: Cornell University Press, 1981.

Czyba, Lucette. "Misogynie et gynophobie dans *La Fille aux yeux d'or*." In *La Femme au XIXe siècle*, 139–149. Lyon: Presse Universitaire de Lyon, 1979.

Davis, Earle. *The Flint and the Flame*. Columbia: University of Missouri Press, 1963.

Davis, Natalie Z. *Society and Culture in Early Modern France*. Stanford, Calif.: Stanford University Press, 1975.

De Batz, George. "History, Truth and Art." *Art Quarterly* 8 (1945): 249–260.

Delon, Michel. "La Fiction immédiate." In *La Mort de Marat*, edited by Jean-Claude Bonnet, 253–269. Paris: Flammarion, 1986.

Dickens, Charles. *A Tale of Two Cities*. London: Penguin Books, 1970.

Dowd, David Lloyd. *Pageant-Master of the Republic: Jacques-Louis David and the French Revolution*. Lincoln: University of Nebraska Press, 1948.

Duthie, Enid L. *The Foreign Vision of Charlotte Brontë*. London: Macmillan, 1975.

Eagleton, Terry. *Myths of Power: A Marxist Study of the Brontës*. London: Macmillan, 1975.

Eigner, Edward M. "Charles Darnay and Revolutionary Identity." In *Charles Dickens's* A Tale of Two Cities, edited by Harold Bloom, 95–106. New York: Chelsea House, 1987.

Felman, Shoshana. "Rereading Femininity." *Yale French Studies* 62 (1981): 19–44.

Frank, Lawrence. "Dickens's *A Tale of Two Cities*: The Poetics of Impasse." *American Imago* 36, no. 3 (1979): 215–244.

Fried, Michael. *Absorption and Theatricality: Painting and Beholder in the Age of Diderot.* Berkeley: University of California Press, 1980.

Furet, François. *Marx et la révolution française.* Paris: Flammarion, 1986.

Galand, René. "Chateaubriand: Le Rocher de René." *Romanic Review* 77, no. 4 (1986): 330–342.

Geertz, Clifford. *The Interpretation of Cultures.* New York: Basic Books, 1973.

Gengembre, Gérard, and Jean Goldzink. "L'Opinion dans *Corinne*." *Europe* 64 (1987): 48–57.

Gilman, Sander L. "Sexology, Psychoanalysis, and Degeneration: From a Theory of Race to a Race to Theory." In *Degeneration: The Dark Side of Progress*, edited by J. Edward Chamberlin and Sander L. Gilman, 72–96. New York: Columbia University Press, 1985.

Gombrich, E. H. "The Dream of Reason: Symbolism of the French Revolution." *British Journal for Eighteenth-Century Studies* 2, no. 3 (1979): 187–217.

Gubar, Susan. "The Genesis of Hunger, According to *Shirley*." *Feminist Studies* 3, nos. 3–4 (1976): 5–21.

Guilhaumou, Jacques. "La Mort de Marat à Paris." In *La Mort de Marat*, edited by Jean-Claude Bonnet, 39–80. Paris: Flammarion, 1986.

Gutwirth, Madelyn. "Corinne et l'esthétique du camée." In *Le Préromantisme: hypothèque ou hypothèse*, edited by Paul Viallaneix, 153–168. Paris: Klincksieck, 1975.

———. "La *Delphine* de Madame de Staël: Femme, révolution, et mode épistolaire." *Cahiers Staëliens* 26–27 (1979): 151–165.

———. *Madame de Staël, Novelist.* Urbana: University of Illinois Press, 1978.

Hertz, Neil. "Medusa's Head: Male Hysteria under Political Pressure." *Representations* 4 (1983): 27–54.

Hogsett, Charlotte. *The Literary Existence of Germaine de Staël.* Carbondale: Southern Illinois University Press, 1987.

Hollander, Ann. *Seeing through Clothes.* New York: Viking Press, 1978.

Huet, Marie-Hélène. *Rehearsing the Revolution.* Berkeley: University of California Press, 1982.

Hugo, Victor. *Quatrevingt-Treize.* Paris: Garnier, 1963.

Hunt, Lynn. *Politics, Culture, and Class in the French Revolution.* Berkeley: University of California Press, 1984.

Jameson, Fredric. "Imaginary and Symbolic in *La Rabouilleuse*." *Social Science Information* 16 (1977): 59–81.

———. *The Political Unconscious.* Ithaca, N.Y.: Cornell University Press, 1981.

Kadish, Doris Y. "Hybrids in Balzac's *La Fille aux yeux d'or.*" *Nineteenth-Century French Studies* 16, nos. 3–4 (1988): 270–278.

———. *The Literature of Images*. New Brunswick, N.J.: Rutgers University Press, 1987.

Kelly, Dorothy. *Fictional Genders*. Lincoln: University of Nebraska Press, 1989.

Knight, Diana. "The Readability of René's Secret." *French Studies* 37, no. 1 (1983): 35–46.

Korshak, Yvonne. "Paris and Helen by Jacques Louis David: Choice and Judgment on the Eve of the French Revolution." *Art Bulletin* 69, no. 1 (1987): 102–116.

Kristeva, Julia. *Revolution in Poetic Language*. Translated by Leon S. Roudiez. New York: Columbia University Press, 1984.

Kucich, John. "The Purity of Violence: A Tale of Two Cities." In *Charles Dickens's A Tale of Two Cities*, edited by Harold Bloom, 57–72. New York: Chelsea House, 1987.

Lacour, Léopold. "Marat féministe." *Grande Revue* (1902): 575–602.

Landes, Joan B. *Women and the Public Sphere in the Age of the French Revolution*. Ithaca, N.Y.: Cornell University Press, 1988.

Lascault, Gilbert. *Figurées, Défigurées*. Paris: Union Générale d'Editions, 1977.

Lehtonen, Maija. "Le Fleuve du temps et le fleuve de l'enfer: thèmes et images dans *Corinne* de Madame de Staël." *Neuphilologische Mitteilungen* 69 (1969): 101–128.

Levitine, George. "Some Unexplored Aspects of the Illustrations of *Atala*." In *Chateaubriand Today*, edited by Richard Switzer, 139–145. Madison: University of Wisconsin Press, 1970.

Lubin, Georges. "George Sand en 1848." In *George Sand Papers, Conference Proceedings, 1976*, edited by Natalie Datlof, 28–41. New York: AMS, 1976.

Magraw, Roger. *France 1815–1914: The Bourgeois Century*. Oxford: Oxford University Press, 1983.

Mantion, Jean-Rémy. "Enveloppes A Marat David." In *La Mort de Marat*, edited by Jean-Claude Bonnet, 203–232. Paris: Flammarion, 1986.

Marrinan, Michael. "Images and Ideas of Charlotte Corday: Texts and Contexts of an Assassination." *Arts Magazine* 54, no. 8 (1980): 158–176.

Marxist-Feminist Literature Collective. "Women's Writing: *Jane Eyre, Shirley, Villette, Aurora Leigh*." *Ideology and Consciousness* 1, no. 3 (1978): 27–48.

McWilliams, John P. "Progress without Politics: *A Tale of Two Cities*." *Clio* 7, no. 1 (1977): 19–31.

Miller, Nancy K. *Subject to Change*. New York: Columbia University Press, 1988.

Minnigerode, Meade. *The Son of Marie Antoinette*. New York: Farrar & Rinehart, 1934.

Mitchell, W.J.T. *Iconology: Image, Text, Ideology.* Chicago: University of Chicago Press, 1986.

Moers, Ellen. *Literary Women: The Great Writers.* Garden City, N.Y.: Doubleday, 1976.

Moses, Claire Goldberg. *French Feminism in the Nineteenth Century.* Albany: State University of New York Press, 1984.

Mozet, Nicole. "Introduction." In *Nanon.* Paris: Editions de l'Aurore, 1987.

———. "Les Prolétaires dans *La Fille aux yeux d'or.*" *L'Année balzacienne* (1974): 91–119.

———. *La Ville de province dans l'oeuvre de Balzac.* Paris: Société d'édition d'enseignement supérieur, 1982.

Nanteuil, Luc de. *Jacques-Louis David.* New York: Abrams, 1985.

Nye, Robert A. *Crime, Madness, and Politics in Modern France.* Princeton, N.J.: Princeton University Press, 1984.

O'Brien, Dennis. "George Sand and Feminism." In *George Sand Papers, Conference Proceedings, 1976,* edited by Natalie Datlof, 76–91. New York: AMS, 1976.

O'Brien, Patricia. "Michel Foucault's History of Culture." In *The New Cultural History,* edited by Lynn Hunt, 25–46. Berkeley: University of California Press, 1989.

Ohmann, Carol. "Historical Reality and 'Divine Appointment' in Charlotte Brontë's Fiction." *Signs* 2, no. 4 (1977): 757–778.

Ozouf, Mona. *Festivals and the French Revolution.* Translated by Alan Sheridan. Cambridge, Mass.: Harvard University Press, 1988.

Paulson, Ronald. *Representations of Revolution (1789–1820).* New Haven: Yale University Press, 1983.

Perrone-Moisés, Leyla. "Le Récit euphémique." *Poétique* 17 (1974): 27–38.

Peterson, Carla L. *The Determined Reader.* New Brunswick, N.J.: Rutgers University Press, 1987.

Poovey, Mary. *The Proper Lady and the Woman Writer.* Chicago: University of Chicago Press, 1984.

Rabine, Leslie. *Reading the Romantic Heroine.* Ann Arbor: University of Michigan Press, 1985.

Rance, Nicholas. *The Historical Novel and Popular Politics in Nineteenth-Century England.* New York: Barnes & Noble, 1975.

Rand, Erica. "Depoliticizing Women: Female Agency, the French Revolution, and the Art of Boucher and David." *Genders* 7 (1990): 47–68.

Respaut, Michèle. "*René*: Confession, répétition, révélation." *French Review* 57, no. 1 (1983): 14–19.

Roberts, Warren. *Jacques-Louis David, Revolutionary Artist.* Chapel Hill: University of North Carolina Press, 1989.

Sadoff, Diane F. *Monsters of Affection*. Baltimore: Johns Hopkins University Press, 1982.

Saint-Pierre, Martine. "Le Bruit des noms." *Etudes françaises* 23, no. 3 (1988): 99–112.

Sand, George. *Lelia*. Translated by Maria Espinosa. Bloomington: Indiana University Press, 1978.

———. *Nanon*. Translated by G. Burnham Ives. Philadelphia: George Barrie & Son, 1901.

Schor, Naomi. *Breaking the Chain*. New York: Columbia University Press, 1985.

———. "The Portrait of a Gentleman: Representing Men in (French) Women's Writing." *Representations* 20 (1987): 113–133.

———. *Reading in Detail*. London: Methuen, 1987.

Scott, Sir Walter. *The Life of Napoleon Buonaparte*. 2 vols. Exeter, England: J. & B. Williams, 1828.

Shelley, Mary. *The Last Man*. Lincoln: University of Nebraska Press, 1965.

———. *Lives of the Most Eminent French Writers*. Philadelphia: Lea & Blanchard, 1840.

Siegel, Patricia Joan. "Chateaubriand, révolutionnaire politique." In *Chateaubriand Today*, edited by Richard Switzer, 177–184. Madison: University of Wisconsin Press, 1970.

Smith, Charlotte. *Desmond*. 3 vols. London: Robinson, 1792.

Staël, Germaine de. *Corinne, or Italy*. Translated by Avriel H. Goldberger. New Brunswick, N.J.: Rutgers University Press, 1987.

———. *Correspondance Générale*. Edited by Beatrice W. Jasinski. Paris: Pauvert, 1972–1978.

———. *Delphine*. 2 vols. Paris: Editions des Femmes, 1982.

———. *Oeuvres complètes*. Vol. 1. Geneva: Slatkine Reprints, 1967.

Stepan, Nancy. "Biological Degeneration: Races and Proper Places." In *Degeneration: The Dark Side of Progress*, edited by J. Edward Chamberlin and Sander L. Gilman, 97–120. New York: Columbia University Press, 1985.

Sterrenburg, Lee. "Psychoanalysis and the Iconography of Revolution." *Victorian Studies* 19, no. 2 (1975): 241–264.

———. *The Last Man*: Anatomy of Failed Revolutions." *Nineteenth Century Fiction* 33, no. 3 (1978): 324–347.

Suleiman, Susan Rubin. "Writing and Motherhood." In *The (M)other Tongue*, edited by Shirley Nelson Garner, Claire Kahene, and Madelon Sprengwether, 352–377. Ithaca, N.Y.: Cornell University Press, 1985.

Thomas, Chantal. "Portraits de Charlotte Corday." In *La Mort de Marat*, edited by Jean-Claude Bonnet, 271–286. Paris: Flammarion, 1986.

Thompson, J. M. *The French Revolution*. Oxford: Basil Blackwell, 1966.

Tinko, Michael. "Splendid Impressions and Picturesque Means: Dickens, Carlyle, and the French Revolution." *Dickens Studies Annual* 12 (1983): 177–195.

University of Essex English Studies Group. "Strategies for Representing Revolution." In *1789: Reading Writing Revolution*, edited by Francis Barker, 81–100. Essex: University of Essex, 1982.

Vallois, Marie Claire. "Les Voi(es) de la sibylle: aphasie et discours féminin chez Madame de Staël." *Stanford French Review* 6, no. 1 (1982), 38–52.

Vanden Bossche, Chris R. "Prophetic Closure and Disclosing Narrative: *The French Revolution* and *A Tale of Two Cities*." *Dickens Studies Annual* 12 (1983): 209–221.

Verbraeken, René. *Jacques-Louis David jugé par ses contemporains et par la postérité.* Paris: Léonce Laget, 1973.

Viglieno, Laurence. "*Delphine*, roman de la Révolution?" In *Hommage à Claude Digeon*, 129–139. Paris: Belles Lettres, 1987.

Wakefield, David. "Chateaubriand's 'Atala' as a Source of Inspiration in Nineteenth-Century Art." *Burlington Magazine* 120 (1978): 13–22.

Waller, Margaret. "*Cherchez la Femme*: Male Malady and Narrative Politics in the French Romantic Novel." *PMLA* 104, no. 2 (1989): 141–151.

Walter, Eric. "Vies et maladies du docteur Marat." In *La Mort de Marat*, edited by Jean-Claude Bonnet, 335–372. Paris: Flammarion, 1986.

Walters, Margaret. *The Nude Male*. New York: Penguin Books, 1978.

Warner, Marina. *Monuments and Maidens*. New York: Atheneum, 1985.

Wildenstein, Daniel, and Guy Wildenstein. *Louis David*. Paris: Fondation Wildenstein, 1973.

Wilson, E. Daniel. "Science, Natural Law, and Unwitting Sibling Incest in Eighteenth-Century Literature." *Studies in Eighteenth Century Culture* 13 (1984): 249–270.

Wittig, Monique. *Les Guérillères*. Paris: Minuit, 1969.

Index